1984

THE ROMANTIC PREDICAMENT

THE ROMANTIC PREDICAMENT

Geoffrey Thurley

St. Martin's Press   New York

ISBN 0-312-69182-3

Library of Congress Cataloging in Publication Data

Thurley, Geoffrey.
   The romantic predicament.

   Includes bibliographical references and index.
   1. European poetry—18th century—History and
criticism.   2. European poetry—19th century—History
and criticism.   3. Romanticism—Europe.   I. Title.
PN1241.T47 1984   809.1′9145   83–15995
ISBN 0-312-69182-3

This book is dedicated
to the memory
of my father
James Thurley

Contents

Acknowledgements

Thanks are due to the large number of friends and colleagues to whose advice I have been indebted. I should like in particular to thank Jonathan Bennett, Bernard Bergonzi, John Colmer, Harry Lubasz and Arthur Terry.

G.T.

1 Defining Romanticism

Romanticism has proved as hard to define as to be rid of. The age of partisanships having passed, it seems appropriate now to look at it dispassionately, yet without losing sight of its peculiar relevance to our own cultural situation. Neither the nineteenth century view (Romanticism as a vast act of liberation after the confinements of the eighteenth century), nor the modernist view (Romanticism as an orgy of subjective destructiveness after the orderliness of the Enlightenment) really stands up to close scrutiny. Contrary to many critics of the modernist period,[1] Romantic art is characteristically as solid in construction, as well-shaped, objectified and energetic as that of the eighteenth century.[2] Contrary to neo-Romantic critics, Romantic art does not have a monopoly of organic form, passion, seriousness or 'the true voice of feeling'.[3] No definition of Romanticism has yet been offered, indeed, which cannot, apparently, be discredited by a host of counter-examples: the characteristics usually thought of as specifically Romantic (subjectivity, nature-worship, distrust of rationalism, hunger for wholeness, pantheism) can all be found in much work that certainly is not Romantic, yet are often absent from much that indisputably is.

Because of such difficulties, some critics have suggested that there is no such thing as Romanticism at all.[4] This view – what we could call the pedantic – cannot, it seems to me, be taken seriously. Romanticism exists, or existed; even if we discredit false notions of it, we are surely obliged to admit that there is or was something which caused these effects, something which needs to be clarified and explained, not explained away. With this in mind, some critics accept that, although we cannot define Romanticism very clearly, we know what it is, and are entitled to go ahead with our evaluations, so long as we take the care to draw two lines across History (one before, one after Romanticism), making it clear what works we are accepting as Romantic. Thus for instance, we will call Piranesi's drawings, German *Sturm and*

1

Drang, Young's *Night Thoughts* and Gray's 'Elegy' all pre-Romantic. The post-Romantic is more difficult to date, and the chronology varies from art-form to art-form. Music critics usually accept Brahms, Wagner and Schumann as Romantic, where literary critics – in England at least – would want to withhold the term from the poets (Browning, Tennyson, Arnold, Swinburne) contemporary with these composers, calling them simply Victorian. Art-historians tend to reserve the term Romantic for the work of the first thirty years of the nineteenth century, beginning, let us say, with Turner and Goya, and ending with Delacroix. Thereafter, as in the history of the novel, Romanticism gives way to Realism, just as Realism in turn gives way to Impressionism, Symbolism or Naturalism. This general way of proceeding – what we could call the Art-Historical – answers the problematic questions about Romanticism by ignoring them. No matter how minutely the formal structures of the work that falls inside the agreed period are examined, its real nature and significance can only be appreciated when we try to define the way in which it intrinsically differs from the work which comes before and after it. The 'feel' of the art of Wordsworth, Turner, Delacroix and Beethoven differs profoundly and significantly from that of any art that came before it: however reductively we try to find equivalents for their individual qualities in the art of earlier periods, there will always remain the Romantic quality of the whole, and this pervasive quality cannot be properly appreciated simply by isolating the work in time and submitting it to the same kind of formal analysis as we apply to the art of the Baroque or the Classical periods, with no consideration of its 'Romantic' properties.

According to another way of dealing with the problem of Romanticism – what we could call the typological – Romanticism is a state of mind, a kind of artistic temperament, the opposite of which is the Classical. This dichotomy is a by-product of the great age of German art-history, and follows the typological dichotomies of Heinrich Wölfflin (*Barock* and *Classical*).[5] What is generally today thought of as characteristically Romantic, in fact, is what Wölfflin called *Barock*, and we can use the two terms interchangeably. Thus, Rubens could be described as Romantic, Van Dyck as Classical; Shakespeare as Romantic, Ben Jonson as Classical; and so on. Alternatively, *Barock* (or Romanticism) can be seen as appearing historically in alternation with its temperamental or typological opposite, according to the needs of man at the time. The classic exposition of this kind of view is Worringer's *Abstraktion und Einfühlung*,[6] though his theory is so complicated by questions of compensation that it is dangerous to apply it outside the areas chosen by Worringer himself. ('Cool' abstraction, for instance, could be conceived as evidence of the Classical temper; on the other hand it could be seen as Romantic, in so far as it is understood by Worringer as a symptom of fear and insecurity in man.) As applied to Romanticism itself, this view of things inverts the error of the art-historical view. If the art-historical view ignores the 'intrinsic' properties of Romanticism by concentrating all its attention on chronology, the typological view ignores the historical dimension of Romanticism by concentrating attention exclusively on certain qualities Romanticism seems to share with the art of other periods. We could grant, for the sake of argument, that Rubens had certain qualities which appealed to Romantic artists and, even, were 'typically' Romantic. But such a view still fails to explain the deep and decisive differences which exist between the art of Rubens and that of his Romantic disciple, Eugène Delacroix, who might, for the sake of argument, be granted to be typologically similar. What was to be explained by the typological argument is thus precisely what remains unexplained.

The most intellectually respectable attempt to define Romanticism – the epistemological – focuses attention on its theory of mind and traces to German Idealist reaction against the Enlightenment–empiricist attempts to reduce the mind to a passive collector of mental traces the quintessentially Romantic conception of Imagination as creative force overmastering the bounds of sensory experience and creating horizons and values transcending mere associationism. Like all the theories I have considered already, this view contains a certain amount of truth and cannot be wholly discounted. Yet by itself it explains little. Poets and artists plunder their philosophers fairly randomly, and there is little evidence that Kant offered the Romantics more accommodating models than Spinoza or Plato. Much of the great Romantic poetry apparently owes nothing to the Transcendentalist critique of mind; nor is there anything especially Romantic in Transcendentalism itself, though there can appear to be, when, as in Emerson, for instance, it is given a Wordsworthian coloration. Rational to the point of neurosis,

Kant himself would appear to be the very negation of the spirit of Romanticism, and his fruitful disagreement with Hume has no real implications for the artist or the believer in deeper-than-rational drives in man. Kantian man is as colourless an abstraction as ever limped out of the pages of a moralist's textbook, and it is hard to see the essential relationship between Transcendentalist theories of mind and the art of Romanticism. This is not to deny that there is a certain structural analogy between Kant's Transcendental Ego and Blake's Poetic Genius, for instance, nor that certain poets (notably Coleridge) exploited aspects of the Kantian critique for their own purposes. Essentially, the Kantian theory of mind affords no more sustenance for the particular hungers of modern man than those of Hume. Value gets into empiricism, as into Transcendentalism, and neither philosophical tradition is intrinsically more charitable to poetry and the human needs poets believed they were providing for. An outstanding proof of this is Kierkegaard's essentially Romantic rejection of the super-Transcendentalist, Hegel. The Romantic conception of the Imagination as redeeming and spiritually uplifting force is quite alien and irrelevant to Kantian Idealism, and owes its origins to a complex of causes both more limited and more remote. The more remote cause I have already touched on: the ancient conception of poetry as spiritual power greater than Reason. The closer-at-hand cause is the social and historical situation in which the Romantics found themselves, and out of the conflict with which they made their art. By concentrating attention too exclusively upon the (undoubted) similarities between Romantic views of the Imagination and Transcendentalist theories of mind, the epistemological view also fails to comprehend the extent to which both Transcendentalism and Romanticism are symptomatic. Once again, the real nature of the Romanticism is neglected.

What we need is an approach which accepts the historical actuality of Romanticism and understands that to analyse Romantic art in its forms and intentions is to explain its historical situation, and vice versa. Such an approach must, I believe, in part accept a sociological element in criticism. The errors of the various views I have considered above stem from their attempts to deal with art in isolation from the general cultural and historical situation in which it is always grounded. This is not to say that I endorse what one might call an archaeological sociology of literature, treating the work of art as the archaeologist treats the stones, broken stelae and fragmentary zephyrs of Troy or Mycenae, as clues to a reality other than themselves. As symptomatic structures, works of art preserve certain homologies with the social and economic structures of their time, and are important sources of information about human history: every work of art is, *inter alia*, an important social document, and it is foolish to think that it can be somehow 'above' such things. On the other hand, art can be seen as something we understand better by its being approached through a prior consideration of the facts surrounding its birth. But whether he accepts art as being explained by the historical facts, or as, on the contrary, itself throwing light on history, the sociologist of literature is guilty of reductivism unless he accepts that the work of art is a source of experience otherwise unattainable and that this experience is its real value. The criticism which fails to take the 'aesthetic' experience generated by the work of art as its first object ignores precisely that quality in virtue of which the work is to be valued. This does not mean that we can ignore the socio-historical facts in our interpretation of the work of art. If we are primarily concerned with the work's 'aesthetic' identity (the source of the identifying experience it offers), we are still obliged to acknowledge that this identity is only to be grasped through the contingent properties which constitute it. That is, though we must study not the *background* of works of art but their formal intensions, we must see that these formal intensions only came into existence in collaboration with time and the historical process. Once the forms come into existence, they pursue their own quasi-autonomous existence, but they are never really autonomous. They can only be enjoyed when they are understood, and they can only be understood when their relationship to the society that produced them is understood.

In the case of Romanticism, it is generally acknowledged that Romantic art is related in some way to the French and Industrial revolutions. The violence of the one set of facts 'explains' or parallels the irruptive nature of the other. We tend to associate – even if we ignore the association in our actual criticism – the despair, the excitement, the solitude and the frequent irrationality of Romantic art with the emergence of the new society out of the ruins of *l'ancien régime*. There is general acceptance, too, of the psychical and societal phenomena variously categorised as symptoms of alienation. A sense that we are living in a 'destitute time', to use Hölderlin's phrase, permeates both the art and the criticism of the Romantic age. It would be foolish to try to deny that this general, imprecise *mélange* of stresses and preoccupations is characteristic of 'Romantic' art and thought. What we must not do is attempt to derive the art and thought (the superstructural features in general) from any precisely defined base. No writer has ever been able to establish any such derivations or generations: the attempt to establish patterns of cause-and-effect between the art of the Romantic period and the various political and historical processes that lie behind and within them must be abandoned as theoretically unsound, yielding merely circular fulfilments of the theorist's own requirements.

Such 'correlations' of history and art are useful only if regarded as symptomatic, as defining properties of art and literature themselves in need of a clarification and understanding. No literature is to be explained by postulation of prior historical, economic or political event. At the same time, the art is itself made up of these events and processes: it is no less than a predicament. The purpose of the following pages is to clarify the nature of the various elements of the predicament that is Romanticism. Certain of these elements have, as I have mentioned above, accurately been outlined and identified: an emphasis upon individuality rather than collectivity, a certain ontological and teleological anxiety – such qualities can genuinely be located within Romantic works, and validly be called specifically Romantic. But these qualities are in turn part of general predicament, and it is with this predicament that we must be concerned in our efforts to understand Romanticism. Obviously nothing less than a description of the total state of affairs – cultural, linguistic, political, societal, economic, philosophical, religious – is really sufficient to accomplish this understanding. Equally obviously, no critic – least of all the present one – is capable of providing such a description. Such a description, moreover, would embrace not only the art and literature generally thought of as Romantic, but all the subsequent art, both the realist fiction that dominates the later nineteenth century, and the modernist art that, apparently, reacts against this realism in the twentieth. Realism falls within the Romantic territory; so does avant-garde modernism with all its devices (irony, fracture, dislocation, dissonance).

This last point is particularly important, because what has become known as modernist criticism has based itself upon a rejection of Romanticism and realism supposedly implicit in the great avant garde artists of this century. If this rejection is a genuine one, then we are confronted with a reaction against the very things which, according to my view of the matter, constitute that historical predicament of which avant garde modernism is itself a symptom. It is with this problem that we must now be concerned.

(i) MODERNIST DISSOCIATIONISM

Modernist criticism, from its beginnings in the Cubist period, has always eschewed the 'positivistic' theory of the 'demon of progress in the arts';[7] yet it has itself generally assumed the reality of a historical process. Its very basis, in fact, reflects the essentially historicistic notion of a reaction against a phase of culture felt to be decadent and anomalous. The myth of modernism derives its persuasiveness from the skill with which its first proponents exposed the fallacies of Romanticism and Realism. The Romantics assumed that poetry – where good – was 'sincere', and the product of a desire or need to 'express' personality or experience; that it is 'the expression or uttering forth of feeling', in Mill's representative phrase.[8] If lyric poetry remained, as in Mill, 'more eminently and peculiarly poetry than any other',[9] Realism, with its quasi-scientific theories of explanation and mimesis, became the ideal of fiction: novels were to be, like Hume's 'ideas', representations surpassed in force only by the reality itself. Modernist criticism has always adopted the reproving attitude to both Romantic poetry and to realist fiction suggested in T. E. Hulme's and T. S. Eliot's earlier essays, but most brilliantly articulated, perhaps, in Ortega y Gasset's little *esquisse*, *The Dehumanisation of Art*. Ortega distinguished between modern anti-realism and impersonality on the one hand, and Romantic seriousness and self-expressive realism on the other. The Romantics saw themselves as prophets – as something *more than* just artists – while the realists' concern for telling the truth about the world constituted a 'maximum aberration in the history of art'.[10]

Both this conviction of an importance outside the materials of their art and the preoccupation with 'reflecting' reality are also taken by the neo-modernist critics as signs of the Romantic-realist heresies. The Romantics, Gabriel Josipovici argues, mistook the nature of language and the purpose of art. They believed that the purpose of poetry was to try to express '*everything*, the totality of experience, unfettered by the rules and limitations of conventions and consciousness',[11] and the attempt was bound, he says, to lead to self-destruction – Rimbaud's retreat into silence, Wagner's artistically suicidal *Gesammt-kunstwerk*. In point of fact, Josipovici believes, language is limited by its rules and conventions, and its purpose is not to commune, but to communicate. The Romantics wanted to dissolve the Self into the Absolute, yet at the same time they wanted desperately to find and be *themselves* – not social beings but individual subjectivities. Such was the Romantics' dilemma and it led them (according to Josipovici) to overstress one of the twin drives of post-Renaissance art (expression) at the expense of the other (mimesis). The Realists made exactly the opposite mistake, overdoing the mimesis at the expense both of expression and of artifice, and mistaking the illusions of the imaginative worlds for the 'truth' – reality, what exists 'out there', as opposed to inside the covers of the book.

Josipovici is unfortunately too miserly with his evidence to permit any very concrete disagreement with his 'assessment' of the Romantics: he moves from Schleiermacher in full flow, wishing to dissolve into the cosmos, to Rimbaud in flight, admitting the whole venture to have been mistaken, by way of Nietszche on Wagner, concluding with a few choice bits of Swinburne to show that the Romantics as a whole disregarded 'meaning' in their pursuit of association and 'music'. He makes no mention at all of the major Romantic poets, of either England or Germany (to say nothing of Russia and Poland), so that the assumption that the Romantic poets did not – deliberately, skilfully and professionally – get their effects through the use not the abuse of language, is never exposed to the text of serious poetry. The same is true of his treatment of Realist fiction. No evidence is offered, we are just asked to accept that the fictions of Dickens, Tolstoy, Balzac and company can be equated with the childish 'imaginations' of Proust's Marcel.[12] Whereas Dickens, George Eliot, Dostoevsky and the rest of them expected their illusions to be taken for reality, Proust knew that there was a difference between the 'imaginative' world and the reality of life. By reminding the reader of the essentially fictional nature of the text and thus of the relations between this text and the reader's own reality, the modernist writer restores the world to the reader, so that he experiences 'a joy as great as that which floods through us when, looking at long last, with Dante, into the eyes of God, we sense the entire universe bound up into one volume and understand what it is to be a man'.[13]

Yet although Mr Josipovici is apt to be carried away (we should not, we are told, be able to *see* Velazquez's *Las Meninas* without benefit of Picasso's caricatures of it),[14] he is an eloquent advocate of the modernist cause, and this cause is widespread enough to require serious criticism. Underlying Mr Josipovici's criticism is the myth of modernism – that of the intelligent Prince Charming who breaks into the fortress of the Western psyche, steals past the cobwebs of Realist and Romantic verisimilitude, and kisses the beguiled reader awake with the touch of his ironies. Yet underlying *this* enabling piece of mythology, in turn, there is a particular conception of language: fundamentally it is to Eliot's dissociation of sensibility theory that neo-modernism is indebted. Eliot's thesis – picked to pieces and left to rot long since – is nevertheless sound enough structurally to withstand its own errors. The underlying evolution that took English poetry from metaphysical conceit and catachresis through Augustan lucidity to Romantic naturalness is accurately enough mirrored in Eliot's scenario, for all its quasi-theological implications of a state of Grace, followed by a Fall and subsequent state of sin. The poetry involved feels roughly as Eliot's theory leads us to expect. The theory can, moreover, be read along different conceptual parameters, as an alienation-theory calibrating deep changes in the Western psyche with changes in the organisation of society, or as a purely linguistic theory describing the rise of realism. Eliot had a foot in two camps of course: he was both intellectualist and modernist. And Cambridge 'intellectualist' criticism shared both Eliot's distaste for Romanticism and his modernist methodological bias: re-directing attention from the emotions and ethical contents 'expressed in' literary texts to the texts themselves and to the nature of the reader's participation in them through the act of reading, they yet hold on to a conception of literature's moral and psychic *telos* – that is, to the notion of a *work* rather than a mere *text*. Richards' pioneering examinations of the act of reading, Empson's archaeological structuralism and Leavis's attempts to structuralise the value-judgement, remain generally and decisively important in the history of modernism.

It was Eliot who crystallised modernism into a historicistic theory of language implicitly or explicitly rejecting the presuppositions of Romanticism–realism. His critical emphasis upon Dante as a fulcrum of European literature, his distaste for Romantic libertarianism in particular and for Whiggishness and 'inner light' Protestantism in general, are accompanied by the rejection of perspectival frame, humanist subjectivism and homophonic self-expression in his own verse. Eliot was at one with Cubism and the new music of Stravinsky and Schönberg in helping Western man put himself outside what were now felt to be the blinkers of self-expressive realism, and it is with the rise of just that characteristic realism that we are concerned in dealing with the Romantic predicament in general. Neo-modernism has drawn on a number of sources to expand Eliot's dissociation-theory in support of the claim that the literature dominant over the two hundred years beginning with the founding of the Royal Society in 1660 and ending, say, with the First World War, had based itself upon a superficial and mistaken view of the nature of language and, therefore, of literature.

Cleanth Brooks it was who, following Eliot, first directed attention to the linguistics of the Royal Society and its role in impoverishing the language of poetry thereafter.[15] It has been fashionable to do so ever since. The Trotskyite modernism of Peter Ackroyd follows Brooks and Josipovici in attributing the divorce of rhetoric and logic directly to the language-theories of Sprat and Locke.[16] Ackroyd distinguishes between the old 'modernism' of the empiricists (Locke's 'new way of ideas') – which is simply the new realism – and a second modernism which has returned language to its pre-Lockean status. Again, in Ackroyd, Realists and Romantics both mistook the function of literature. They assumed that literature was made by individual men working upon individual experience through a common language to produce novels, plays and poems: they thought that books should not just *be* something; but be *about* something. In Mr Ackroyd's version of the modernist myth, we were awakened from the tedious moralistic humanism of Baudelaire, Wordsworth, and the rest of them, by the kiss of de Sade, Kierkegaard, Nietzsche and Mallarmé. With Marcel (Proust)'s lecture to Albertine to guide him, Mr Josipovici was able to accommodate certain Realists and show that they were really uninterested in their ostensible content, being really concerned with the illusion-reality problem. Mr Ackroyd has no room for such right-wing revisionism. They are all swept out – Goethe, Tolstoy, Baudelaire, the lot. Even T. S. Eliot is only a genuine modernist in bits: when he talks about 'the human condition' ('each in his prison thinking only of the key') he writes 'very bad poetry indeed'.[17] For following Roland Barthes's (interrogative) tip that the verb 'to write' is intransitive (though the N.E.D. says it's transitive as well), Ackroyd indicts almost every Western writer of the past two hundred years of failing to understand that the writer's task is not to produce poems, plays and novels *about* things, but simply to make a *littérature* – self-generating, referent-less, purposeless.

Now, the reason why the Realist writers all went so badly wrong, we are told, was that they followed Locke and the empiricists in misapprehending the function of language. Sprat had insisted that 'Words . . . are to be stamped in the image of things; they are to be plain and they are to be transparent. They are to reflect "things".'[18] (Transparent *and* reflecting? Windows and mirrors? This sort of confusion doesn't occur in the empiricists.) Locke, for his part, demands recognition of the fact that 'Words are man-made and derived from natural objects', so that language is 'the result of an artificial contract'.[19] (Can a contract be other than artificial? It is another revealingly slack phrase.) From these ideas, Ackroyd argues, arose the notion of 'autonomous meaning'. Inventing 'meaning' for language, the empiricists (and rationalists, for their mathematically orientated semantics preceded empiricism here) robbed language of its autonomy and so paved the way for the Humanist literature of the following two centuries: the Humanists assumed that poems and novels were bag-like things holding contents, because the empiricists had argued that words were glass-like things showing meanings: 'the banishment of language as autonomous and as an object of knowledge makes way for the primacy of Man'.[20]

This anti-humanism is clearly in line with Eliot's Anglicanism and Josipovici's (implicit) Catholicism. In each case there is a distaste for scientific liberalism and a suggestion both that the Romantic–Realist tradition somehow *chose* its predicament, and that the basis of their choice was Protestant wilfulness – the hell-for-leather drive towards Truth. As it is, we have been landed with a literature of contents, fostered by a linguistics of 'meaning'. Now such a view, condemning Romanticism and Realism as being too concerned with certain ethical and psycho-spiritual contents to understand the true function of literature, makes certain assumptions as to the nature of the language and the possible role of language within the modern period. But it makes equally important assumptions about literature and the role of language in the *old* world – the world before the vitiating influence of the empiricists and the experimental scientists of the Royal Society robbed the Word of its 'sacramental status'.[21] The neo-modernist position assumes, in fact, a certain pre-Lockean language (autonomous, an 'object of study in its own right', sacramental) and postulates a pre-empiricist literature (self-sufficient, referent-less, contentless). Are these assumptions justified?

(ii) LANGUAGE AND ITS ORIGINATION

Modern linguists tend to regard the question of the origins of language as being beyond testing and therefore simply too speculative for serious study.[22] Whether we adopt a purely utilitarian view of the matter, however, and trace the beginnings of language to man's perception of the possibilities in grunts and howls, or take a higher sacral view, there is little doubt that names once had magic status. It is feasible to describe the whole course of man's emergence into his humanity in terms of his religious consciousness – his primal discrimination of sacred and profane areas of experience as reified first in the concept of *mana* ('the minimum definition of religion'), then in the 'momentary gods' described by Usener.[23] In this process, the role of language is absolutely essential. The momentary God is named – in awe, fear, reverence – and the name then pursues its own existence, independent. Such is the nature of language that its symbols, though initially formed in response to a particular situation, can be used in other circumstances and at other times. Language, let us say, begins with things, events, powers outside itself, yet becomes self-contained, so that the word appropriated from external reality (without which it would not have come into existence) now behaves as if it had its own identity and reality.

However, the word retains some of that primal mythic quality when, in Ernst Cassirer's words, 'it is not a mere conventional symbol, but is merged with its object in an indissoluble unity'.[24] The momentary God that had sprung into existence (neither 'in' man's consciousness, nor outside it) from a particular situation of shock, a confrontation with death and fear, continues to exist afterwards in the Word, so that He can be 'invoked'. Such is man's respect for the God that His reality or spirit appears or becomes present when His name is mentioned. This feeling persists in the higher religions, in their laws against blasphemy and taking the Lord's name in vain, and in the ritual of baptism, where the child is bathed '*in* God's name'. So close is the identity of language and religious feeling, Cassirer observes, that it may be said 'that the concept of Godhead really receives its first concrete development and richness through language'.[25] Even today, as Bernard Shaw noted, the hard-swearing atheist, with his 'Gods' and 'Christs' and 'Damns' pays homage to the power within the words he uses. Such a feeling persists also in our sense of meaningfulness and appropriateness of speech. Even people who do not know the rules (illiterates and children) adhere to the underlying laws of right relations between word and world. Nonsense is a kind of blasphemy, and Nietzsche's perception that to believe in grammar is to stick with God goes right to the heart of our language venture.[26]

Man's very essence as man, then, is deeply involved with his use of language, so much so that he has been called, with some justice, the language animal.[27] Yet such a description surely does less than full justice either to the truth or to man himself. For it becomes clear in examining the sacramental view of language that man's capacity for language is contingent on his prior capacity for what we must call a religious response to existence. The sacredness of the Word itself in the earliest religious phases testifies to the power not of language but of the *mana* or *tabu* thought to reside in things, in places or in events. It was *mana* and *tabu* that generated the word, not vice versa, and the word retains its magic or sacramental status only so long as man believes in the forces behind or within it which generated the name in the first place.

Such a belief, as we have already noted, persists in apparently trivialised forms in our own blasphemous speech, and our vague unease when God's name *is* taken in vain; more interestingly in our deep-seated, ineradicable respect for the forms of right speech. But these very exceptions to the general scepticism governing our current use of language force upon us a certain conclusion. Whether we account for the rise of language in terms of gradually clarified systems of communicative grunts passed among hunters, or in Cassirer's more exalted terms of religious crises of *mana*-discrimination, language is instrumental in its very essence, and never has been and never can be autonomous. The modern de-sacralisation of the Word, therefore, is not a by-product of the empiricists' faulty view of the functioning of language but an inevitable by-product of western man's changing *Weltanschauung*. What Eliot's 'dissociation of sensibility' theory really charts, that is to say, is the evolution of man's beliefs about the universe. This evolution can be described in terms of man's changing view of language, but only if it is recognised that in so doing we are talking about his underlying views of reality. The new theories and critiques of language which began to appear in England during the later seventeenth and earlier eighteenth centuries should not mislead us into attributing to language itself the causation of the intellectual and cultural developments of the next two hundred years. The new language theories are, to the contrary, a by-product of a fundamental re-orientation in man's relations with reality. The new realism of language does not fix these relations, it reflects them. (Though it, in turn, becomes an influence of course.) The process was irreversible and inevitable. When belief decays, it does so for reasons over which man has no control: we cannot choose *not* to believe in God, any more than we can choose *to* believe in Him. And to explain *that* fact it is not sufficient to analyse our use of words (as linguistic analysis used to suppose that it was); we must look to the psychological, spiritual and other facts informing our use of the words.

To believe that man could control the way his *Weltanschauung* and his views of language developed in the modern age is the characteristic delusion of the more sacramentally inclined modernism, with its conviction that the once unified sensibility of western man was wilfully split asunder by pig-headed protestants who misapprehended the nature of language. A number of men have made significant contributions to our understanding of language – Locke, Hume, von Humboldt, Frege, Russell, Wittgenstein, Saussure, Austin and Chomsky spring to mind; but the room for manoeuvre available to these men has always been strictly limited: there are certain conditions which can neither be ignored nor created.

Primary among these is, of course, the growth of scientific materialism and the concomitant decline of traditional religious belief. Now this process, again, was slow and inexorable. It is invidious to select any single cause or group of causes. There were no causes in fact, only symptoms. Mr Josipovici pins the blame on rebelliousness, taking the year 1264 as the high point of Church authority, with a slow decline, continuous but given a fillip now and then from Luther and others – until our own age.[28] But the rejection of Rome's authority was a symptom, not a cause. In point of fact, it was the pantheism of such men as Giordano Bruno and Tommaso Campanella, and the naturalism of Bernardino Telesio rather than the protest of Martin Luther that really spelt out the deterioration in Christian belief.[29] The primal religious phase of *mana* postulates a clear separation of sacred and profane, of significant and non-significant. And such a discrimination remains part of religious belief. The Christian church has always been hostile to the notion that God is not only every*where* but every*thing*. Such a phase (pantheism as we usually call it) is distinctly decadent, and was outlawed by the Church as heretical: Bruno was not only excommunicated by the Church of Rome, but by the Calvinists.[30] In annihilating the distinction between the sacred and the profane, Bruno degraded the Word far more troublingly than Luther's rebelliousness did. Here we find the seeds of that 'hideous hypothesis' the atheist Hume found so disgusting in Spinoza, *deus natura*, or, where all is God, nothing is God. God is reduced to his *materia*, and here begins His dying.

This is, of course, to hang far too much upon Giordano Bruno, who is not important except as symptom. What matters is that we do not mistake the nature of the empiricist revolt. When the empiricists, following the rationalists, stipulated that words should be clear signs standing for clear ideas, they were in no way deviating from the principles of all philosophical practice. In no previous philosophical literature will we find any tendency to treat language as autonomous, or to regard words as other than clear signs for simple or complex entities. The great epistemological debates of classical philosophy (those between Platonists and Aristotelians, for instance, or realists and nominalists) cast no doubts on the *function* of words: what they were at odds about was the status of the entities referred to in their words. In all cases, we notice, the natural assumption in linguistic theory is that language primarily concerns itself with names for things. Empiricism and rationalism are orthodox in this. What is new in the empiricist critique is the underlying feeling it reveals as to the function of language. In all previous philosophy, the function of language is assumed. Contrary to what Mr Ackroyd says, indeed, it was only with empiricism that language came to be studied as an object in its own right. Saussure's debt to Locke is openly acknowledged in the *Cours Générale de Linguistique*. What is less readily recognised, perhaps, is the significance of the fact that the first suggestion of the need for a semiology occurred in one of the great empiricist landmarks. It is no accident that man's first attempt at a theory of signs accompanies the rise of empiricism and philosophy of science. On the contrary, it is absolutely crucial. What undid the knot of rationalism – that nexus which had made it possible for Descartes to get from the *cogito* to the outer ends of the universe by logical steps – was the empiricist suggestion that our words are merely signs. With Locke's critique of language, the signifier slides away from the signified as a child's transfer slides away from the coloured picture somewhat fuzzily left on his wrist. If our words *are* mere signs, mere learned conventions, with no reality behind them, our confidence in what we can sensibly assert is far more devastatingly shaken than it had ever been by the questionings of sceptics and materialists. Neither scepticism nor materialism, in fact, is singular to empiricism. None of the empiricists was a sceptic in the strict sense of disbelieving in the existence of the material world or of anybody but himself, though Kant mistakenly assumed that they were. And there is a long history of materialism in both East and West, beginning with the doctrine of *lokayata* in India and the atomism of Leucippus and Democritus in Greece.[31] Nobody actually believes that the material world does not exist, or that nobody exists outside himself, or that there are not serious differences between mind and matter: such opinions are always really about the use of terms. What Hume and Locke did was much more damaging than such scepticisms: they threw in doubt the tool of language itself, suggesting that words are mere signs agreed on by contract, and then, in consequence, that whatever 'meaning' they hold is literally put there by man. It is once again, exactly the opposite of what Mr Ackroyd says: far from inventing meaning for words, the empiricists destroyed the capacity for words to embody meaning. It was only a matter for refinement and time for 'meaning' to emerge as either the structure of the word (structuralism) or its use (linguistic analysis). Of course, when men turned to find ways of giving weight to their utterances in the new dispensation, it was to find that the only criterion they trusted was that of sense-experience. It was not merely the philosophy of experience but, gradually, our whole Western way of looking at things that accepted that words *stand for* nothing, but are signs for the interpretation of which we have only sensory experience as a guide. And both structuralist linguistics and linguistic analysis take place inside the scope of empiricist philosophy. It is not important that these disciplines have severally widened and subtilised the empiricist account of language and meaning: Saussure, Wittgenstein and Austin merely opened up the study of linguistic behaviour. None of them gives any reason for abandoning the principles of meaningful utterance laid down by Hume, that if a statement contain neither 'abstract reasoning concerning quantity or number', nor 'experimental reasoning concerning matter of fact', it should be committed to the flames.[32] This theory of meaning has held good for two hundred years: it still defines the extent of our beliefs about the universe. No serious man today thinks it possible to revive the metaphysical entities destroyed by Hume, Berkeley and Locke, though we sometimes evade the issue by exaggerating the discrepancy between empiricist meaning-criteria and the actual possibilities of verbal behaviour.

In general, our social, political and philosophical behaviour acknowledges the force of the empiricist critique: the empiricists destroyed, in turn, the notion of 'innate ideas', the notion of a substantial Self, of inherent and necessary causes in things, of God and all other 'metaphysical' substance, of moral absolutes and aesthetic norms. It is not only philosophers who adhere to the letter of empiricist law: the man-in-the-street's general mental and moral behaviour also tells us that the world the empiricists helped bring into being is, for better or worse, *our* world.

The notion common in some critical circles that the 'new' realism of English empiricism represents some kind of aberration in man's relations with language that can be reversed by 'once more' treating language as a self-sufficient and independent

entity, therefore, is a mere pipe-dream. The empiricist demand
for 'clear signs' standing for clear meanings is as old as
philosophy itself. All that the empiricist critiques testify to is the
fact that certain procedures in philosophy and in common
parlance made demands that could no longer be met, that some of
the counters peddled by philosophers and metaphysicians now
seemed to be monopoly money, with no reality to back them up.
That the empiricists – and with them, eventually, Western man
in general – felt this, was of course entirely a matter of man's
general development: once again, the problem is not primarily
one of language, but of *Weltanschauung*. In earlier philosophy, we
may say, although the need for terms to be clear, unequivocal
and referential was recognised as fully as it was by the
empiricists, the Word was undoubted, it was not felt as a *sign*, but
as a reality, and this *un*awareness of the function of language was
the guarantee of philosophical processes.[33] And this meant that
things were accepted in their integrity, as backed by God.

(iii) LOGIC AND RHETORIC

What *The World and the Book*, *Notes for a New Culture*, *Logic and
Rhetoric*, *Modern Poetry and the Tradition*, *The Order of Things*, *The
Disinherited Mind*, and all the other dissociation-of-sensibility
books really register is awareness of the change that comes over
western writing and culture over the two hundred years between
the middle of the seventeenth and the middle of the nineteenth
centuries. This change, to say it again, *is* (rather than is due to)
an inexorable and irreversible change in *Weltanschauung*, in the
way we think the universe ticks. Literature, as part of this
process, takes on new forms as the period evolves. Now these new
forms and methods were noted by the dissociation-of-sensibility
critics as if they were part of an aberrant decline, that was both
willed and yet blundered myopically into. Logic got divorced
from rhetoric, much as Pope forecast in *The Dunciad* (itself an
accurate barometer of cultural change and the first real statement
of the dissociation-of-sensibility theses):

There foamed rebellious Logic, gagged and bound,
There, stripped, fair Rhetoric languished on the ground.

'Dullness' – the new monarch – is poetry without rhetoric. It was 'dullness' which Byron, Pope's Romantic acolyte, castigated in the bard of the new realism:

> Next comes the dull disciple of thy school,
> That mild apostate from poetic rule,
> The simple Wordsworth . . .
> ('English Bards and Scotch Reviewers')

If 'the simple Wordsworth' represents poetry without rhetoric, 'gentle Coleridge' can stand for poetry shorn of logic, to whom 'obscurity's a welcome guest', and who 'takes a pixy for a muse'.

Now in fact, a certain tension had always existed between logic and rhetoric, and we would do well to question the hypostatised whole or non-dissociated sensibility that is so often supposed once to have existed. Aristotle, we remember, recommends the use of enthymeme (incomplete syllogism) in a speech, rather than syllogism proper, because enthymemes are easier to follow, i.e. more persuasive.[34] This incompatibility between the needs of persuasion and the demands of logic remains unresolved in Aristotle, as in every later writer. Truth and right-thinking should be enough to convince, yet as Gorgias – and Hitler – demonstrated, the wrong case can be argued as persuasively as the right. Rhetoric was never, of course, allowed to be a full account of discourse and its fluctuating popularity follows the graph of social and political history. At its strongest in the Greek free cities, it declines to the forensic in repressive Republican Rome, and still further to the academic in the dictatorship of Imperial Rome, where it had already become a conscious cultural game, requiring imitation of classical models.[35] Obviously when our modern critics use the word, they are thinking of the elaborate inventories of linguistic effects made up by the theorists of Renaissance Italy. But when Petrus Ramus – generally credited with bringing about the end of rhetoric – isolated Quintilian's *inventio* and *dispositio* (roughly the argument and logic of the case) from style and delivery, and stipulated the latter alone as the true concerns of rhetoric, he was only exaggerating a schism that had always existed. A sense of the competing claims of 'truth' (to which a plain style was better suited) and manneristic delivery (making rhetoric an 'art in itself') goes back to ancient Greece, with Aristotle's uncertainties and the analysis of Lysius's manipulative rhetoric in the *Phaedrus*. Certainly, rhetoric died under Ramus's ministrations, but its demise could long have been predicted.[36]

There would seem, then, never to have been any marriage (ideal or otherwise) of rhetoric and logic. It had always been felt that logic in rhetoric made for a better argued case, but this applies to the art of persuasion (i.e. oratory), not to all literature. In fact, as I have suggested, the history of rhetoric needs to be related to social and political history, rather than to literary theory proper. To treat the rhetorical textbooks of the fifteenth and sixteenth centuries as containing a formula for a sound literature is certainly wrong. The mannerism of late sixteenth and early seventeenth century poetry (in England, Spain and Italy, most notably) seems now to have been a brilliant carbuncle on the skin of European literature rather than deeply characteristic of it.

Michel Foucault's version of the dissociation-of-sensibility thesis, 'The prose of the world',[37] proffers the analogical hypertrophy of sixteenth century thinkers such as Campanella and Paracelsus as if they represented the kind of ideal union of reason and emotion, sign and meaning, which T. S. Eliot postulated in Shakespeare and the Metaphysical poets. In fact, the mania for establishing an order based upon similitudes which we witness in the pseudo-science of Paracelsus (doctor and alchemist, visionary and charlatan) is anything but secure; it is rather a neurotic attempt to hold onto the faith that had passed, and which required no intellectual vindication of the kind attempted in the *Liber Librorum*, the *Traité des signatures*, and the *Realis philosophiae*. Here is that decadence diagnosed so acutely by Huizinga,[38] the analogical mania neither religion nor philosophy, calling upon the gods of alchemy and pseudo-science alike, and, inevitably recurring to that neo-Platonism which has surfaced regularly in European thought at moments of doubt and uncertainty. For the rest, M. Foucault's imprisonment within French tradition leads him to ignore the really decisive moment in European philosophical history – the advent of Locke and the empiricists. Foucault's virtuosity has impressed a number of English theorists, such as Peter Ackroyd, but I can see no significant addition in Foucault's work to the lines laid down by Eliot fifty years ago. To invoke the associationism of Paracelsus – a mode of thought reaching its truest forms in the mysticism of

Jakob Boehme, the paranoid parallelisms of Swedenborg, and finally in the delightful mystifications of Sir Thomas Browne – is to weaken the argument for a linguistic wholeness existing before empiricism.

For does not the example of Petrus Ramus tell us that it was not the empiricists who split rhetoric from logic, poetry from truth, metaphor from statement, but the drift of Western society itself? That, once again, we are concerned with an 'inexorable' process of evolution and change, which we must fail to understand if we apply to it the wrong methods of explanation? In relation to human history, literature can always be treated indexically as a series of fragments telling us 'how it was' at any particular point in time. It is the fallacy of archaeological sociology of literature, I have noted above, to treat all literature as if it were nothing but indexical. Yet the fallacy of imputing to indices or symptoms an excessively causative role is, if anything, still more damaging than the archaeological fallacy. Literature did not 'decline' (if indeed it did) because Luther questioned Rome's authority, or Bacon regarded metaphor as a kind of lie, or Sprat said that 'words are to be stamped in the image of things'. Undoubtedly, Protestantism itself is more than a mere index: it is itself 'the way things went'. My contention here is that nothing could have stopped things going that way, that Rome was challenged because it was challengeable, that the pantheistic heresies of Giordano Bruno and Tommaso Campanella, quite as much as the arrogance of Luther, showed how much of its power the Christian Word had lost. Of course, the part played in this by Galileo was considerable: we may judge how far things had gone by contrasting Duns Scotus's emphasis on the limited nature of reason and the dangers of thinking that we can ever explain or understand the Almighty with out intellects, with the sixteenth century intellectual's embarrassment at Rome's patent inability to explain the physical universe as well as Galileo.[39] It was of course the sight of Rome being 'caught out' that was so disastrous. Galileo's demonstration of the inaccuracy of the Christian account of the universe, as much as anything, finally destroyed the old authority of the Church, but it also confirmed that new reliance upon judgement and observation which the empiricists were to make their own. So much is commonplace cultural history. How then, in the face of so manifest a 'drift' of the tide, can we attribute the evolution of our literature in the past two hundred and fifty years to inadequate theories of language, or a wilful disobedience? The split between faith and reason is already far advanced before the sixteenth century draws to its close, making necessary a dissociation of the judging mind and the believing soul: our values and our reason were set asunder long before Bacon put pen to paper.

(iv) THE FALLACY OF MODERNISM

If the 'dissociation-of-sensibility' theorist replies to all this, 'Yes, I know; I just hate the way things have gone, even though I admit there was nothing anyone could do to prevent it; Dante is my ideal writer, and the fact that the circumstances (notably the union of faith and reason) which made for his synthesis simply disintegrated into others less suitable for it, doesn't concern me at all', [the position, incidentally suggested in T. S. Eliot's essays on Blake and Dante] – then he is unimpeachable. It is the position – more or less – of what we might call the entire Hegelian tradition, which has concluded, both in its Marxist and non-Marxist forms, simply that the conditions required to produce great art no longer obtain. This is that 'disinherited' state so eloquently described by Erich Heller:

> The notorious obscurity of modern poetry is due to the absence from our lives of commonly accepted symbols to represent and house our deepest feelings. And so these invade the empty shells of fragmentary memories, hermit-crabs in a sea of uncertain meaning.[40]

All dissociation-of-sensibility theories are covert alienation-theories, and it is alienation, in whatever form, which provides the underlying unity of bourgeois modernism. With the basic contentions of Hegelian alienation theory I do not wish to quarrel: I shall be concerned to demonstrate its accuracy. Certainly, modernists like Josipovici would do better to acknowledge their own cultural Hegelianism: they assume a process of 'decline' as inexorable as deplorable. But in their more reasonable forms, such theories reflect much that is actual and important.

What is to be questioned, though, is the assumption that, with

Romantic art and its characteristic realism and subjectivism, we enter upon a phase of art which falls away from the high ideals of earlier creation not through historical evolution (which is what Hegelian theories assume) but through false intellectual models, fallacious theories of art and thought and a generally myopic philosophy of mind. It is one thing to say that 'things' in their most general sense, have turned out badly for man. Quite another to suggest that they could have turned out otherwise if some of us had thought a bit more carefully. What I am concerned with in the present book is the general condition in which modern man exists, and the cultural consequences of that condition. I have suggested referring to Romanticism as a predicament because doing so helps us to avoid the solecism of either looking for hidden keys to a Romantic quality or, to the contrary, concluding that there is no such thing. But if the Romantic predicament is ours also, then the whole scenario of modernist theory must be abandoned: the idea that there is a right of way of thinking about language and art (i.e. non-naturalistic, non-mimetic), to which modernists like Mallarmé returned us after the exile of Romantic realism, must emerge as the greatest fallacy of recent cultural history. Modernism itself, to the contrary, will be seen as the logical and inevitable evolution of Romantic theory and practice – as the adaptation of modern writers to their peculiar cultural circumstances.

It is from this point of view that we must understand the modernist reaction against Romanticism and Realism, as a contrary movement within a general and unalterable tide. No less so must we understand the identifying characteristics of nineteenth century art itself. If we are to make sense of Cubism and Abstraction, of stream-of-consciousness and ironic displacement, we must first make sense of the imaginative condition of the great Romantic poets and Realist novelists and dramatists. If their characteristic subjectivism and realism are not to be dismissed (as I have tried to show that they cannot) as the aberrations of an ignorant and sentimental age, they must be so analysed that their role in the general cultural predicament becomes clear.

2 Romantic Subjectivity

(i) THE LEVELS OF THE TEXT

It was the various ethical, moral and psychological interests of the Romantic and post-Romantic writers which led to the modernist repudiation of their work as something of an artistic disaster. Consistently, both proponents and critics of Realist fiction and poetry had dealt with literature as if its value lay in its veracity, its faithfulness to certain experiences and social facts. When the modernist reaction took place, the first object of attack was the 'seriousness' of the Victorian writer-sage; the next was the wrong-headed preoccupation of critics with the life and opinions of the writer instead of with the discourse, the rhetoric of the work he produced, the writer's 'literature' – literature without contents such as was thought by some critics to have flourished in the days before Locke and company upset the apple cart. In fact, we nowhere locate the hypostatised literature without contents, existing for itself alone. In each case, we find that there is present, either avowedly or subtensively, a content, transpersonal, shared, societal. Whether or not the writer uses such contents to say something else, the content is always present: Dante's cosmology, Milton's wish 'to justify the ways of God to men', Shakespeare's themes of power and kinship, death. In every case literature is seen to revolve about a declared or implicit content. Certainly literature is also *en soi*: it always ends in something which is ultimately irrelevant to the original purposes and contents out of which it is made. But this does not mean that it can ever be produced *pour soi* – for itself alone. On the contrary, it cannot achieve its strange independence without having gone through the contents it must necessarily propose for itself.

We can describe the relationship of these themes and contents to the words on the page as we will. But there is, I submit, no intrinsic difference between the problems involved in such a description in relation to older literature and those aroused when we turn to Romanticism.[1]

24

The question of describing the contents of Romantic literature, is not one that presents any particular theoretical difficulties for the critic. Indeed, there are gains from having to make Romantic literature coherent with the classical and Renaissance literature, that preceded it, and the modernist literature that followed it. Art-historians have generally been more reasonable in this area than literary critics. The literary critic searching for guidance today will find more assistance, I believe, from Burkhardt, or Worringer, Wölfflin or Panofsky, than from any literary historian. Perhaps this is because of the manifest nature of pictorial symbolism: we cannot look at Giotto or Raphael and doubt that they were using certain conventionalised references and systems of reference based upon the social and religious life outside the artist himself. Such references have been well described by Erwin Panofsky.[2]

Panofsky discriminates between three layers of content in a painting. At the most basic level are the fundamental materials of representation – this stands for woman, that for shoe, and so on. (Significantly, in talking about painting we usually find ourselves saying, not that represents a woman, but 'That *is* a woman'.) The next level is that of iconography – the realm of motifs, symbols archetypes, which *uses* or draws upon the elements of the lower layer – Christian symbol, pagan mythology and so on. At the third and highest level, Panofsky refers to the actual work – that is, the particular use of both earlier layers to make a 'unique' work of art which has a particular meaning for the artist as for the viewer. This is the realm of 'intrinsic content'.

Such a schema makes it perfectly clear that when we speak of a great work of art we necessarily assume the existence of the first two layers of visual semantics: we accept, that is, the overtly objective and public contents along with those more 'personal' mannerisms, rhythms or emphases that compose these contents into the third order, a work of art that moves us deeply, or affects us as so many other works, which exploit the same contents, fail to. With incomparable common sense – common sense equalled only by his sensitivity – the great art-historian penetrates to the centre of that misty void in which so many modernist critics get lost. Certainly the work of art draws upon, *contains* objective formations or contents. But it is not reducible to them. The work of the literary or art-critic may begin with the distinguishing of the elements of the works's iconography. But it does not, *pace*

Northrop Frye, end with it. The work of art, I have said elsewhere,[3] is a hierarchy of contents (a hierarchy, indeed, of *sorts of* content), and the critic must show himself aware of the relations between these different sorts of content. Or rather, to be precise, he must show himself aware of the fact that the literary or artistic symbol belongs simultaneously to several different types or order of symbolism.

Thus, for instance, the jealousy Hamlet feels for his step-father belongs to the 'archetypal' order of symbols, in which men play out, unwittingly, a timeless battle of generation and renewal. But it also belongs to the realm of psychology in which the young man both loves and hates his father. Further still, it plays a leading symbolic role in the drama of personal despair and disillusionment. From this latter point of view, Hamlet's role as psychoanalytical 'case', or as incompetent persecutor of seasonal rites, is irrelevant: these lower levels of the textual hierarchy serve as mere providers of fodder for the ultimate 'expression' which is the work of art. In this sense, each speech in the play is read (or heard) both as final statement and as instrument of deeper purpose. The prince's disgust at his mother's behaviour with Claudius exists – clearly – to express an ultimate *Weltschmerz*. To understand this emotion, we have certain norms of acceptable behaviour assumed in the play. In a society in which it was normal for wives to re-marry so soon after their husband's deaths, Hamlet's bitterness would be incomprehensible. Some critics *have* found Hamlet's feelings either incomprehensible (as in T. S. Eliot's essay on the play) or immature (as in L. C. Knights).[4] Alternatively, they have found the imbalance between cause (Gertrude's re-marriage) and effect (Hamlet's despair and disgust at all things) as evidence of Shakespeare's real meaning – the Oedipal situation and the dread of incest.[5] From this (Freudian) point of view, Hamlet's over-reaction is good art, since without it the *re*pressed content could not be *ex*pressed. Yet again, the Romantic critic heeds neither the Oedipal nor the archetypal aspects of Hamlet's role, but concentrates purely upon Hamlet as culture-hero – he who knows too much, feels too much, and therefore rejects the 'normal' world and its values. From this point of view Hamlet's 'excessive' introspectiveness, sensitivity and anxiety are proper responses to the essentially disgusting world of society and materiality. Again, from such a critical standpoint Hamlet's over-reactions are entirely justifiable both as artistic elements of the play (which utters the essentially tragic vision of ultimate despair) and as moral response to existence.

The example of *Hamlet* proves that our critical rationalisations depend upon our world-view. But it also demonstrates with particular clarity the nature of the formal hierarchy of the literary text. T. S. Eliot was – in my view – wrong about the play, but he was wrong, as it were, for the right reasons: the 'emotion' for which Hamlet's sumptuous analytics provide objective correlatives is precisely that tragic emotion which undercuts the more easily definable discontents to which Eliot wished to confine it. For the articulation of *this* tragic emotion, the whole hierarchy – from seasonal rite, through political dissent to 'Freudian' disturbance – was necessary. In a good literary work, the elements of the formal hierarchy or structural pyramid hold strict relations of dependence with one another. In the good work, there are no 'pegs' upon which imagery is hung. Eliot could achieve his reading of the play only by bracketing out the work's intrinsic content and reducing it to its iconography, that is, by choosing to regard it as a failed Revenge Tragedy. In point of fact, Shakespeare's greatest triumph in the play was to shift its fulcrum, with the utmost subtlety, from one region of interest to its outer limits when it appeared as the common intersection of many other spheres, so that we are constantly responsive to different claims, without disregarding any of them. Out of this web of competing claims and intersecting levels, Shakespeare generates the invisible centre which is the play's real 'content' – i.e. its form.

It will be clear that the archetypal level of symbolism, the psychoanalytical, the existential or the historico-political, could each be described as 'objective'. At these levels, one is discussing thematic and objective contents which could appear in other works. These various thematic layers correspond to Panofsky's first two interpretative levels – iconography and iconology. It is characteristic of certain types of structuralist and modernist criticism that it wishes to confine interpretation to these two levels. Northrop Frye's famous anatomy leaves no room for 'personal' or 'unique' features of works. Pierre Macherey, from a different ideological position, has dismissed the artist's individual performance as 'parody':[6] the work merely parodies the objective, thematic contents of which it is made. But this is in fact both to say nothing and to repeat the obvious. The question is, what is the nature of this parodying? What is the difference between the parody in *Hamlet*, and the parody in a standard 'Revenge' tragedy?

Erwin Panofsky, significantly, recognises this problem. He refuses to allow us to remain at the level of iconography and iconology. The work of art, if it is composed of elements and themes objectively shared with other works, and created for the artist by tradition, history or discourse, must surpass these elements in order to achieve what Panofsky calls the third level of interpretation, that of symbolical values or intrinsic content. Panofsky is here catering for that phenomenon glaringly absent from Macherey, Foucault and Frye: the unique work of art itself. The problem is to describe the pyramid of contents which is a work of art, so that we are led plausibly up the hierarchical ladder from the level of the basest, most inchoate contents, common to all human utterance, up through the so-called objective or thematic formations (Panofsky's iconographies and iconologies), finally to arrive at the finished, unique work. The critical act properly encompasses the whole sweep of this upward movement, 'reading' the work's surface by informedly interpreting its objective contents, and appreciating the minute differentiations by which the artist effects the final work.

If we confront the question openly and honestly, we shall see that the process which takes us from the shared, general objective levels of a text to the final 'unique' level of Panofsky's intrinsic content, is one of progressive particularisation. We begin with an archetypal hero, flung into an age-old predicament: he does not choose his humanity, nor his parentage, nor the state of the times. We end with *Hamlet*, a poem like none other, unique, individuated.

Even a second-rate writer must give us some individuation: unless he reproduces an earlier text (itself an individuated version), he must make his hero speak lines invented by the poet, even if of a wooden predictibility, a soporific banality. The artist's 'symbolical values' are those of the text he makes, the picture he draws, the tune he inscribes. Thus, even in the most conventional, least original work, we are forced to confront Panofsky's third level – the actual words, marks or notes of a text. The fault of Frye, Macherey and others is to pretend that they can pierce through to a general, objective level of contents that annihilates the final marks, or, at least, to play down the importance of the individual nature of these marks. This is, of course, a matter of emphasis. Sometimes we want to be reminded of the archetypal or objective derivation of a poet's characters or situations, and this was the task taken on by the Jungian and Frazerian criticism of the 1930s and 1940s (a school of criticism, note, more or less absent from French culture). But this is only to say that the existence of these objective contents ought to be acknowledged, that they must be 'read' before the text can be understood. It does not alter the fact that the final text represents the end-point of a process of progressive differentiation or individuation, and that appreciation of the nature of the poet's particularisation must form part of a total critical act.

(ii) THE 'PROBLEM' OF THE SUBJECT

Note that such a belief need not rest on any particular understanding of the human subject or the human individual. Much recent criticism has devoted its energies to destroying a so-called 'humanist' individualism. Erecting an 'untheorised' concept of the 'free' individual, 'bourgeois humanists' (these include Sartre, as well as all the great philosophers of the Western tradition), fail to understand that there is really no such thing as the 'subject'. The human individual becomes a mere meeting-place of material forces, ideological formations, or whatever. Now this view is, we must emphasise right away, simply a *parti pris*. In Foucault, for instance, it is merely asserted that 'man' is a meeting-place of discursive formations'.[7] Foucault shows no evidence whatever for accepting his view that a work of art can be regarded as having come into being as if by accident, or at the behest of some cat's cradle of forces oblivious to the author's intentions. As a matter of fact, Foucault's view is fantastical – the kind of philosophical rococo that finally overtakes any long established view (in this case the kind of Hegelianism that ran the gauntlet of Marxism). Moreover, nothing has been gained: the 'author' has been obliterated only in theory: it amounts to nothing more than a rule-book for philosophical behaviour, the concept 'author' being outlawed.

Foucault's later concessions fail to make any serious impact on the problem: having observed, with laughable pomp, that 'the subject should not be entirely abandoned', he goes on to say that 'the subject (and its substitutes) must be stripped of its creative rôle and analysed as a complex and variable function of discourse'.[8] Why should it be stripped of its creative role? No reason is forthcoming: it just should, otherwise our theoretical pagodas will come tumbling down. The architecture of these pagodas is Marxist, and the purpose of adopting the anti-humanist *parti pris* is plain: without it, the Marxist is left with the embarrassing fact of a phenomenon (creative art) which eludes all determinist and materialist theory; while Marx and Trotsky and others were prepared to accept this as a fact of life, the new Marxism is not.

It is important to note that my concern in the present book is with the nature and status of the marks that make up works of art – with symbolic meanings, in Panofsky's sense. I am not interested in theories of the 'subject'. Until it is demonstrated (not merely assumed dogmatically) that in order to speak of the *value* of the forms of artist it is necessary to abandon the concept in present use of a creative subject (equivalent to the millions of creative subjects to whom the work speaks), then I shall continue to follow the common sense code of 'bourgeois' humanism, dispensing with the more ponderous and ridiculous periphrases by which Eagleton, Foucault and others have tried to replace the 'subject'. The only serious attempt so far made to write the subject out of the contract, that of Jacques Lacan, cannot be regarded as other than a merely elaborate series of arabesques, a brilliant if often absurd performance, resting upon foundations long familiar from the great writers of the nineteenth century who gave Freud so much of his theoretical framework. It is no news that the unconscious dominates much of our behaviour, and often makes a fool of the ego, or that the self itself is constituted by interaction with mother and father. So far Lacan merely follows accepted practice. His further contentions, that language as it were constitutes a Symbolic Order – necessarily patriarchal – which thrusts identity and gender upon the unwilling individual is more fanciful than convincing. It is too dependent on the exploitability of the signified-signifier distinction to be other than pretentious: it depends upon a theory of meaning and language that could only be cooked up within an intellectual tradition more or less devoid of genuine linguistic analysis, and reliant upon formal linguistics to solve problems that are properly the province of the philosopher. Too many realities, too many uncancellable brute facts are airily written off by Lacan for his endless discourse to be much more than an intellectual plaything for a bored bourgeois intelligentsia with revolutionary aspirations.

The view offered here has much in common with that offered by Sartre in his *Problems of Method*, a book which anticipates a remarkable number of subsequent absurdities. His postulation, in particular, of a 'hierarchy of mediations', of which the last is that of the author or individual mediating between the work of art and the social structures, is eminently sane.[9] Unlike Sartre, however, I am not concerned with the psycho-biographical facts that are inscribed in the work of art, preoccupation with which inevitably leads to the kind of terminal psychical investigations represented by Sartre's own study of Flaubert. The purpose of postulating the mediation of the individual is other. We are not concerned with quirks of uniqueness, with what makes Flaubert's psychic world different from Balzac's. That properly belongs to History. To this extent, the view offered here is Aristotelian: poetry is different from history in being concerned with the general and externalised, rather than with the uniquely individuated. The authorial individuation with which I am concerned is not that accidental uniqueness of one private psyche as opposed to another. If a poet had an accident as a child when passing a brewery, and forever after associates pain with the smell of malt, it is irrelevant to his poetry, unless he effects upon the fact a transformation bringing it within the scope of all readers.

Thus, the authorial participation I am invoking is not a deviation into biography. It is, to the contrary, an acknowledgement of the common ground occupied by author and reader: the ground of a common humanity. The essential feature of this humanity is, precisely the fact that the meaning of much of what we experience is divulged to us in the privacy of our own consciousness, and that the boundary between our own consciousness and that of our neighbour (however that consciousness is constituted, by whatever ideologies) can, in important respects, never be broken down. This is true of all human beings, of all periods. The inadequacy of Marxist theory is an inadequacy of its conception of human experience itself.

(iii) AUTHORIAL PARTICIPATION

It will need no great strength of the imagination, then, to discern in this progressive individuation, the participation of the artist himself: it is he who must decide what to select and what reject from the wealth of motif offered by convention and tradition. It is he, too, who must inscribe those actual marks – give the phrase trenchancy, the line pungency, the chord memorableness. If the process of the art-work from objective formations and themes to final uniquely individuated form is to be understood, then it must be in terms of the individual artist's participation. This much is obvious, and equally obvious is the fact that it must apply to all work of whatever period – from the Cycladean idol to the Action painting, from the anonymous hymn of an early cosmogonist to the allusive lyric of a Symbolist poet. The process by which objective formations and contents become, in the final stage of execution, the living 'work of art' can be understood only in terms of a certain subjectivisation. This is so, no matter whether the work is anonymous and 'primitive'; or authorial and modern. This fact is reflected in our use of the value-judgment even with primitive and archaic art.

We recognise the varying degrees of 'life' and 'vitality' even in neolithic and palaeolithic art. We acknowledge, that is to say, the anonymous artist's success in making the inherited and public themes and contents *important to us*. We say that the unknown cave-artist or mediaeval sculptor has made his themes and ikons 'come alive'. In doing so we pay silent homage to the artist's skill in subjectivising the objective. For the process by which common stock-in-trade (carvings of devils and angels, corn-dollies or sketched reindeers) are 'brought to life' is the result of the artist's personal experience or feeling about them. This may be itself the projection of a *general* emotion or scepticism – as witness the preference in many art-historians for palaeolithic to neolithic art;[10] what we witness in looking at dead or mechanical art may well be the degeneration in the 'mind' of a whole society. Or it may make more sense in terms simply of the spiritual and imaginative vitality of the individual man – in terms, that is, of 'genius'.

It is this last, of course, which modernist criticism has found so hard to swallow. Yet there is really no alternative. The objective themes and contents must be experienced subjectively before a work comes into being, and this applies to the drawings on a cave-wall in Altamira as much as to the apparently arcane hieroglyphics of a Paul Klee; to the courtly *chanson* of a fifteenth century Burgundian composer as much as to the intensely 'personal' symphonies of a Tchaikovsky. What, then, accounts for the differences between the poetry of ancient cultures such as is represented in the hymns of the Rig Veda or the Old Testament, and that of nineteenth century England or France?

This is a question which cannot, it is plain, be answered within the de-historicised parameters of mainstream modernist criticism. It cannot, that is, be answered in terms of an aberrative subjectivity (that of the nineteenth century) intruding between the objectivity of 'the past' and the restored sanity of anti-subjectivist modernism, though this is the cherished belief of much modernist criticism. Eliot's essay, 'Tradition and the Individual Talent' was not isolated in its rejection of Romantic subjectivity. The vices of Romantic self-expressiveness form the burden of modernist criticism from Remy de Gourmont and Ortega y Gasset to the Cambridge-influenced New Critics, with their fastidious disdain for any questioning as to the poem's 'human' meaning, and neo-modernists such as Josipovici and Ackroyd. It is a trend which has been reinforced by the bias of Marxist criticism towards an 'objectivity' based on the facts of economic and political history. From the Marxist point of view, Romantic subjectivity is self-ignorance. In fact governed by class-prejudices and ideological formations, the Romantic poet believes himself to be at the centre of the universe, thinking 'his' thoughts and feeling 'his' feelings. Romantic subjectivity achieves its philosophical apogeum in existentialism, that essentially 'bourgeois' plea for individual freedom and a truth based, in Kierkegaard's classic formulation, on subjectivity. The schizoid self-division manifested in the existentialist and Marxist phases of Sartre dramatises the situation admirably.

Yet all art, as we have seen, (all thought, indeed) is necessarily born in subjectivity, as, in the final analysis, it is received in subjectivity. Even the members of a culturally unified audience (that of ancient Greece, for example, or sixteenth century England) experienced a play or ritual in the privacy of their own consciousness. It may be as well – it may be necessary – at times – to ignore this dimension of the cultural experience in our analyses of the products, just as it is necessary to ignore it in psychological and philosophical analyses of perception and sensation. It was as a corrective to what T. S. Eliot usefully called the critical impressionism of late Romantic criticism,[11] in which the work of art was forced to play the role of chance instigation of the critic's private fantasies, that modernist criticism first came into being. Often, it is not important to stress the uniqueness or individuality of a given work: criticism must generally concern itself with shared properties and structures. But this trend must not be allowed to dictate its own dogmas, so that the real nature of art is obscured. However many shared formations it has, the work of art has its own finally differentiated signature, its emergence into 'form', its achievement of what Panofsky calls 'intrinsic content', the stage at which content dissolves into form, and nothing can be said of content which is not a comment about form, and vice versa.

This final stage of the art-process is not, of course, private: no work of art can be private. But the final differentiation of the work is achieved only by the author's participation, and this presents us with a direct parallel to the way we ourselves receive it in our own consciousness. The important point is that this is no less true of the poetry of, say, Alexander Pope, the high-priest of Augustan objectivity, than of Wordsworth, in whom the new Romantic subjectivity is first manifested. This essential participation is allowed for in the critical formulations of the Augustans' critical ideologue, Dr Johnson. Johnson's theory included the important category of Wit or Genius – the faculty which enables the true poet to transform and bring to life or simply *make important*, the themes, truths, precepts or world-views of contemporary society. It is difficult to find anything 'original' in the 'Essay on Criticism' or the 'Essay on Man', in the sense that little if any of the abstractable thematic content can be shown to have originated with Pope himself. Everything is second hand, *rechauffée* – as hostile critics felt it to be – of Shaftesbury or Boileau. Yet only Pope's 'genius' made possible those luminous transformations which have proved so memorable. Pope's genius for saying 'What oft was thought but ne'er so well expressed' is the only proper faculty of the poet. The genius of the poet is not to create *ex nihilo*, but to produce formulation which forbid traffic through itself, neither iconic and opaque, neither communicative nor transparent. The statement of the poet is thing-like in that it resists translation into other words of the same language, but language-like in opening up vistas beyond itself, making us forget the words when we are most admiring them. Jakobson and others have defined poetic language as that use of language which proffers its code as its message, which draws attention to itself as language not as communication of meaning.[12] Yet we do not admire nonsense as we admire poetry, and most of us habitually discriminate between poetry which 'says something' and poetry which is mere fine writing – Parnassian, in Hopkins's word. The poem's words do not, *pace* Jakobson, call upon us to admire themselves for the sake of their form or their code, but only in the act of saying something which seems important to us.

Of this essential quality of poetry, the work of Pope is one of the most remarkable instances. What Johnson called Pope's Wit or Genius, I am simply proposing to call the exercise of his subjectivity; it is what cannot be predicted or determined from outside by history or ideology or any other force. We can reduce Pope's 'content' to its sources until there seems nothing left; but we cannot analyse away its Popeness, its breath, its life, its poetry:

> Damn with faint praise, assent with civil leer,
> And without sneering, teach the rest to sneer.

We think we have merely dropped in upon a particularly felicitous expression of what we always knew about literary society; but it is the peculiar gift of Pope to generate this illusion: it is in this way that his 'form' is 'content', his 'structure' 'meaning'. We have been told something, and it is the error of much modern criticism to believe that we have been told nothing, but merely asked to admire the code.

Pope's poetry, of course, appeared to the Romantic themselves as the very negation of poetry – something so cold and impersonal as to fall short of the genuinely imaginative. This account, in turn, bred the fierce contempt of modernists such as T. S. Eliot and F. R. Leavis. Yet this reaction was, in its own way, just as imbalanced as the Romantic rejection itself. If the Romantics were wrong to think Pope's poetry devoid of feeling and personality, the modernists were as emphatically wrong in holding Romanticism to be excessively and aberrantly subjective. Somewhere between the two positions the truth lies.

After all, the most celebrated formulation of the idea that the poet should 'Look into the heart and write' derives from the later sixteenth century; and Aristotle, for instance, assumed that the poet wrote from 'the heart of a genuine passion'. He also believed that the poet dealt not with the particular of History but with the general. But this duty devolves upon all poets, no less on the Romantic or Symbolist than on the Augustan or the Caroline. What, then, is the explanation of the change in tone and meaning that comes over poetry after about 1780? For the poetry of the Romantic period undeniably is more 'personal', more 'subjective' than that of Pope and neo-Classical France. The great writers of the Augustan age were almost stridently and trenchantly individualistic men: Swift and Pope, Johnson and Voltaire seem still, at a distance of two hundred years, vibrant egotists. Is the impression of greater impersonality in their writing the result simply of their power to suppress their individuality in their art? Did they sacrifice their individuality to the social body with a firm-mindedness denied to the weaker Romantic egotists?

The answer to this is, clearly, no. Pope does not suppress his individuality in the interests of his art or of a social vision. On the contrary, his themes enable him to give free rein to an egotism at times bordering on the maniacal:

> Let Sporus tremble – A. What? that thing of silk,
> Sporus, that mere white curd of ass's milk?
> Satire or sense, alas! can Sporus feel?
> Who breaks a butterfly upon a wheel?
>
> ('Epistle to Dr Arbuthnot', ll. 305–9)

We shall find nothing so intensely animated by personal animus (revenge, dislike, contempt all mingled together) in any of the Romantics. Byron, for all his spleen, strikes us as either calmer or less poetic. For the really remarkable thing about Pope's lines is that their malice is equalled by their artistic success: it is good poetry. The same goes in general for Swift, whose masterpiece surpasses all Romantic art in its intensity and personal animosity, yet still seems a great work of art, not a warped diatribe.

There is no point, then, in trying to disguise the naked subjectivity – the personal animus and bias – of Pope and Swift;

neither is there any point in seeking to downgrade their art. Yet the differences remain. When we turn to Wordsworth and Byron, Keats and Shelley, it is to find an art that wears its subjectivity, as it were, on its sleeve. We are obliged to repeat that Romantic poetry is no more and no less subjec*tive* than that of Milton or Pope: the Renaissance epic, the Elizabethan play, the Metaphysical love-poem or the Augustan epistle, were brought into being through the minds of individual men working on material part-public (the so-called objective contents described above), and part-personal (the writer's own miseries, hopes, disappointments, awareness of age). We need only consider Villon's or Donne's poetry, to say nothing of Milton's, to see that the difference between Romantic self-expression and the expressions of earlier poets is no absolute one, and that in a very material sense, all poetry seeks, and always has sought, to be an expression of self and society. The subjectivism of Romanticism, therefore, cannot be explained as a sudden collapse into self-indulgent egocentricity by men no longer capable of achieving the 'objective' strength of earlier artists. It is at this point that our postulation of an essential subjectivity in all art stands us in good stead. For we can now see that all art – the meeting-point of subjectivity and objectivity – consists of a subjectivity *working upon* certain formations or contents. These contents we are obliged to describe as objective: they were not created by the poet, they cannot be 'private'. They must be, in some sense, given. This applies to Romanticism as much as to any other art. We can therefore describe the difference between Romantic and pre-Romantic art in terms of the different objective contents proposed to, and available, to the poet. The Romantic predicament is to be defined in terms of the particular amalgamation and interaction of objective elements in a given historical phase.

The nature of this amalgamation will be clarified, I think, if we distinguish right away between subjectivity and subjectiv*ism*. Let us agree that all art is basically born and experienced in subjectivity, and that this subjectivity is repeated and manifested in the uniqueness of 'form'. Let us then agree to call subjectiv*ism* a particular set towards the purpose and content of writing characteristic of a given historical phase, namely the Romantic. This will enable us to preserve the essential relationship between Romantic and pre-Romantic art, and at the same time to

describe Romantic art within its historical situation. Subjectivism
will then emerge as a stylistic feature of Romantic art, one in no
need of apology, and certainly not such as to disqualify it from
serious consideration. Our analysis so far has brought us to a
kind of neo-Hegelianism: the work of art takes place at the line
between subjectivity and objectivity, between the received and
worked-upon public content, that is to say, and the artist's
consciousness of them. Our task now is to describe that shifting of
mental frontiers that resulted in the peculiar artistic condition
known as subjectivism.

(iv) THE NEW INDIVIDUALISM

What gives rise to the impression that Pope is a more 'objective'
writer than Wordsworth is simply the fact that Pope's thematic
material is different from Wordsworth's: Pope is working upon
objective contents concerned with *what is true of man as a social being
rather than as a private individual*. Pope does not suppress his
individuality in the interests of a social vision. On the contrary,
as we have seen, Pope's intellectual parameters enable him freely
to indulge, at times, almost maniacal egotism. He feels free to
denigrate, sneer and attack his enemies with no constricting sense
of the needs of fair play. 'Fair play' in fact is a definingly
Victorian notion, admirable in itself, but advertising a certain
loss in confidence, and consorting easily with sentimentality – the
literary vice totally unknown to Pope (though appearing already
in the new 'bourgeois' poets, Philips and Carey).
    Such was Pope's belief in the social and intellectual values he
expressed in his verse that he was able to give them the
untrammelled force of his genius in expressing them. When we
turn to Romanticism, it is to find, among other things, that,
paradoxically enough, a new kind of stringency has been forced
upon poets: they cannot any longer give free rein to an intensity
of personal animus to produce the vicious yet pure satire that is
perhaps the greatest product of Augustan poetry. When they
attempt satire, it is to fall into one of two lesser postures: they will
produce either the angry self-righteousness of Byron (who lacked
none of the wit or technique to write great satire), or the
vituperative lampooning of Shelley. Byron's satire is bad because
uninformed by any deep conviction of rightness in the 'values' he

is upholding. There are no values at all in 'English bards and Scotch reviewers', in fact, only a pointlessly caustic rancour at any rival or elder. Shelley's political poems are excellent lampoons: but they are not on the level of his greatest poetry. Again, the explanation lies in no soft-mindedness or sentimentality on the poet (Shelley and Byron were intelligent and tough-minded men), but in the nature of the predicament in which they were writing. The particular feature of the predicament we are now concerned with is the absence of that sense of cultural community, of man as a social being with a defensible and proud identity to be defined and advertised in appropriately stylish and refined verse.

The problem may here best be seen in sociological terms. We are concerned with the evolution of a new kind of social man. The pity of it is that western man only achieved his subjective individualism when it was too late for him to be able to channel it in a homogeneous society.[13] Of course, man was no less 'individual' in the sixteenth century; think of Hamlet, of Francesco Sforza, of Leonardo. What Marx meant was that the order of society had altered so that human subjectivity was put into an entirely new situation. What we are concerned with is the disintegration of the old organic, quasi-familial society which, for all its social injustices and oppressions, had enabled man to live and work in meaningful relations with his fellows, and its replacement with the agglomeration of individual units which is the societal result of the division of labour and the onset of capitalist economy.

This development has two faces. Looked at negatively, it is called alienation, and has been treated exhaustively so often as to need little comment here. Suffice it to say that the processes of modern production and social organisation result in an unsatisfying state of being, in which the workman feels alienated from himself because he does not perform a whole, coherent task each day, but only contributes a meaningless fragment of a task completed by many others like himself. The bourgeois feels alienated because he is conscious that his well-being depends upon the unjust exploitation of the workers. Positively, modern social development can be seen as the emergence of individualism. In differentiating between primitive and modern societies, Emile Durkheim observed that primitive man is bound to his fellows by 'mechanical solidarity', and cowed by many punitive laws.[14] Modern man is held to his fellows by 'organic solidarity', and his laws tend more to be cooperative and restitutive than punitive and coercive. A further aspect of this dual development is the sameness of primitive men, and the greater diversity of modern men. With the growth of modern transport and education and the spread of centrist ideas, Durkheim remarks, there grows the tendency for our societies to resemble each other. England becomes more like France, France more like Germany. This process has of course been accelerated to an almost infinite degree in our own time. But alongside this growth of sameness, Durkheim observes, there is the increase in individualisation within each society:

> Indeed, it is even true that each province tends to lose its distinctive feature, but that does not deny that each individual partakes more and more of what is personal to him . . . the diversity which the last, taken as a unit, present, continues to grow. For if some provincial types which used to exist tend to merge with others and disappear, there remains, in their place, a very considerable number of individual types.[15]

From this angle, modern society appears as a machine for securing more and more freedom. Durkheim allots a smaller space to the 'pathological' symptoms of the division of labour – the 'Anomic division of labour'. The fiction contemporary with Durkheim's book – that of Dickens and Zola, for instance – placed a great deal more emphasis on the alienating effects of the process than Durkheim, who rather mildly remarks simply that 'at certain points in the organism certain functions are not adjusted to one another.'[16] Nevertheless, the very fact that Durkheim's positive view of modern social evolution places the same emphasis as Marxist theorists, underlines the fact that the most prominent feature of this development is the emergence of modern individualism. The lonely world of alienated man with his nuclear family, boxed-off from the other lonely nuclear families around him, is only Durkheim's world seen negatively rather than positively. And if Durkheim occasionally appears rosy with satisfaction at the state of things, Marxists too often seem incapable of acknowledging that within the isolation, exploitation and anomy of modern society, human life in its rich, positive aspect still goes on.

What we are concerned with is the collapse, through socio-economic evolution, of the hierarchical society. Writing of the society of the late middle ages, J. Huizinga observes that 'Medieval political speculation is imbued to the marrow with the idea of a structure of society based upon distinct orders. . . . That which, in mediaeval thought, establishes unity in the very dissimilar meanings of the word, is the conviction that every one of these groupings [the various orders of which society was made up] represents a divine institution, an element of the organism of Creation emanating from the will of God, constituting an actual entity, and being, at bottom, as venerable as the angelic hierarchy.'[17] Such a society persisted long after its economic foundations had changed, because, as Huizinga remarks, 'for the history of civilisation every delusion or opinion of an epoch has the value of an important fact'.[18] It was not until the eighteenth century in England that this view of society really changed. If the mediaeval conception of society was, as Huizinga says, 'statical not dynamical', it was not only under the influence of economic evolution that social vision as well as social process became dynamic. It is not only the emergence of the dynamic, mobile society of modern capitalism that governs the forms of literature and philosophy in the eighteenth century, but also the loss of the idea that society was an organism 'emanating from the will of God'.

Romantic subjectivism, then, far from being a spurious bourgeois retreat from the social and objective realm to the private and subjective, constituted a proper response to the changed condition in which Western man lived in the late eighteenth century. The poetry written before the Romantics was, as we have seen, really no less mediated by the subjectivity of the poet than Romantic poetry. But this subjectivity – the necessary subjectivity of art – was externalised in iconography, or 'carried by' the objective themes of the age. The so-called objectivity of the Augustans is nothing less than the expression of a different social order, one which was still pyramidal and hierarchical, centred upon the court, such that the animus or egotism or subjectivity of the individual poet could still be absorbed within the purpose of the social power-structure or 'objective mind', in Hegel's term. More inward and spiritual, Milton's profound egotism found ample satisfaction in the Christian world-view he inherited. Of course, it is not simply a matter of there being imperative objective themes available. It is also a matter of how men conceived themselves. With the growth of modern individualism there grew also new objectivities. As late as Pope and Johnson, Bach and Voltaire, man was and felt himself to be, part of that greater social pyramid, that god-given hierarchy which determined his ends and gave him his personality. Their art tells the truth of this condition.

Romantic subjectivism is nothing less than the acknowledgement by the original writers and artists of the late eighteenth and early nineteenth century that the conditions in which man lives have altered. Romantic subjectivism is thus a new content forced upon the writer by social and historical circumstances. An authentic poetry in the first generation of the nineteenth century had necessarily to partake of this new subjectivism. The difference therefore between Augustan 'objectivity' and Romantic subjectivism is largely to be explained in terms of such a shift in contents. The situation could be summed up by saying that for the Romantics, subjectivity has entered the realm of structure. Subjectivism, in other words, is the only authentic objectivity of the period: it is the no less general truth of the new individualist condition.

This is what I meant by asserting that Romantic subjectivism was necessary. It would not however be true to say that it was inevitable. This would be to commit oneself to a spurious critical determinism. As a matter of fact there were many writers in the early Romantic period (they were probably the majority) who did not embrace Romantic subjectivism, but continued to draw upon the bankrupt stock of Augustan objectivism. Most of Crabbe's poetry, despite the 'Romantic' turbulence of its subject matter, is Augustan in this way. So is much of John Clare, and the later Church poetry of Hurdis and Corrington. There was nothing inevitable about the emergence of Romantic subjectivism; as always, things were in the hands of a few men of integrity and intelligence. Romantic subjectivism, in other words, had to be fought for. It did not emerge automatically from the historical circumstances, though it was in a sense demanded by them. The mediation of the artist was required, and this, as always, meant active vigilant effort. The mediation of the artist is no more inevitable than the expression of the political and social structures embedded in contemporary society. In point of fact there is never anything inevitable about the artistic expression of any age.

There is much bad art in any period, and the successful work (which always has the decisive influence) is pretty much of a miracle. In the case of Romantic subjectivism we can say that what was required of the artist was a reorientation of the creative self.

(v) CONTENT-SHIFTS

Thus, the Romantic predicament can be defined in terms of a certain shift in objective contents. Briefly put, Romantic subjectivism is to be explained as a shift in contents, by which certain ranges of feeling and perception themselves became objective: subjectivity – the mind's processes and movements – itself becomes objective. The purpose of the present is to describe some of the reasons for this particular shift of contents; to explain why it was that these apperceptive feelings and emotions themselves became objectified; how it was that subjectivity became objective. Right away we can see that much of the explanation must be couched in negative terms. When a certain range of contents or themes become available to the artist, it is because a whole range of *other* contents becomes unavailable: the objective contents and formations of one age go dead on the artists of a later. It is this consideration which is so damagingly absent from Northrop Frye's account of literature. In retailing the 'eternal' themes and modes of literature, Frye failed to see that the inherited themes and archetypes of literature (of any art) do not persist unaltered within the body of culture and history. Themes and contents lose their force: literary forms change because man and society change; what is vital for one generation is dead for the next, so that a content-shift has to take place within literature. There is no 'human condition' unchanged and unchanging, waiting for the artist to bring his subjectivity to bear on it, and bring it to life. No work of art ever came into being without the maximum expression of the author's subjectivity: to this extent, all live art is subjectively born, even the Egyptian fresco or the cave-drawing in Lascaux. In this Romantic art is orthodox.

This subjectivity, however, is itself constituted both by the historical conditions and by the *Weltanschauung* of the society in which the artist is born. The necessary subjectivity of art is subject not only to the general laws of consciousness – which dictate that although each of us is in one sense unique, in others we are limited by physical and environmental laws beyond our choosing – but also to the laws of art; the laws, in particular of generality and objectivity. The poet does not deal in the particular non-recurring facts of History, nor in the private data of the diarist or the psychotic. Thus, the artist's subjectivity is of a representative order, and it must be stimulated and impelled by themes and contents which are objective and societally alive. These objective themes and contents need to have a certain imperative quality before they can function as proper root-themes of art. The decline of painting with overtly Christian themes over the course of the seventeenth century may be taken as an example. The lambent power of Raphael's Madonnas, or of the dynamically dramatic 'illustrations' of Christian incident in Tintoretto and Bellini, for instance, reflects at the deepest level the strength of Christian belief even in a century of scepticism and humanism. Obviously, even within the ages of Christian faith (an impossibly elastic phrase) there are wide variations: there is a great difference between the eleventh century Byzantine Fresco and the rich, realistic humanism of Raphael, for example, who worked at a time close to the effective demise of Christian unity. Yet the greater authenticity of Raphael's Madonnas over such execrable pieties as Rembrandt's 'Christ at the marriage of Cana' (a hypocrite such as Luis Buñuel himself would have been proud to create) is surely related to the more advanced stage of philosophical and social scepticism reached in the seventeenth century. By the time we reach the vapidities of Tiepolo a century later, it is clear that Christian iconography no longer has the power to impel the creative mind as it once had. Good art cannot be created with an outworn iconography. This axiom can be applied to all the possible contents of an art-form at any given time. This general law I shall call the law of availability:[19] the artist is limited to and by the contents available to him at the time when he is working. This is a matter of the way men in general, and the artist as representative man in particular, feel about the universe. It is a matter of belief.

This must not be regarded as simply a matter of substituting one substantial content for another, as if an empty bag were to be filled. That kind of content-shift is generally less significant in art-history than is often supposed. To extend 'subject-matter' (generally in the direction of a broadened social range of increased sexual explicitness) is generally the work of lesser talents working within new territory marked out by greater minds: we are concerned rather with attitudes towards subject-matter. In the case of Romanticism, we are confronted by what is perhaps the most radical content-shift in the history of art. It is a shift that corresponds directly to the altered societal and philosophical conditions of Western man at the end of the eighteenth century. Erwin Panofsky spoke of the difficulties confronting the critic of Romantic art, the art produced, that is, at a time when 'the whole sphere of secondary or conventional subject-matter is eliminated'.[20] The critic of such art can no longer concern himself with the analysis of iconography, of conventional symbolism of the sort so richly witnessed in the painting of the Renaissance. What is he to make of this new art, in which, as Panofsky says, a 'direct transition from motifs to content is effected'[21] – in which, that is, the artist's subjectivity, which formerly had worked upon iconographies and conventional symbols, is working upon 'content' itself – on that intrinsic value formerly generated out of conventional motifs? That is the problem facing the critic who wants to make sense of Romantic art, and that is what explains its apparent lapse into subjectivism. Social and political circumstances had altered in such a variety of ways as to undermine permanently the range of political, social and imaginative contents available to the artist. Not at a stroke certainly, but swiftly enough, a whole range of conventional, traditionally compulsive contents became useless to the artist. It is the purpose of the present book to analyse some of the consequences. Here the concern is with the new subjectivism which can at first strike the reader fresh from Milton or Pope as narcissistic or self-indulgent. In point of fact, Romantic subjectivism is nothing more than the acknowledgement of the more advanced artists of the time that the objective themes of Augustan literature had gone dead on them. This awareness produces no less startling results in the realm of form. We have now to study that transition from 'content to motif' of which Panofsky spoke, as it appears in poetic language.

3 Romantic Language: the Rise of Object-Dominance

(i) INTRODUCTION: A CRITICAL REACTION

When the reaction against Romanticism took place in England in the early decades of this century the principal objection raised against the poets so beloved of the Victorians was not, in the first instance, their excess subjectivity, but their use of language. Critics orientated towards a Marxist reading of social history, did, it is true, take Romantic poets to task for a specifically 'bourgeois' subjectivity, but in England, where such a tradition was underdeveloped, the main error of the Romantics was felt to be a certain paucity of verbal texture. I. A. Richards found them largely lacking in irony as a result of a limiting simplicity of language.[1] William Empson admitted that the Romantics 'were making a use of language very different from that of their predecessors' – especially the admired Meta-physicals. 'One might expect', Empson went on, that they would not need to use ambiguities of the kind I shall consider to give vivacity to their language.'[2] The poverty which Richards had diagnosed as a lack of ironic complexity becomes, in Empson, an absence of 'vivacity', so that the approach to them should be 'psychological rather than grammatical'.[3] Empson was shrewd enough to sense that something in Romantic poetry was evading the sort of grammatical net he and his confreres were casting; but that net is surely meant to be taken as the appropriate one to cast for real poetry. The Romantics are being given over, rather scornfully, to the psychiatrist, in accordance with the general view of them as interesting neurotics rather than serious poets. That this is Empson's general view is confirmed a little later when he offers what now seems a disastrously simple-minded psychoanalytic explanation of Byron in terms of his unresolved love for his half-

46

sister:[4] the implication is not only that this is the appropriate mode of approach to Byron's poetry, but that Byron's 'failure' as a poet (confidently assumed by now) can be given just such a concrete psychological explanation. It is a short step from this account to F. R. Leavis's *Revaluation* (1934),[5] possibly the most influential single work to have appeared on Romanticism in the past forty years: here it is assumed that the Romantic poets are naïve men, lacking adult self-awareness, and, with few exceptions, linguistically uninteresting as poets. The assumption implicit in Leavis's book, too, is that the absence of the sort of metaphoric involvement and verbal 'density' which we see in the Metaphysical poets is both a reason for rejecting the Romantics as a whole, and a sign of a general lack of mature honesty about 'life'; poetry should be textually complicated because emotional experience requires it, and the Romantics fail on both scores.

Now this critical revolution in fact comprehended a profound self-contradiction within itself. On the one hand, the new critics valued a kind of logicality in verse – demonstrable in semantic terms without appeal to 'inspiration' –, yet at the same time they valued a particular order of sensuousness, concreteness, *thereness*, which was not, so the polemics ran, to be found in the Romantics. To be sure, the assumption was that the tough-minded logicality of Donne, who could subject his emotions to 'secondary consideration' or irony, who could follow out a conceit or an argument in verse without losing afflatus, who could allow the play of wit (intellect) without becoming sterilely cerebral – this intellectuality was precisely what gave rise to the concreteness. In Leavis, the most methodologically consistent of all the new critics, it was constantly stressed that the choice of a dense, Anglo-Saxon vocabulary went hand in hand with the intellectual poise.

Nevertheless, there is a certain uneasiness here. We see it also in the poetic avant-gardism which preceded the Cambridge critics of the 1920s. The rejection of Milton by the Cambridge critics had been anticipated, and perhaps suggested, by Ezra Pound. Spurred on by Ernest Fenollosa's researches into Chinese poetics, Pound also opted for a certain 'concreteness', a concreteness supposedly absent from the bookishly abstract Milton and the vapid Romantics. He elected, as is well known, for a poetry of image, shorn of all abstractions, and even of the use of passive verbs and the copula. Pound passed on to Eliot not only a distaste for Romantic 'tushery' and Miltonic 'grandeur', but also a sense of the value of concreteness. This concreteness was eventually located, ideally, in the English Metaphysical poets. Pound himself had singled out Donne for praise and it became customary to use Donne's imagery as a kind of criterion for poetic concreteness. Yet Donne is in fact highly typical of his time and, in all essentials, his use of imagery is similar to Milton's: the opposition erected by Pound and the new critics between Miltonic 'abstractness' and Metaphysical 'concreteness', is largely spurious. Consider the following lines of Herrick's:

> Like unthrifts, having spent
>> Your stock, and needy grown,
> Ye are left to lament
>> Your estates alone.

What could be the title of these lines? 'To Debtors', perhaps? Clearly not, for Herrick uses debtors as the vehicle of the analogy, not the tenor. What is the tenor? – Something – anything, perhaps – that provides the structural relation of better-to-worse, of deterioration-through-waste. Whatever we concluded, we should have every right to be surprised, if not to feel cheated, to be told that the actual title of the poem from which these lines come, is 'To Meadows'. Such a title in a volume of modern poems – by Robert Frost, let us say, or Edward Thomas – would lead us to anticipate, with a smacking of the lips, an orgy of exact perceptions. Now Herrick gives us no such orgy; in fact, there are none of the insights we should call 'perceptions' at all. The poet tells us nothing about 'meadows' *qua* meadows that we don't already know. And what we call a 'perception' in a modern poem is just this new insight into the way natural things look – *and therefore are*. Now this anticipation of ours is in fact a highly revealing one.

It is precisely the point of Herrick's poem that the poet tells us nothing about 'meadows' that we do not already know. For what the poet wants to tell us about is not meadows (a 'mere' natural phenomenon), but time, and human life in relation to time. In fact the natural subject, upon which the poem is hung, must be presented in its general, accepted qualities, otherwise the poet's cleverness in showing us the 'moral' in it would be lost on us. In this Herrick is wholly typical of the seventeenth century. He is, of

course, a notoriously sunny poet, a kind of psychological opposite
to Milton. His pages are sprinkled with natural titles of the sort
we might expect in Edward Thomas or William Barnes – 'To the
Willowtree', 'To Daisies', 'To Blossoms', 'To Daffodils', 'The
Primrose', 'To the Western Wind', 'To Violets'. Nature – the
world of trees, flowers, skies, weathers – breathes through
Herrick's pages as ravishingly as through those of any of the
Romantic poets. And yet Nature in Herrick is used entirely to
furnish types and examples of human life: the 'Blossoms' of 'To
Blossoms' are 'Fair pledges of a fruitful tree', and in them we
may 'Read how soon things have/Their end'. The behaviour of a
sickly primrose ('This sweet infanta of the year' – a beautiful
instance of Herrick's vivifying use of the language's conventional
resources) is to 'discover/What fainting hopes are in a lover.'
Herrick's pagan morality is paralleled in Herbert's Christianity.
In Herbert's 'Virtue', Nature – also freshly alive – is seen as the
example of mortality, against which only the non-Natural faith is
proof. A more forthrightly 'descriptive' poem such as Marvell's
'Thoughts in a Garden,' suggests the background of a Van Eyck
altar-piece rather than an actual garden in Middlesex. It is the
play of wit that matters, not the peculiarities of the subject itself:

> The nectarine and curious peach
> Themselves into my hands do reach.

The peach is doubly 'curious' – it is not only strange
(unaccustomed in England), but inquisitive, as if thrusting itself
to be picked. The choice of the adjective – at once bookishly
abstract and playfully witty – is characteristic of the whole piece,
which moves towards its centre of gravity with the reflection upon
reflection which is what the experience of being in the garden
principally suggested to Marvell:

> Meanwhile the mind from pleasure less
> Withdraws into its happiness;
> The mind, that Ocean where each kind
> Does straight its own resemblance find;
> Yet it creates, transcending these,
> Far other worlds, and other seas;
> Annihilating all that's made
> To a green thought in a green shade.

The poem later extends its scope to find in the garden the type of Eden, but the modern has chosen to remember these lines about the mind's symbol-making capacities. And rightly so, for Marvell is, I think, significantly self-conscious about the way people's minds operated in his time: it is not the things of the natural world (or the 'kinds' as Marvell calls them, with significantly Aristotelian generality) which find their resemblance in the human mind, but the human mind which makes analogies for everything it beholds. (Marvell expresses his time here, or rather, perhaps, comments upon its weakness for systematising its knowledge by means of structural analogy-making: 'Studious Observators', Sir Thomas Browne remarks, 'may discover more analogies in the orderly book of nature, and cannot escape the Elegancy of her hand in other correspondences'.[6] Sir Thomas Browne's learned disquisition upon the quincunx requires only a slight change of theoretical stance to stand forth as the paradigm of the structuralist anthropologist. I have referred to the question elsewhere.[7])

The garden, that is, certainly told Marvell something he did not know before he entered it, but what it 'told' him concerned not the trees and flowers but the nature of his own mental faculties, and he did not learn it through observing things, but by bouncing off the *idea* of them. Now such a notion is anathema to our way of thinking. We are supposed to dislike and disapprove of a linguistic abstractionism; we are accustomed to setting our sights on what modern critics call concreteness, or fully realised encounters not with ideas but with things – experiences 'rendered', as the phrase goes, so as to present us with the thing itself. If this way of thinking may be most notoriously associated with F. R. Leavis, it is so generally pervasive in Anglo-American criticism after the revolution of the twenties as to defy any attempt to run it to its source. Neither is it an idea confined to criticism in English.

An excellent parallel is afforded by one of Antonio Machado's Notebooks, in which a famous Spanish poem of the seventeenth century, Calderon's sonnet 'Estas que fueron pompa y alegria', is criticised on grounds familiar to English and American readers: 'One has to recognise', he writes, 'that Calderon has taken too easy a way in order to achieve the de-temporalising end of art.' (The de-temporalising end of art, one must interpolate, is, in Machado, very similar to the kind of 'inspiration' the

English Romantics aimed for.) Calderon is being criticised for getting there too easily, by using 'concepts and conceptual images, images which are thought not intuited, (lying) outside the psychic time of the poet, outside the flow of his consciousness'. 'The whole charm of Calderon's sonnet, if it has any, lies in its syollogistic correctness, poetry here does not sing, it reasons, it discourses around a number of definitions – it is like all or most of our literary baroque – outdated scholasticism'.[8] Now, of course, this last jibe tells us of the different literary landscape in which Machado is working. What is interesting is the similarity between Calderon's sonnet and the little poem of Herrick's (*our* 'literary baroque') we have noted above as so significantly typical of the seventeenth century. Calderon too can reason, discourse around a number of assumed definitions. Eliot merely praised the quality (Machado) dispraises: what they are talking about is the same – the predominance of idea over image. Rosemund Tuve has observed: 'It is clear that images designed to assist in the poetic statement of values would not succeed in this by virtue of their sensuous precision. Poets well understood the role of a credible vividness in accomplishing such intentions, especially in certain genres; but profound suggestiveness or logical subtlety is likely to displace sensuous accuracy in the images.'[9]

This may at first seem unsatisfactory; the poetry written a century and a half after the poetry of the Elizabethan and Metaphysical poets which Tuve was describing also effects 'the poetic statement of values', but by the use, precisely, of 'sensuous precision'. 'Sensuous precision', in fact, is just that 'concreteness' valued in modernism. Tuve was nevertheless right: the 'credible vividness' of a Herrick or a Calderon was of a different order from the 'sensuous precision' of not only the Symbolist but of the Romantic poets, and her observations justly describe the involved, logical poetry of the seventeenth century poets, who, even at their most lucid (in the Carolines and in Herrick) never allowed an interest in the actual nature of objects to prevail over the 'profound suggestiveness' of the meanings they intended to convey. The general absence, in the seventeenth century of the kind of sensory interest in things we have grown accustomed to demand from poets, derives in fact from a bias of mind which is deeply, perhaps ineradicably European; the shift, such as it has been, in the direction of a different kind of poetic, one based upon 'sensuous precision' as an aesthetic ideal, corresponds to, and constitutes, a deep and irreversible change in the European mind and culture. To understand this change, we must abandon the criticism of parochial preferences, which establishes a mode of poetry congenial to itself, and then sets about looking for examples and styles from the past that fit the bill, electing Donne, for instance, to flatter our sense of ourselves as tough-minded libertines, or Dante because he appeals to our hunger for an objectified Oneness. We must turn instead to the study of the historical processes enacted by and within our cultural traces which lead us, eventually, to ourselves.

(ii) FROM FIGURE TO SYMBOL

The change in European consciousness that can be traced over these centuries is reflected in a growing European self-consciousness. The first objective statement of the real nature of European writing comes from Coleridge: 'In all modern poetry in Christendom', he wrote in the course of a lecture on Milton, 'there is an under consciousness of a sinful nature, a fleeting away of external things, the mind or the subject greater than the object, the reflective character dominant.'[10] No one yet, to my knowledge, has approached the incisive accuracy of this characterisation, much less improved on it, and it is surely significant that it was in speaking of Milton that Coleridge made his discovery. Milton can stand as the quintessential European poet, from several points of view. It was Milton who served as principal scape-goat in the critical revolution of the twentieth century. Yet what had seemed in his style a wilfully idiosyncratic disregard of the way things appeared, and a preference for the obscurely bookish over the clearly perceived, was in fact nothing but a deeply characteristic and typical European-ness. Contrary to what critics like Pound, Eliot and Leavis said, the sound does not take precedence over the sense in Milton, but the sense itself has 'the reflective character dominant' and the 'under-consciousness' of which Coleridge spoke has become an *over*-consciousness – that 'sinful nature' itself providing Milton with the theme which had to be exorcised in being expressed. Thus, when the Imagists, modernists and intellectualists put Milton in the dock it was European literature itself which was really on trial, and the critical revolution was merely putting the finishing touches to a lengthy historical process. Shakespeare, Dante and Chaucer were all variously offered by critics such as Pound as 'objective', non-Miltonic poets, by whom to measure Milton's delinquencies; but in point of fact, these poets are just as 'subject-oriented' as Milton, and they offer no true contrast with him. We are confronted – once again – by a deeper, underlying development, one which concerns Western man's relations with his environment and with himself, rather than with any purely literary matter. For the process that took Western philosophy from Christian rationalism to atheist empiricism, and from rhetoric to realism, also enforced upon Western poets a new way of using language. Coleridge – one of the prime practitioners involved – was merely articulating that awareness of its own internal nature which in a sense determined the form these new ways were to take.

The first important stage of the development towards Miss Tuve's 'sensuous accuracy' took place in the neo-classical eighteenth century. The practice of the century is important for two reasons: first, the general reliance upon the conceptually-hinged simile, replacing the inwardly realised conceit and catachresis of the seventeenth century, and second, the rise of the 'descriptive poem'. The dissociation-of-sensibility critics regarded eighteenth century simile as sure evidence of neo-classical rationalism, replacing a proper conception of metaphor with the (empiricist) notion that its purpose must be 'To point a moral and adorn a tale.' Yet in setting tenor so distinctly apart from vehicle, Pope – the supreme exponent of neo-classicism in Europe – was in fact preparing the way for a new welding.

As much may be said of Pope's descriptive poems. *Windsor Forest* is a significant departure from classical Georgic, and its formalism in no way detracts from its impact as nature poetry. Nature breathes through Pope's elegance, though – tone and gesture at all times remind us – in a most unRomantic way; it is the human mind and, more, its civilised sense of order, which enables the symmetry of Nature to be apprehended. Later in the century, Erasmus Darwin was to observe the 'words expressive of (the) ideas belonging to our vision make up the principal part of poetic language'.[11] The dominance of the eye in our sensory machinery became obvious, of course, as soon as the empiricist philosophers started focusing attention on the nature of our experiencing. Yet although Darwin's remark is pedestrian, and his further recommendations naïve, his emphases are significant, for there are no real 'descriptive' poems before the eighteenth century. The idea of a poem made up of description and not much else besides would not have made sense to the Renaissance theorist. There had been, of course, a long history of various country poems – idyll, Georgic, pastoral – but these had always had a rationale of custom and agrarian husbandry. Thomson's *The Seasons* is neither idyll nor Georgic nor pastoral, but a description simply: like the modern novel, it is a new species that has outgrown its genus. And if it is significant that a poet should have thought it worth while executing such a project, it is no less significant that he should have made a success of it. Vivaldi's famous musical 'descriptions' of nature show, incidentally, how general the development was. The raw materials of Vivaldi's musical symbolism (tremolos, pizzicatti, the elaborate repertoire of string devices) were, of course, created within the craft itself by composers such as Monteverdi and Purcell. But, once again, it is significant that what had been isolated effects and technical capacities, useful for enriching and extending the expression of other emotions (love and war, power and death), should be gathered together to make a description of the world with no other rationale, and therefore made themselves to assume the expressive burden. It is common for literary critics to speak of 'mere' description, and even to dispense with the adjective altogether and use the term to denote a lesser literary activity. Yet the emergence of the 'descriptive' poem was in itself an important event in the history of Western literature. It led directly to the Romantic and thence to the Symbolist poem, which is not descriptive precisely, yet is nothing else. We can, again, illustrate the general trend by comparing a seventeenth century poem with a Romantic one on the same subject.

Let us compare, for instance, Herrick's daffodils with Wordsworth's more famous ones. Herrick's flowers are steady symbols of our own transience: 'We have short time to stay as you,/We have as short a spring' and so on. The mechanism is in fact deceptively complex, as even these lines show. Seeing daffodils is part of a 'spring' experience, and Herrick wants to exploit both the fast-fadingness of the flowers and the zest and thrill of the season: the flowers, too, have their youth. The complexity accrues throughout the two stanzas, and it derives substantially from the sureness with which Herrick can assume the meanings in the symbol, the confidence with which he knows we can cast them in their role. The daffodils are poignant because they come and go much faster than we do, and, in reminding us of our own equally bitter brevity, precipitate comparison with a still faster process of dissolution. There is a crescendo of rapidly increasing transience, leading from man (who provides the whole context of contemplation), through flowers (who have their own epi-cycle – life/spring), to summer's rain; finally – briefest of all, – to morning dew. The scale thus reads: man–daffodils–rain–shower–dew. Since the theme is transience, the scale of increasing brevity is also a scale of intensification. Enfolding the whole poem is the assumption of the recurrence of the daffodils: unlike us, they will be back next year. Herrick does not mention this, and it would be a different (and probably less good) poem if he did. But it is there. The poem is apparently unthinking in its reliance (itself daffodil-like) upon conventions of interpretation among the readers. Yet its strength stems just from this. Formally, the poem is less slight than it appears. Graceful and wasp-waisted as it is, 'To Daffodils' is supple and sinewy. And of course, daffodils were not especially symbolic or emblematic of transience: it is not the figure itself that is conventionalised (the freshness of the poem tells us that the flowers have really been encountered), but the mode of symbolically reading nature for its significances.

'I wandered lonely as a cloud' is no less of a 'performance' than Herrick's piece; it is, as is well known, a doing-over of a really much more quick and vital prose passage from his sister's journal.[12] Yet, although Dorothy captures the freshness of the experience better than her brother, his version *is* a poem (which, given some twentieth century assumptions, it ought not to be, freshness of notation being all). One way of accounting for the differences between Wordsworth's poem and Herrick's would be, of course, simply to say that they were different poets and leave it there. Yet their ways of approaching or responding to the same phenomenon are really much more fundamentally distinct than a mere difference of temperament would dictate. We note first that with Wordsworth's gain in 'doing' (where Herrick merely names or points to the flowers, Wordsworth spends a stanza and a half 'evoking' them, with what it used to seem easy to call immediacy), there is a corresponding loss in complexity. This loss cannot be handled with the dissociation-of-sensibility concept, because there are compensations involved. Wordsworth's rationale is, I think, weaker than Herrick's: and the consoling nature of the drawing-room recollection in his last stanza has just a touch of unconvincing bathos to it. Structurally, it cannot be dispensed with; it is simply less strong than Herrick's. Herrick's poem rests upon the implication of death; Wordsworth has to make do with a kind of consoling day-dreaming, which comes across as less strong a reason for rejoicing. By means of this formal modulation, Wordsworth achieves satisfactory resolution of the experience, and this is what distinguishes his poem from Dorothy's rave in the *Journal*. Yet the real heart of Wordsworth's poem is less the celebration of the experience (Dorothy had already done justice to that), than the apprehension of the kind of significance such experiences have for us. The real difference between Wordsworth's poem and Herricks's (and the difference between the two centuries, the two contexts in which the poets were writing) lies in this fact. For the Romantic poet, the natural sight or phenomenon has to be made into a symbol by the poet's attention, by his act of apprehension. Wordsworth's poem is intrinsically Romantic in the way that the object (the flowers) has to be made into a meaning through the mediation of the poetic imagination. In the seventeenth century poem, no such act of attention is necessary: it is the meaning (life's transience) which the poet has to re-feel, not the phenomenon. The seventeenth century poet poeticises the 'meaning' by the exercise of his subjectivity. The nineteenth century poet makes the 'thing' into a symbol; the seventeenth century poet turns to the thing in order to illustrate a meaning or feeling that is an idea (separation, anxiety, love, immortality).

We have then a complete reversal of position. Where the seventeenth century poet tries to understand man's place in the plan of things, the Romantic contemplates nature to try to find out if there *is* a plan. This explains the rise of nature-worship in the Romantic period. Nature was simply the world, and this had become an object of attention instead of a mothering situation.

In this sense, we can say that, from this time onwards, things – phenomena, objects – begin to exist in their own right and for their own sake. The poet's concern is still with meaning, we note, not with natural history. But in order to gain meaning – to be poetic – the poet now requires the thing to be itself, not the emblem of some anterior world-order, and this, as we shall see, marks off his work from that of earlier poets. The phenomenon must now be realised as itself in order that the poet may enquire of its essence and its *raison d'être*. And this is not the maverick wilfulness of a handful of poets, but simply their recognition that our human situation has changed and that our modes of enquiry must reflect that fact. We no longer recognised ourselves in the external world, and Romantic poetry registers the fact.

The situation may be summarised in the following way. If the seventeenth century poet draws upon the object of his experience (remembered more often than encountered afresh) in order to illustrate the phases of human life or some idea – the waxing and waning of life, its impermanence or whatever – the Romantic poet can create 'scenery', in the words of John Stuart Mill, 'in keeping with some state of human feeling; so fitted to it as to be the embodied symbol of it, and to summon up the state of feeling itself, with a force not to be surpassed by anything but reality'.[13] T. S. Eliot had only to paraphrase Mill's definition to give the twentieth century its principal critical concept – the objective correlative. Mill was describing the poetry of Tennyson, but in Tennyson we have only the perfection and refinement of a new way of feeling, one which we must, following Mill's lead, call symbolism. It is this new way of feeling we see evolving over the hundred and fifty years between Herrick and Wordsworth. Wordsworth himself made the greatest contribution to the development, I think. He carried out a new act of poetic fusion, welding the percept (the 'descriptive' image of the eighteenth century poets) to the concept – the image to the feeling. The welding is now carried out from the opposite direction. Where the seventeenth century poet draws the outer image (usually typical and simple in form) into the orbit of his own intellection, the Romantic poet prays upon the outer until it yields a symbol of the inner. Where the neo-classical poet selected from among the objects of the outer world in order to lend plasticity to his thought, the Romantic poet searches among the phenomena of the outer world for significances which exist as yet only in any inchoate sense of meaningfulness. The meanings, that is to say, come into existence only through the mediation of the outer world. This means of course that a new weight is placed upon the outer or phenomenal, which is now presented shorn of its iconographic significances.

The rationale of poetry was now provided by the logic of

image, which, instead of metaphor, after the seventeenth century pattern, formed symbols with their own intricate inter-relatedness. Shelley, in the lyric 'When the lamp is shattered' conducts his 'argument' along a line of surmounted and superimposed images. The images are sequential rather than consequential, each one suggesting the next and exploiting the space created by the last to usurp it with its own. The broken lute begets the ruined cell, which in turn begets the empty nest, which itself begets the key-image of the poem, the starkly effective parallelism of reason as a wintry sun:

> Bright reason will mock thee
> Like the sun from a wintry sky.

It is natural to move from this to the 'eagle home', and the nakedness to 'laughter'. The mechanism, by which the successive images are 'begotten' is what troubled Leavis and the New Critics, who had their geiger-counters set for the wrong things – the kind of surface-connectedness which can be given an apparently 'logical' demonstration. The truth is that the images of poetry always sustain an inner connectedness, a justifiability which depends in the last resort on a right-feelingness: they can, that is, only be justified by what Croce called intuition. In fact, this applies as much to the metaphoric sequences of much Shakespeare and in the denser passages of Herbert ('The Collar', for instance). What is different in the Romantic poem is the reliance upon images which are, as Mill put it so early, symbols, objective correlatives. In the case of the Shelley lyric, sound and rhythm ensure that the images are fixed with clarity and fierce persistence, but essentially the images themselves engender their own powerful undertow: the poem *is* their sequence, a montage comprising an empty nest in a ruined cell beneath a wintry sun. The reasoning logicality of the seventeenth-century poem has been left far behind; a mastery of psychological action – helped into existence, I suggest, by the subtle analyses of Hume and Berkeley – has replaced the conceptual wit of the earlier age.

(iii) EAST AND WEST

It is in this sense that we can say, with Poe, that a poem does not mean something, but *is* something. Of course, in another sense this had always been true: what the poet made out of his philosophical, moral or religious material had always become something other than them, so that his poems had always *been* something, rather than *meant* something *else*. In point of fact, Poe's dictum has contributed to a good deal of critical confusion in this area. If we want to account for the different qualities which Romantic and Symbolist poems possessed, we must look to their bases, not to their surfaces. Then we shall see that the tendency towards the pure Symbolist or Imagist poem is inherent in Romanticism itself, and that the most significant feature of Romantic poetry is precisely its use of imagery as symbolic, in the new sense defined above.

The situation is, in fact, exactly the reverse of that described by Jakobson, who observed that 'The primacy of the metaphoric process in the literary schools of romanticism and symbolism has been repeatedly acknowledged, but it is still insufficiently realized that it is the metonymy which underlies and actually predetermines the so-called "realist" trend, which belongs to an intermediary stage between the decline of romanticism and the rise of symbolism and is opposed to both.'[14] On the contrary, the 'metaphoric process' suffers a severe curtailment under the impact of Romanticism, both in the Russia of Pushkin and the England of Byron. Jakobson's terms, and the distinction presumed to be beneath them, are virtually useless in any serious literary discussion. The symbolic landscaping which Mill perceived to be the essence of the new poetic style of the nineteenth century is fundamentally opposed to the kind of metaphoric involvement characteristic of the seventeenth century. What we need to consider is not the rhetorical category of the effects in a poem but the direction in which the poet makes his connections. Any work of any length, of any period, has perforce combined linguistic elements in the way Jakobson insists on calling metonymic – that is, according the laws of mimesis and syntagmatic organisation. To say that Anna Karenina's handbag is a 'synecdochic detail', or, still more bizarre, that the ladies' 'bare shoulders' in *War and Peace* are, simply runs counter to the rules of use: these are simply not synecdoches.

What Jakobson does is to lump all non-metaphoric devices together as metonymies, with total disregard to the actual work done by them in a specific literary context. The work done by, for instance, the physical details in a realist novel is rarely to be described as metonymic: these 'symbolic' details – the train that kills Anna Karenina, the river running past outside Emma Bovary's death-chamber, Clarissa Dalloway's nun-like bed-room – acquire their meaning both through what Barthes called connotation[15] – accumulation of inter-relationships inside the text – and secondly, by denotation, exploring properties within those objects and phenomena which can be associated by the reader with such abstractions as death and fate. Neither of these processes is metonymic.

The resonances and meanings of the 'imagery' in a poet like Wordsworth are not dissimilar from those of novelists like Flaubert and Tolstoy. The wonderful freshness of 'Westminster Bridge' is eminently poetic, yet has only one – dead – metaphor ('And all that mighty heart is lying still'). 'It was a beauteous evening' ('Calais Sands') offers a magnificent simile ('The holy time is quiet as a Nun/Breathless with adoration'), but rather than depending on a substitution, the effect calls upon deep reserves of what we can only call animism – the human response to the sacredness of the universe. It is this fund of emotion the poet taps, and he may do so either by metaphor, or by some other literary figure, or, as in the case of the Wordsworth sonnet, by simple description:

> The broad sun
> Is sinking down in its tranquillity;

What do we call this – animism? Metaphor certainly is not here ('sinking' is another dead mataphor). And when Wordsworth says that the 'mighty Being is awake', how is that to be taken? It is not a metaphor, nor yet a personification. It is an assumption of immanent value – in life – in what is presented. It is, in Yeats's meaning of the word, a symbol: ('for metaphors are not profound enough to be moving when they are not symbols.') It is better to ask of a figure, what work does it do? than what is its rhetoric.

Jakobson's general dichotomy, then, is more hindrance than help. It really simply draws attention to the existence of metaphor, and calls everything non-metaphoric metonymic. This point is taken by Lodge,[16] one of the writers who have spent time chasing Jakobson around. But rather than waste time trying to decide whether simile, for instance, is more metaphoric or more metonymic, as Lodge does,[17] it would be better to jettison the whole business, and admit that Jakobson's theory does nothing to throw light on literary texts. This is especially true of its relationship to Romantic and post-Romantic texts, in which there is a predominance of object-dominated figures, and in which poetic argument is carried out by superimposition of significant images, not by metaphoric logic. It is even more spectacularly the case when we come to the case of an entire poetic literature which knows little of the metaphoric processes Jakobson believes to be definingly poetic.

An interesting and important aspect in the historical process with which we are concerned, is the rapprochement over the course of the nineteenth century between the poetry and religion of the East and of the West.

The emergence of chinoiserie and japonaiserie over the course of the nineteenth century has generally been set down as unimportant, a matter of facile attractiveness – cherry-blossom, kimonos, Lafcadio Hearn and Cho Cho San, the whole phenomenon aptly being given its final and due level of importance in *Chu Chin Chow*. The literary critic, in England especially, tends to be scathing on the most serious literary result of the influence of Oriental poetry – and up to a point rightly so. Time has still not weakened the 'unfortunate belief', in Fenollosa's phrase, 'that Chinese and Japanese poetry are hardly more than amusement, trivial, childish, and not to be reckoned with the world's serious literary performance'.[18] Yet Pound was right, and there is more to the oriental influence than the ideograms in *The Cantos* and a few minor reputations acquired with little effort.

There were, in fact, profound parallels between the basic aesthetic of Chinese literature and the Western European literature that had come into being since about the middle of the eighteenth century, and Pound was right in sniffing out a relevance in Ernest Fenollosa's theories. This contention is borne out in the curious fact that modern English readers find a conspicuous and unaccountable modernity in the poetry of, say, sixth century China or seventeenth century Japan. The short lyric of Tu Fu or Li Po, the *haiku* of Bassho or Bunson, seem to us, quite simply, modern poems, not merely because of the generally loose free verse in which translators since Arthur Waley have chosen to render them, but, more legitimately, in their very action – the strategy of image by which their meanings and emotions are conveyed. The pleasure a modern Western reader without Chinese derives from the free renderings of what was extraordinarily exact and tightly structured poetry, may be vague, but it is legitimately aesthetic: what we respond to in Chinese poetry, often written a thousand years ago, is very close, in respect of movement and inner logic, to the poetry we have come to expect from our own contemporaries. Our poetry has become, in important respects, 'oriental', and this is not a matter of influence, but of the inward development of our own society and language. We could put this process simply by calling it the dominance of the object – the thing named, the sight seen – in our poetic language. In the way that they make use of objects (natural or manufactured) to express, set off and dramatise emotions, Chinese classical poets are remarkably close in method to Western poets of the twentieth century. It is only certain accidents that obscure from us the fact that the movement towards this state has been going on for nearly two hundred years, and that the Romantic poets themselves use a symbolic method closer to that of the Chinese than to that of Dante. As if by remote control, in fact, Western poetry has groped its way towards the condition of Chinese. The actual coming-together – as close as it could ever be – does not take place until the first decade of the twentieth century, with Ernest Fenollosa's discovery of Chinese poetics. But Fenollosa's researches only complete the process. Not only the short Romantic lyric, with its argument by image, but the longer Romantic poem with its narrative of scenery, significantly demonstrates the new dominance of the object in Western poetry, and it is just this object-dominance that characterises Chinese and Japanese poetry. It may seem a long way from the pictural clarity of Pushkin, Byron and Heine to the spareness of Imagism, but just how close the theories of Romantic critics like Mill were to certain central currents in Chinese poetry may be gauged from the following extract from the eleventh century theorist, Wei T'ai:

> Poetry presents the thing in order to convey the feeling. It should be precise about the thing and reticent about the feeling, for as soon as the mind responds and connects with the thing the feeling shows in the words: that is how poetry enters deeply into us.[19]

On three important counts, Wei's passage is identical with post-

Romantic thinking in Europe. First his insistence on the clear presentation of the thing conveyed (a requirement that would have made full sense to Mill, in fact, but little to Dr Johnson). Second, his stress on the dominance of the object over the feeling (recalling Eliot's impersonality, and also the insistence of *fin de siècle* theorists in Paris on 'I' impression'). Lastly, the evaluational criterion implicit in the idea that the 'feeling shows in the words' as soon as 'the mind responds and connects with the thing'. The implication is that the excellence or the success of the poem is not to be demonstrated in any logical consistency of image or metaphor, nor in any concordance of moral with illustration, but only in the intuitive response of the reader. When the poet 'has seen' or felt the thing, this will 'show' in the work and the only justification a poem needs or can have is the reader's intuitive response: in intuition the poem was born, in intuition it will be appreciated. In Wei's passage, therefore, we have the technical emphasis of the Imagist critics allied to the empathy-theory of Romanticism proper, and this confirms the general drift of the argument being offered here.

It appears, then, that Western poetry begins to approximate to Eastern not only in methodology, but in its very theory. This can be seen even more clearly by turning to the poetry and poetics of the Japanese *haijin*. The greatest of the *haijin*, Basho, greatly admired those among his predecessors (Saigyo in particular) who had based themselves on the works of Li Po (Pound's Rihaku). The Japanese *haiku* can in fact be regarded as a refinement of Chinese T'ang poetry, much as Imagism itself is a refinement of Symbolism-Romanticism. There could be no closer parallel to the poetry and poetics of post-Romanticism than in Basho's teaching:

The Master once said: 'Learn about pines from pines, and about bamboos from bamboos.' What he meant was that the poet must detach himself from his will. . . . . 'Learn' means to submerge oneself within an object, to perceive its delicate life and feel its feeling, out of which a poem forms itself. A poem may clearly delineate an object; but, unless it embodies a feeling which has naturally emerged out of the object, the poem will not attain a true poetic feeling, since it presents the object and the poet as two separate things. Such a work is artifice made by the poet.[20]

It is not a short jump, but no jump at all from this to *Biographia Literaria*, with its characteristic dichotomies – imagination and fancy, mere will and true possession. Basho is certainly clearer and more coherent than Coleridge. His account of the way the poet 'merges with' the object in order to be able to reproduce its essence in words is wholly consistent and lucid: he does not flounder with Organic Analogues, as Coleridge did. But, of course, Basho had behind him Buddhism, and in particular that brand of Buddhism known in China as Chan and in Japan as Zen. His poetic methodology assumed a whole series of spiritual exercises and techniques of meditation: its theory was, in fact, as ordered and intelligible as the Thomism that lay behind Dante. Like Wei T'ai, Basho insists on the elimination of the personal and the subjective, but he can do so because the individual's subjectivity is constituted in a world-view it implicitly accepts, and is therefore made objective. What we see in his most admired poems is the operation of wit, the detonation of relevance in the notation of the phenomenon perceived. This phenomenon itself is usually so common as to be almost conventionalised. If we read a commentary by a Japanese scholar on the poetry of the *haijin*,[21] we are struck by the fact that the images of Basho or Bunson do not take place in a vacuum formed out of the innumerable possibilities of ocular experience: they stand as elements in an image-system. The moon for instance, always signifies the harvest moon; the crow signifies autumn desolation; flowers always mean cherry-blossom; Mount Fuji stands for the peerlessly beautiful; the plum-blossom means spring. One *haiku* of Basho depends for its effect on the reader's knowing that the cuckoo sings at dawn; others on the fact that it was customary for people to stay up admiring the harvest moon, to join each other in admiring snow or the cherry-blossom. In general, the *haijin* could rely upon a whole calendar of social behaviour and associated images, and unless one knows something of the correlations one can hardly read the verse at all.

Such a background is more or less totally absent from Western poetry in the Romantic era. Yet there is unquestionable similarity of poetic methodology between the poetry written in the West by Wordsworth and his successors and the classical poetry of Japan. There was an important similarity in the first place in the conception of the creative process. Beginning with Coleridge – an important influence again, via *Edgair Po* –

Western poets felt that a new relation subsisted between the poet and the objective world. The notion now arises that, however stubbornly the critic may attempt to give a poem a subject – the decline of modern civilisation, social disintegration – all reaction to poetry consists at bottom in a feeling of something symbolised, unspoken. Something lies in the text, not, as in discursive prose, *through* the text. In Japanese poetry of the seventeenth century the material was plain and pastel, the means the purest 'imagism'.

It has been argued that, in Imagism, there is nothing but the snapshot, the illegitimate cultivation of the Image as picture; that a general reduction in scale and seriousness is indicated by the change of name from Symbolism to Imagism. But in fact, Imagism is only a refinement of Symbolism. The Imagists, like the Acmeists in Russia, thought of themselves as being in reaction against the cloudy indefiniteness of the Symbolists. Yet their ideal of 'direct treatment of the "thing", whether subjective or objective'[22] – is not fundamentally different from Mallarmé's statement that 'it is not description that can unveil the efficacy and beauty of monuments, seas or the human face . . . but rather evocation, allusion, suggestion'.[23] For the indefiniteness urged by Mallarmé did not mean inexactness (what Pound found in Swinburne, who, untouched by the real spirit of Symbolism, developed the verbal density of the early Romantic to the point where the meaning was submerged in the associations). On the contrary, Mallarmé wanted to refine the instruments of language ('Donner un sens plur pur aux mots de la tribu') to the point where they could frame the *otherwise inexpressible*. 'To create', Mallarmé observed, 'is to conceive an object in its fleeting moment, in its absence.' We have only to read Pound's description of his own *haiku*, 'In a station of the Metro', to see how close he was to the spirit of Symbolism: 'In a poem of this sort', he wrote, 'one is trying to record the precise instant when a thing outward and objective transforms itself, or darts into a thing inward and subjective.'[24] For Pound and Mallarmé, as for Basho, the question is of the relationship between the outer and the inner. In Japan, the task of 'capturing' reality was almost institutionalised in a number of concepts. The most important of these perhaps was that of *yugen* – the inner beauty of things, which both implied a conception of the outer world as in some sense illusory, and imposed upon the poet-dramatist the obligation to secure 'a momentary hold of hidden truth', exactly as Mallarmé stipulated,[25] and Wordsworth suggested in *The Prelude*. The Japanese poets rested securely upon the foundations of religious belief. The pursuit of *yugen* was akin to the Buddhist pursuit of *nirvana*, or the Zen quest of *satori* – momentary accessions of 'reality' such as the young James Joyce called epiphanies, Wordsworth 'gleams like the flashings of a shield' and Rimbaud 'Illuminations'. Makoto Ueda observes of the dramatist Zeami: 'His ideal [of *yugen*] is the union of the subjective and the objective, the observer and the observed, in the sphere of the scientifically impossible. The union is made possible only when one recognizes some super-human soul latent in all things of the universe. An artist ought to catch this invisible spirit and present it through the things visible.'[26]

This is a precise enough description of the aims and intentions of the Western poets of the past hundred years to need no commentary. The difference between the Japanese poets and their modern Western counterparts is, of course, that the western poet lacks precisely that secure foundation of religious belief as well as that unspoken community of responses around him. And it is this which has made so many neo-modernist and Marxist critics sceptical of the Romantic and Symbolist poets. Mallarmé himself warned against *Le demon d'anologie*.[27] Yet a conception of an 'invisible spirit', a super-human Soul in the universe, informs all the poetry of the modern era in the West. The logic of the Symbolist poem, with it subtle observations and detonations of meaning, depends upon a belief (momentary or otherwise) in just such a latent spirit, a principle of significance continuously to be revealed by the poet's disciplined vigilance. Thus although everything was now to be revealed, as Maurice Bowra observed, 'in metaphor and symbol', it was not the case that 'all that (mattered) was the subtle re-creation of mood and atmosphere'.[28] In Symbolist poetry, the images are held together by the syntax of the inexpressible. This has become the principle of modern poetic modes, and it is the sense in which we can justly speak of the poet's attempting to 'circumscribe reality'. The sheer uncertainty in the absence of any general religious belief such as backed up the poetry of the Japanese *haijin* imposed upon Western poets a considerable burden of anxiety, but it did not invalidate what they achieved. To think that it did is to misunderstand the whole nature of modern language and literature. The absence of a general belief, is itself an index of social change, and together, the two things – social disintegration and religious scepticism – help to define the condition of the poet in the modern age.

(iv) CONCLUSION

We can say that the rise of object-dominance in Western poetry runs parallel to the development of philosophical materialism, and the decay of the hierarchic social order noted elsewhere. The paradox in this case is that Western man, as it were, loses his 'under-consciousness of a sinful nature' only when he loses his religious faith. In this, he approaches, I have said, the condition of Chinese and Japanese poetry. This rapprochement, though fortuitous, is real, and it suggests a rather different reading of general cultural history than is orthodox. The orthodox view speak of the mystic east and the materialistic west. The domination of Western scientific method, we are encouraged to believe, expresses Western man's generally materialistic and unspiritual nature, a regrettable triumph of the empirical and the pragmatic over the spiritual and the other-worldly. This is almost the exact reverse of the truth. The truth – as the foregoing analysis of poetic language suggests – is that Western man remained swathed in a spiritual and moralistic miasma until the late seventeenth century. His literature expressed this in its metaphor-bound, over-rhetorical self-involvedness. It is almost impossible to imagine an educated and sensitive Chinese deriving much pleasure from the great European poets, unless the poet in question happened to have a narrative structure (the Shakespearean drama, Dante's dramatic Hell, the events of the Trojan War) which in some sense alleviated the general opacity of the language. We know, on the other hand, that it is very easy for Europeans to enjoy Chinese and Japanese classical poets in translation, and we can accept that this enjoyment is not entirely spurious. We can enjoy T'ao the Hermit, Li Po and Basho simply because their subtle but simple pictural logic is more like the methods of twentieth century European poems than it is like our own classical poets.

Chinese poetry was, from the very beginning – from the *Book of Odes* in Confucius's edition, at least – practical and down-to-earth: by contrast with the misty depths of Celtic and Norse poetry and with the guilt-ridden metaphoric patterns of the Attic drama, it is solid and concrete in its pictures and in the philosophical models it proposes. The Confucian social philosophy – so significantly to appeal to Pound, that subtle, but simple-minded extrovert – admirably supports the poetic methodology. The subtlety which even a foreigner with no Chinese can appreciate in the great T'ang poets, is the natural refinement of a way of thinking and feeling by and large free of the tortuous self-involvements of Judaeo-Christian tragedy: in Li Po it is the material world which must be made to divulge the mystery of existence. And this is the way of our own Symbolists and Romantics. It would therefore make more sense, generally, to speak of the mystic West than of the mystic East. Western science itself is a triumph primarily not of severe practicality, but of inwardness and meditation. The practical mind invents the wheel, the clock and gun-powder. The scientific mind guesses at gravity, relativity and sub-atomic particles. The consequences of the Western scientific revolution have obscured, in their triumphant subjugation of the material difficulties accepted hitherto as inevitable concomitants of life on earth, the true nature of the thinking that went into the making of that revolution. From Aristotle to Heisenberg, the Western tradition (if we can speak of such a thing) has united logical generalisation with an intuitive acuity capable of yielding insights which may later be submerged into a consistent theoretic framework, but which could not themselves have been reached on strictly experimental or pragmatic grounds – which, indeed, provided field and direction to the later pragmatic researches.

As far as literature is concerned, the rise of object-dominance has brought about a fundamental change in the organisation of literary works (or rather, to speak more accurately, it has constituted such a change). The question of the contents of literary works has exercised many minds recently. The misunderstanding of Romantic literature I have referred to above could indeed be treated purely from the point of view of content: it was the relations between word and meanings that critics like Leavis and Empson mistook in their dealings with Romanticism. The matter may be clarified again by considering the schema suggested by Erwin Panofsky in approaching Renaissance painting. Panofsky, it will be remembered, distinguishes three levels of content in art works: first what he calls primary or natural subject-matter (shoes, trees, men, women, etc.), which must be recognised before the picture can be understood at all; secondly, conventional subject-matter – the world of 'images, stories, and allegories': to understand which the viewer must know something about Judith or the Medusa or Saint John; thirdly, 'intrinsic meaning or content' – the world of 'symbolical values'. It is this last which is most interesting, for it is nothing less than the actual way the previous layers of meaning are used, and amounts in fact to the 'meaning' of the particular work itself as an expression both of its time and of its author in that time. Panofsky admits, however, an important area where such an approach is dubious: the analysis of the images and allegories of painting would seem to be an indispensable element of the correct analysis of the third type of meaning – the intrinsic or subjectivised meaning of the particular work, unless – and it is a most significant rider – 'we deal with works of art in which the whole sphere of secondary or conventional subject matter is eliminated and a direct transition from motifs to content is affected, as is the case with European landscape painting, still life and genre, not to mention ''non-objective'' art'.

The development I have been trying to describe in this chapter is nothing less than the elimination of what Panofsky calls 'secondary or conventional subject matter'. In Romantic art, the motifs (things, people, houses) themselves stand forth as content: they do not 'mean' anything else, they are not in that sense symbolic or allegoric. And it is precisely from this new condition that what we call symbolism developed: in losing their conventional or agreed significances, (through social development), things and objects ('rocks and stones and trees') had to disclose and conceal, at the same time, the significances or value with which the poet is always concerned. It is in this way that we are to understand the development of symbolism in the novel and drama, and the new symbolic landscapes of poetry. Meaning is carried not by agreed social convention, but by the forms of the everyday things we experience in common.

The new language-situation was largely engineered by empiricism. The new element, we remember, was this: words may not have magic properties, they may not stand in mystic relationship to things, but they acquire their meaning through a process of experience and the collaboration in social discourse and intercourse of all the verbal experiences common to man. Verbal experience is common and inter-subjective. What we have in language therefore is the opposite of a divisive thing ensuring that each of us remains in his own cell. It is, on the contrary, that by which we can guarantee to know that others feel as we feel, think as we think. Language is man's self-transcending triumph, the basis of Objective Mind. This is what is behind Romantic and Symbolist imagery, which now emerges as the reverse of solipsistic: it is unifying and objective. The point is, of course, that this objectivity is achieved through the exercise of our subjectivity. Our experiences are subjective (nobody can have my sensations but myself); but language, as Wittgenstein showed, is not. Language is like the juggernaut's spy-in-the-cab: unless we pervert and misuse language, we can never be fully alone if we know language. What the Romantic poets did, quite properly in the circumstances, was to confine their poetry and their language, to the area that all men had in common. That is, to their 'personal' experiences.

It is in this light that we are to understand Wordsworth's new language – the language of a man speaking to men, a language without rhetoric, without arcana.

The heart of the new literature, as of the new world-view, was the new status of the object. European literature had developed from the high religious faith of the early Middle Ages. In describing the poetry of Dante in the high noon of Christian civilisation, Gabriel Josipovici is moved to exclaim, 'Never has there been such faith in the phenomenal.'[29] The strength and coherency of Dante's poetry, he argues express (rather than derive from) 'an assured correspondence between meaning and appearance'.[30] Yet did not precisely this faith, this assurance of meaning in the phenomenal, keep Western man from really *seeing* the phenomenal? The faith that the world was a book written by God, precisely, made everything in it symbolic. We might even counter-assert that there had never been such an evacuation of the phenomenal as in the Middle Ages. When we say that a thing 'means' something, we rob it of its thingness. It ceases to be in-itself; it becomes a sign, whose lineaments we scan for its meaning, its place in the eternal design. It is this eternal design we really read and observe in the *Divine Comedy*, and, in an intensified form, in *Paradise Lost*.[31]

The inherent tendencies in Thomist thought were early diagnosed by Duns Scotus, who attempted to stem the tide of 'symbolism'. Scotus wished to replace St. Thomas's analogical view of the universe, in which we did not see God but inferred His presence, with what he called 'univocitas' – the presence of reality in things we could actually know, by first-hand acquaintance. The 'fundamental weakness in the mentality of the Middle Ages', in fact, was precisely 'this tendency to reduce all things to a general type', owing to which 'the power to discern and describe individual traits was never attained'.[32] This is a state of decadence, to be sure, but decadence is only an exaggeration of a healthy state; the 'health' of Dante's world-view also was purchased at the expense of a regard for 'things-in-themselves'.

What we are concerned with in the development of a Romantic rhetoric, in fact, is the poet's adaptation to the new world-view and to the new language. The language was now without internal or intrinsic significance, in the sense that it was backed by no God or inherent meaningfulness in the world, and therefore had come to be seen merely as learned sign. What distressed the dissociation-of-sensibility critics was simply the fact that modern man could no longer hold a world-view which was intrinsically meaningful and religious, that he had come to acknowledge the fact of a physical universe which had no imperative claims on his moral or emotional being.

Yet man remained man. That is to say, the Thomist world-view which seems, to some literary scholars and historians, so admirable a thing, had itself to be conceived: after all, we no longer assent to the literal truths St. Thomas and Dante were prepared to assent to. We do not therefore think them fools. What then is the significance of their philosophy and art? Are we in the position of in fact implicitly wishing to be fooled? Are we claiming that the poets and painters of the Middle Ages were deluded as to the nature of the universe, but that this was a good thing for culture? To read much modernist criticism one would think so. But is not the real point not that we willingly suspend our disbelief, but that we now feel that there must be something in man that is able to conceive of such values and such meaningfulness? That this itself is not only the source but the substance of meaning?

4 Meaning and Meaningfulness

The analysis of the evolution of language in the modern world reveals a troubling paradox at the heart of our dominant philosophy. The empiricist philosophers enjoy a dual personality. In England and America, they are celebrated as the founders of modern philosophy, because of the way they exorcised the various religious and metaphysical ghosts from the human machine. On the Continent, on the other hand, they are generally thought of as solipsists, men who reduced the world to private sensation.[1]

This dual personality of empiricism is strangely typical of the whole development of Western man. In expelling the ghosts and gods of traditional religions, the empiricists would seem to have reduced the world to natural objects and processes, thus laying the foundations of the common-sense philosophy and philosophy of science by which modern man lives. Yet in reducing the world of real things and processes to bundles and sequences of sense-impressions, they withdrew from Western man the very certainty they ought to have secured with their emphasis on sensory evidence. So it is that we find, throughout the nineteenth century, the constant antiphony of optimism and despair. On the one hand, scientists and politicians trumpet the coming of light and certainty after centuries of darkness; on the other, are heard cries of despair, as the traditional certainties are eroded by empiricist scepticism. The more we know, the less certain we feel: that is our gloomy discovery.

This crisis generated in the Romantic period the first questionings of the existence of meaning – not the meanings of particular things and statements, but of meaning itself. The question the Romantics asked was, not 'What is the nature of the meaning of the universe?' but, 'Is the universe meaningful at all?' This new question, or series of questions, is deeply, disturbingly characteristic of the Romantic predicament. The question of the meaningfulness of the universe is something vitally important to us today. The logical opposite of 'meaningfulness' is 'meaninglessness'. Meaninglessness, or the possibility of meaninglessness, bothers us so much that we constantly quest not for any particular meaning to life, but for meaningfulness itself. What we wish to be assured of is not the truth of any particular meaning or philosophy, but simply that the universe, and therefore our lives within it, has meaning – any meaning, and therefore value, since the one implies the other. What frightens us is not evil but nothingness, sheer materiality, with no 'meaning' whatever. So much is this so, that some of our philosophies have tried to frighten us into meaning by forcing us to acknowledge this materiality and the facts of our mortality. But these philosophies (existentialist) only testify to the same central hunger for meaning. And this is not a hunger or concern of any age before the Romantic.

The danger for modern commentators is to assume our own preoccupations in the artists and philosophers of the past. To read the literature of the past as if it were designed to answer our own doubts and anxieties is one of the great fallacies of modern criticism. Gabriel Josipovici, for instance, observes that 'To read the Scriptures figurally is to affirm that history, and our own lives, have meaning, and it is to understand God's plan for mankind and hence for each one of us.' Going still further, Josipovici interprets the life of Christ, too, in this way: '(Christ) deliberately plays out his life in order to guide us to the meaningfulness of the universe'.[2]

Now this is pure twentieth century thinking, reducing the past to what we can see from our own angle. In point of fact neither the Scriptures nor the life of Christ teach us anything of the sort, though they may have come to *mean* that for some people. It was not the meaningfulness of the universe which Christ wished to illustrate or dramatise, but a particular course of events constituting a truth from which man, through greed, stupidity and wickedness, had strayed. In Christian theology, the wicked go to hell; hell exists just as truly and, therefore (to our way of seeing things) just as meaningfully, as paradise or the earth.

Again, Mr Josipovici observes that 'The Scriptures were proof that every man's life had meaning.'[3] They were nothing of the kind. Such a statement can be made only in answer to the implied question, 'Does every man's life have meaning?' And this question can never be put into the mouths of the contemporaries or predecessors of Christ. The question, 'Does life have meaning?' is a purely modern one. It is emphatically *not* the question implicit behind the writing of the Scriptures or the living of the life honoured in them. Man was to be saved from wickedness by Christ, not redeemed from meaninglessness. In the same spirit, Josipovici interprets the *Divine Comedy* as an existential quest poem: 'In Dante and Langland the narrator-hero goes in search of meaning.'[4] But Dante's hero does *not* go in search of meaning. As a matter of fact, he does not set out for anything; he is waylaid by the truth, the Word of God he had lost sight of through human weakness. His relationship to this Truth is more like that of the ephebe at Eleusis to the Mysteries into which he is about to be initiated than that of the existential hero to the 'significance' (authenticity) he doubts the existence of. Dante, like Langland and the Eleusinian ephebe, already knows of the existence of the mysteries. This is a very great difference. Both Christian and Oriental religious doctrines are radically different from modern existentialism here. In Christianity, man is blind because he is sinful; in Buddhism he is sinful because he is blind. That is a radical difference, but both views are aligned by the implicit acceptance of the meaningful and value-bound universe, and differentiated from the post-Romantic philosophies in the fact. In Dante and Langland, the mysteries wait to be revealed, not to be created, as they are in Nietzsche.

Neither is it as significant as Mr Josipovici says it is that Bunyan lacks the so-called 'objective' basis for his allegory that Dante has. We shall come to this objectivity in due course. For the moment let us point out that the Light which Bunyan's hero so sturdily sets out to find is as real and as fully believed-in – the universe is thus as fully meaningful – as it is in Dante.

It is no less wrong, in my view, to assert as Mr Josipovici does, that in the *Comedy*, Dante escapes 'from a false and subjective view of the world'.[5] This again is simply to turn the poem into a modern one. The very notion of the subjective would have meant nothing to Dante. To ellide the Mediaeval notion of Pride with the modern one of egotism (or subjectivity) is false. The frameworks of the two concepts are quite different. In the Mediaeval notion, there is no doubt that the sinner, though he may be confused and in need of instruction, also at the same time *knows* that he is: he assumes a context of God's plan or Book. The modern subjective man makes a mistake – according to Mr Josipovici – as to the nature of the universe, believing his own solipsistic illusions to be real. That is quite different. The process of Dante's poem is to restore to man the right way of life, to instruct him in the true relations of the universe. Like Milton's determination to 'justify the ways of God to man', Dante's intention is to dispel, through imaginative enactment, the confusions and heart-aches of human life, and this is totally and categorically different from the modern writer's desire to show that life has *some* meaning, *some* value. The Protestant poet's need to 'justify' is, of course, different in important respects from the great Catholic poet's certitude. Nevertheless, both poets were at issue not with a possible meaninglessness of existence, but with human declension from the 'right path'. And again, as with Bunyan – only with interest –, we must note that Milton's protestant dogmatism testifies to a cultural and intellectual predicament different from Dante's, but is not therefore invalidated. On the contrary, as the floreate centrelessness of most Italianate art of the seventeenth century shows, it is the sign of Milton's authenticity. 'Light' governs Milton no less powerfully than it governs Dante.

My argument here incidentally is not to be confused with another moral position. I am not saying that 'value' or goodness or right consciousness needs to be striven for in any age, and that virtue is just the old world's way of describing what we today would be inclined to call authenticity. Men had to strive to regain God in the middle ages just as we have to create our values afresh today. This is not the point at issue. In the old world, those men who were wicked, slothful or worldly, *knew* of the existence of God: they knew that they were sinful and accepted the fact. The existence of Confession proves as much. The Confessional meant little to the Protestant because he was aware that man can say one thing and 'mean' or feel another. It means still less to us today for the different reason that the absolution we crave is not to be obtained in any Confessional. We can grant the therapeutic effect of Confession, but, if we are deeply serious about our own souls and 'the meaning of life', we feel that the fact of being made to feel a little easier in our minds by confessing every now and then weighs very little. On the contrary, it is likely to make us feel inauthentic, by accepting a balm we do not deserve, so that our minds' ease may keep us from pursuing authenticity. The situation may be summed up by saying that the sinful modern materialist disregards God's way, he knows of no God or Good. The trouble is that the modern good man knows of none either. This is the real difference between then and now. It has little to do with Protestant inwardness and Catholic outwardness: after all, Catholic writers have failed to secure that Dantesque clarity no less emphatically than Protestant or free-thinking ones.

Thus the real nature of the process that has brought us from Dante and Langland to Beckett and Sartre is not merely the loss of faith in any particular doctrine. We are concerned with a more radical, more recalcitrant shucking. Significantly, Gabriel Josipovici himself remarks that 'the idea of the universe as itself meaningful, because an object created by a rational being, is not necessarily a Christian one'.[6] No indeed. It is, in fact, exactly the opposite: a cosmogony lies at the root of every known human culture. This means that the cosmogonic consciousness precedes all cosmogonies, just as immanence precedes the naming of the 'momentaner Götter'. The construction of culture and even of language itself is a product of a meaningfulness felt in nature. This is not to say that primitive man was aware of meaningfulness itself as an idea, as a concept; exactly the reverse in fact. Precisely what he did not feel was that there was 'meaningfulness': what he felt was specific immanence, overwhelming *mana*, imperative force outside himself, force which must be placated and worshipped. This is to say that language could not have come into being except through the exercise of an attribute we can only call the meaningful. It was not the makers of myths who persuaded men that the world was meaningful. On the contrary, they merely articulated the pre-existent feeling of meaningfulness. Once again, we must be careful to differentiate this *sense* of meaningfulness from our own *concept* of the meaningful, the logical opposite of which is the *meaningless*. Not even the Son of God created religion.

Christ lived amid competing philosophies. Christianity is always asserted as *the* way among ways. Other ways exist. Its existence is defined by the other religions it outdates. This is the defining property of any religion. Its religiousness cannot be created *ex nihilo*, but only, by definition, selected from a religious feeling greater than and prior to itself. This conception explains a number of otherwise puzzling phenomena. In the first place, the fact simply that the Great Religions are grouped both historically and in philosophy. I refer to the derivation of both Islam and Christianity itself from Judaism, and of Buddhism, Sufism and Jainism from Hinduism and Vedanta. There is, moreover, the common origination of various forms of Shamanism from a root-religion of central Asia and possibly of Iran.[7] Obviously a parallel of sorts exists with our languages. Secondly, there is the matter of the egregiously rapid conversion of kings and empires throughout the early history of Islam, Christianity and Buddhism. No reader of history can have failed to be impressed by the rapidity with which great leaders (and together with them, their subjects by the thousand) assented to the religious propositions of crusading Christians or Muslims. Why? Did they 'See the light'? What had they to gain? Were people simply more impressionable than they are now? One would have thought years of drip-feed necessary. People are still 'converted', and even, under the ministrations of a Billy Graham, in their hundreds. Yet this phenomenon belongs rather to the history of hysteria than to that of religion. We have no real equivalent to the speed and thoroughness with which Cnut or Attila became good Christians, permanently re-directing the course of the political history of their peoples.

Does not both the readiness (the indecent haste, almost,) to be converted of great leaders in the past, and the genealogies of the Great Religions, together suggest that there has to be a common stock, a general reservoir of 'religious' feeling before any particularised religious philosophy can emerge? In the Bible, John Hick points out, 'The reality of the divine Being is assumed throughout as a manifest fact. For within the borders of living religion the validity of faith in divine existence, like the validity of sense perception in ordinary daily life, is simply taken for granted and acted upon.'[8] (The validity of language, we might add, is similarly taken for granted, as Wittgenstein strove to show throughout his life.) This tide of 'validity' has receded: our religion is no longer, in the sense intended by Hick, 'living'. The apparent exceptions in the modern scene, I think, confirm my general point. When waves of religious conversion take place, they do so because a still-existing vein of religious feeling is being tapped: it is not new religious world-views that command reverence but Christianity, Islam and various forms of Hinduism. The teaching of J. Krishnamurti, for instance, derives substantially from Vedanta, and Indians generally find

his 'success' in the West puzzling. The reason why such
phenomena remain short-lived or cultish is simply that religious
feeling does not exist in modern man in the same way as it did in
those days. The intellectual's equivalent of the popular
Christianity of our own day is the reasoned view that religion
must be the answer.[9] This view is far from absurd; on the
contrary, it springs from a profound perception of human needs.
Yet it is an expression of despair. Such a view is in competition
not with other religions (as Christianity and Islam were) but with
other world-views – science, communism, materialism. This is a
greater difference than might at first appear.

Can the view (correct as it is in certain respects) that a religious
answer is necessary for man, *be* really religious itself? Christianity
asserted an enlightened monotheism, but it was backed by the
religious world-emotion in general. In other words, the
particularised, defined lineaments of Christianity partake of the
substance from which they came, and *of which they are a part*. The
embattled nature of Judaism surely confirms this general account
of things. The Gods of the Babylonians and Assyrians have a real
life in the Old Testament: they are treated as enemies not as
illusions. Jahwe is the 'God of Gods'. A great religion shapes the
religious feeling of its age: it does not create it from nothing.
Certainly, the enduringness of the Great Religions testifies to the
higher philosophical theory they enshrine. The vengeful, jealous
tribal deity of the Old Testament gives way to the all-embracing
azure divinity whose love rules the cars in the New. But the
suggestion of an 'improvement' here in this view should not be
pushed too far. For the essence of religion requires, we might say,
a certain 'illogicality'. That is to say, it depends ultimately upon
the asseveration of value, and value implies both a transcending
of the purely logical, and a distinction between the more and the
less valuable. Thus, we could say, from the comparative point of
view, that Christianity shares the underlying contradiction of,
say, the religion of the Central Asians for whom God is the sky,
or a Lord dwelling above the sky – who created the world, yet is
not part of it. It was the doubtful distinction of Spinoza – a Jew –
to resolve the contradiction of Christianity by defining God in
terms of nature. But this 'hideous hypothesis' (in Hume's phrase)
effectively destroyed Christianity, and we might assert that one of
the defining characteristics of religion is the presence of just such
a contradiction between the all-powerful Creator and his

Creation as we witness in Christianity and in the religion of the Chukchee or the Samoyed.[10]

The religious asseveration of our own time, whether of the intellectual variety or the commercial ('Jesus Lives'), in fact partakes of the rationalised therapeutic materialism of the age. Thus, it is not truly religious, but clinical. This is the sad truth. The question once again turns upon the notion of value. Whence derives value? We see with the same eyes, we see the same things – *mutatis mutandis* – which Dante and Aquinas saw.

In pre-Lockean philosophy, I have observed, the Word was undoubted: it was not felt as a sign at all, and this unawareness of the functioning of language was precisely the guarantee of philosophy. This in turn was so because the backing of things in their integrity, was simply accepted. The idea of Faith was necessary and inevitable because there was a situation of immanence. Even in the earliest revelations and declarations God had to be revealed, through a Burning Bush or however. Yet this revelation – so it seems to us now – was itself the product of a *response made by man*. That is, although we talk about the objectivity of Faith at the time of Dante, for instance – about the fact that the world-view exists outside Dante's own will – what we really believe now, since no one holds to the Thomist view of the universe any more, is that the response made by Dante (and his contemporaries of course) was such that it could be elaborated in intellectual terms without ceasing to be belief. After all, anyone could, theoretically, construct a World View such as we see elaborated in St. Thomas's *Summa Theologica* and imitated in the *Divine Comedy*. If it is logicality we are after, it is to be had. Yet of course, it is not what we are after: what we are concerned with is not logicality *per se*, but something else, something closer to what I have elsewhere referred to in the concept of availability.

For it was just this faculty for constructing logical systems that began to appear as inadequate towards the end of the seventeenth century. Spinoza, and, to a much lesser extent Leibniz, were the last great system-builders in Europe.

Why?

After all, inner coherency and logicality of the Spinozistic order are still attainable, still within our reach, given the intellectual power of the great philosopher. That Spinoza had this power no one has ever doubted. Yet the difference between his *Ethics* and Kant's *Critiques* or Hume's *Treatise* is not to be described in terms of greater or less intellectual coherency. Why did Kant not avail himself of the rationalist logicality? Because, obviously, his general feeling about the world and about his own experience of it was not satisfied by Spinoza's postulations. Spinoza's system remains as logical today as in 1672 when he first published the *Ethics*. It remains no less inter-related and consistent, yet it seems to us now, as it did to his English contemporaries, to be inner, merely willed, not to 'correspond with' reality. In Spinoza, in other words, the terms of the system, its postulations, are to some extent arbitrary. Now it was just this arbitrariness in metaphysics – an arbitrariness we do not feel in St. Thomas's *Summa* or in Plato's *Symposium* – which drove first Descartes, Spinoza's predecessor, then Locke, his exact contemporary, to question the fundamental bricks of language. The sense that words are signs which can stand for whatever we choose – this excess of liberty in language and linguistic usage – gave rise to the algebraic universe of Spinoza's *Ethics* and Leibniz's *Essay*. 'Let x be such, and y be something else; therefore z must be the case.' Why doesn't this work any more?

Spinoza was solving an old problem – the oldest, perhaps, known to theology – the inner contradictoriness of maintaining that God is somehow different from the world, yet *is* that world. His solution was rational enough – to ellide the two things, and identify God with nature, giving rise to the mechanistic deism of the Enlightenment, with its cheap, and cheaply memorable, rationale from Voltaire, 'If God did not exist, it would be necessary to invent him.' Is it necessary to invoke the tired literature of existentialism to dispel the credulous demon of such rationality, to show that 'God' can no more be invented than destroyed? Long before Giordano Bruno, still longer before Spinoza, the Gnostics had early bid for the soul of Christianity by suggesting that to those who 'knew', God was in all things (or *was* all things). Orthodox Christianity quite properly expelled this heresy by strenuously insisting upon the separateness of God, yet at the same time destroying the claim of all secret Ways, all dark societies, all mysteries. Christianity made it necessary for the soul of man to rise to God, and the Gnostics would debase Him to the level of the occult. That which is entirely open, yet which demands the highest and best of which man is capable – such is the God of Christianity.

Yet this description itself suffers from the inevitable circularity of rationalised descriptions of religious feeling. We cannot prescribe ourselves a God, and those well-meaning attempts to do so – to go one better than the traditional Gods, in the manner of Matthew Arnold – are doomed to reflect nothing but our hunger. Arnold writes from a background of honest empiricist scepticism, and his God is a fabrication. The fact is that our Gods, like our values, cannot be invented, are not open to logical analysis without ceasing to be gods or values. What we see in Romanticism is the crisis of that moment at which our values – our sense of meaningfulness – suffered an unalterable shift from the realm of structure to that of content: 'meaning' which had been immanent, in the beholding mind, became an object of study.

It is no accident that literary Romanticism was accompanied by the first great historiographies. Man begins to wonder whether History itself has a purpose. Hegel's attempt to establish that mind is the last manifestation of matter, that History is a striving organism fulfilling itself in space and time, is deeply characteristic of post-Lockean man. How could it, we must ask ourselves, ever have occurred to earlier historians or writers to question the purpose of the world,[11] or, which is to say precisely the same thing, to suggest that history or the world *could have a purpose*? The purpose or fundamental meaningfulness of existence was given, in pre-Lockean culture.

Taking his cue from Kierkegaard's analyses in *Either/Or*, Gabriel Josipovici contrasts Hegel's attempt to find a pattern, a meaning in history, with the actions of Cromwell or Luther or Napoleon, and deduces that Hegel was wrong because life is lived forward rather than backwards'.[12] This is, perhaps, rather like taking the plot of a Dickens novel to task because it has order and structure whereas life has not, and life is lived *ad hoc* rather than as part of a grand design. Life is life and history is history, and the significance of Hegel's attempt to find a pattern and meaning in history is not that he sees history as like the plot of a novel, but that it is evidence precisely of that newly felt lack in Western man: man in all his fields and divisions had, as it were, ceased living forwards under the impulsion of a meaningfulness felt to inhere in things, and had therefore adopted (or showed in his new cultural activities that he had already adopted) a new stance towards himself and his past. Kierkegaard's reaction against Hegel is in fact itself a characteristically Romantic reaction to 'existence'. Kierkegaard's demand that man live under the mandate of a perpetual choice in order to confer meaning upon existence is akin to Hegel's attempts to establish meaningfulness by incorporating human existence into some design that, holding meaning itself, conferred meaning upon whatever formed part of it. As a matter of fact, it is a mistake to regard Kierkegaard's philosophy as being essentially a reaction against Hegel. Hegel may have given Kierkegaard his occasion and suggested by opposition the mode by which to investigate existence. We might say that, dialectically speaking, the concept of existence itself was suggested to Kierkegaard precisely by its absence from Hegel's sweeping design, which so powerfully failed to convey that quality present in every moment of our lives, precisely in trying to give our lives some purpose. Thus, Kierkegaardian *existenzphilosophie* could well be seen as antithetical to Hegelian design, just as Aquinas's *Summa* dialectically generated Wycliffian inwardness. Yet to see Kierkegaard purely as a reaction against Hegel is superficial; it is the same error as to reduce Romanticism itself to a reaction against eighteenth century rationalism. In each case, there is a relation of dialectical opposition, relating the two terms by the same process as separates them. The Romantic reaction against the Enlightenment view of man is essentially dialectical. What is important is the direction of the dialectical vortex. In this wider perspective, we can see Kierkegaard's philosophy, like Hegel's, as a response to something much broader than Hegel himself – to the modern predicament, and Romanticism not as a local 'reaction' to a series of philosophical doctrines that can be accepted or rejected, but as a further adjustment to a situation essentially mapped in those philosophical doctrines. We must always bear in mind that, hostile in spirit as Romanticism may sometimes appear to be to everything the Enlightenment stood for, there is no essential discontinuity in Enlightenment and Romantic philosophies: there could not be any such discontinuity. The appearance of discontinuity can be explained in dialectical terms.

Perhaps the greatest instance of the antithetical relationship of Romanticism to the Enlightenment is the philosophy of Kant in relation to that of Hume. For the very irreversibility of Humean empiricism drove Kant to conceive his 'Copernican' revolution. Kant accepted in all essentials the philosophical revolution laid out by Locke and Hume, merely bringing to it his own revisionist notion of the categories. It is a big 'merely' and many would argue that the conceptual instrument introduced by Kant equals in significance the original tools of the revolution itself. But this is not important. The main thing to accept is that there was *no going back*: Kant accepted empiricist man and his condition. The quarrel between Kantian and empiricist philosophers is not one of base but of superstructure – of what is acceptable cultural and intellectual behaviour. We have to accept that empiricism gave us our new conception of 'the human condition', or at least that it articulated that condition. The main features of this condition are as follows:

1. We only know what we know through our senses. (Kant accepts this, merely adding that our way of organising what we see is monitored by regulative reason, itself empty but guaranteeing sequences of temporal and spatial logicality, and allowing in an unspecified way 'descriptive knowledge' of things-in-themselves.)

2. There is no metaphysical realm of 'meaning'; there are no super-sensible entities which we might know had we senses fine enough. (Kant's postulation of such a world – that of the noumena – is one of the things modern thinking has rejected: the contradictory nature of his whole enterprise is reflected accurately in his inability to drop the notion of a metaphysical world even when he admits that there is no way we can ever know it.)

3. There is no God in the sense intended by traditional theology. (Kant turned God into an 'exemplar i.e. a pure intellectual concept: we can conceive of a perfection of all perfections; therefore it exists. His intention was to strengthen belief in God, but the only way he found to do so was to destroy all metaphysical proofs of His existence, yet to continue to assert a kind of 'God-feelingness' in man.)

4. There is no moral realm guaranteeing us certain values and standards: ethics shifts over into the realm of psychology, and moral absolutes become descriptive statements of 'approval' (Hume) or 'inclination' (Kant). (Kant however posits a 'heilige Wille', or moral sense, which does know what it always ought to do. In this regard, we must note that, though modern philosophy has refused Kant's option here, modern man as a whole continues to behave as if he were right.)

5. There are no necessary causes, guaranteeing that if one event happens a second is bound to occur. Relations of cause and effect reduce to merely probable sequences, begetting a new science, that of probability. (Kant's 'Second Analogy' – which was supposed to 'answer' Hume on cause – in fact emphasises temporal sequence, precedence and succession of events, in a way which necessitates no modification of Hume's account.)

6. Conclusion: there is really just stuff-behaving-in-time, and man is just another piece of stuff-behaving-in-time. (Kant invokes teleology, but admits that it forms 'no proper part of theoretical natural science' and has to be relegated to 'theology': Kant effectively says that man needs a teleological sense to understand his sense data: i.e. we go on behaving as if things had purpose, even though we can not locate any objective purpose in nature.) Once again, Kant's categories emerge as ways of behaving which man has not yet outgrown, and indeed his entire philosophy may be described as assuming a rational and meaningful structure in the world and in human life at the same time as it proceeds remorselessly to destroy every argument upon which that inherited structure had traditionally been established. In executing this programme of destruction, Kant's philosophical method might be described as systematically incremental – the exact reverse of modern reductivisms. Where a reductivist philosophy, for instance, might want to reduce God to our own experience of father-son relationships, Kant on the contrary uses our own experience of such a relationship to make it possible for us to understand the notion of God – by analogy. The notion of God, like those of a purpose in nature, of good and evil, of causation and of the existence of an 'intelligible world' of things-in-themselves, are assumptions which are so natural to Kant that he could happily spend the whole of his adult life destroying the rationalistic foundations upon which such concepts depended. Methodologically, Kant was an empiricist; in *Weltanschauung* he was a rationalist.

Kant presents us, throughout his work, with a very Kantian phenomenon: systematicness without system. What he was up to is evident enough from his general use of the categories as regulative instruments, empty ideas, and, in particular, by his use of the Analogies by which man's practical reason helps him make sense of, say, the idea of God. We think of God by thinking of the relations of father to child. This does not give us any knowledge of God, but it gives us a 'concept of the highest being adequately determined for us'. The categories, in other words, are simply Kant's way of preserving the structure and meaning-likeness of the old pre-Lockean world, whilst admitting the force of the empiricist revolution. As critic, Kant destroyed every vestige of the old Leibnizian metaphysics. As constructor, he merely *postulated* the mind's constructive faculties, something comforting but irrelevant to the aim of the empiricist, emerging as a kind of Gestalt psychologist with no support whatever for his own claims to have established philosophical certainty in spheres threatened by empiricism. In other words, man inherits certain structures and expectations, patterns of thought and feeling from the past: these he projects automatically onto the present situation even when his own belief in the reality of this world has failed.

This contradiction of Kant is deeply characteristic of Romanticism in general. It was to be sixty years before Nietzsche would proclaim that God was dead, but that the news had been slow getting about. Yet this aphorism is really already implicit in the *Critiques*. What do they mean, if not that God *is* dead, but that, because we cannot function on the assumption that he is, we continue, like Kierkegaard and Hegel, finding different forms for our God-feeling to manifest itself? The same is, of course, true of our sense of value. Essentially, the elements of the Absurd are present in Romantic thought. Yet the feeling of value persisted, expressing itself in large-scale forms with beautiful God-given structures braced by the despair generated by the disparity between the inherited shapes (heroic, beautiful) and the absence of true belief in them. I shall be considering the most fundamental result of this situation later. Here, I wish to draw attention to one example – the Romantic 'interiorised quest' poem, to use Harold Bloom's convenient expression.[13] There is a fundamental and absolute difference between such quests as the Red Knight's in *The Faerie Queen* and those of Shelley's 'Alastor' and Byron's *Childe Harold*. There is an equally great gulf between these latter quest-poems and those of Browning ('Childe Roland to the dark tower came') and Tennyson; an equally great one again, between these mid-Victorian allegories and those of the 'last Romantics', Yeats, and, above all, Rupert Brooke, whose poem 'The Flight' may be said to put a full stop to the whole tradition. It is a mark of Harold Bloom's indifference to the sociological and historical factors that he is able to treat all these various offerings as if they are performing the same sort of function all the time. (The work of this remarkable critic, in fact, takes literary criticism void of any socio-historical context about as far as it can go.)

In point of fact, the whole essence of the Romantic quest-poem is really lost if it is not understood socio-historically – in terms of the Romantic predicament and the shift of contents. For the point of Byron's 'Childe Harold's Pilgrimage' is that it consists of a voyage from nowhere to nowhere, and that the hero finds nothing, as he in effect looks for nothing. That 'the going is the thing' is a message we are more accustomed to meet with today than people were in Byron's time. But that is what the curious conflict of form (the poem as voyage-quest) and content (the hero searches for nothing) condemns us to believe. Shelley's 'Alastor' merely takes this to its conscious conclusions: Death, welcomed and accepted, is the logical end to this quest for nothing as it was to be for Proust. Browning's version ('Childe Roland') brilliantly takes this into the realm of the inchoate: not only is the quest *for* nothing, it is also shrouded in a mysterious deformalising darkness that paradoxically almost convinces us that there *is* something there. In Browning, the element of Allegory – lost in Byron and Shelley – is restored: the world is a scrub-land, the enemies have to be identified before they can be fought; the goal is – the goal is what you have to find out. It is clear that this has come full circle from Spenser where the absent allegorical centre draws the hero vigorously and confidently through trials and combats no longer as real as they were in Mallory and even Tasso: teleological clarity gives Spenser's poem a hard contour even where its incidents and events belong to the realm of allegory rather than that of *figura*.

The transformation of the quest-motif illustrates better than anything else, probably, the real nature of the Romantic predicament as a shift in contents. Each generation, probably, supplies itself at the expense of the next. More accurately, we might suggest that it is in the nature of consciousness and of cultural structures to explore the relationship between consciousness itself, in the sense of subjectivity, and these forms and formations of which it appears to consist. The formations are not unchanging and external to the individual; they are not wholly objective. If the individual subject is 'made up of' these formations – language, culture, nationality, group-identification – he is not determined by them, nor does he reduce to nothing if they are all subtracted from him. Again and again in cultural commentary we shall find the error of cultural reductivism being committed. Cultural reductivism attempts to reduce man to the sum of his isolable formations – to all his cultural 'influences' and socio-economic determinations – without understanding that man has a degree of freedom and autonomy which allows him to use these formations, and to consider itself apart from them, no matter how strong they may be. This is what I have been referring to as subjectivity: without subjectivity we can account for nothing human.

The Romantic poets' conflict of form and content in the quest-poems is paralleled in philosophy by the despair of thinkers who retained the language of the old world to voice the predicament of the new. In general Nietzsche's despairing formula, 'God is dead', gives the game away. What the words mean (amount to) is that there is no God, which means in turn that the traditional belief in God was hogwash and moonshine. But if that belief *was* hogwash and moonshine, if there is no God, there is no need for either rejoicing or lamentation. That is why Nietzsche put his formula as a comment on human cultural assumptions rather than as straight description of the state of things. For of course to say that God has died is to imply that he once lived, a statement which is incomprehensible if taken as a statement about Reality or Nature, but deeply understandable if taken – as it must be – as a comment on human expectations. What Nietzsche meant, was 'Oh, dear, there is no God', meaning. 'There's a leak in the roof, where before it was so warm and cosy.' He should have meant: 'Oh, we were wrong. So?' What this, in turn, entails is that there is a culture-lag, a disparity between man's (intellectual) beliefs and his ways of feeling. Some such formula (a gap between reason and emotion) is of course a commonplace of cultural criticism and history. But the formula is often proffered as if there were a culpable wilfulness in the Romantics, almost as if they were not trying hard enough. Those who push the process farther back historically, dating modern man's apostasy to Zwingli's doubt of the Sacrament's reality, or to Luther's questioning of authority, generally do so with a disapproving reference to Protestant insolence, as if it had been within anyone's control. In fact, what the Romantic agony testifies to is simply the culture-lag between man's new intellectual and linguistic predicament and the inherited cultural presuppositions he finds it so hard to shrug off. There is strictly speaking no justification whatever for Nietzsche' anxiety, or the *Angst* or *ennui* of existentialist thought in our own time. The paroxysm of Romantic and post-Romantic despair, like the Absurd of existentialism, is nothing but the disparity between what we accept as fact and what we feel, through our inherited culture, measured in terms of uncertainty. Sartre's atheism is the rage of the seminarist defecating against the seminary walls. If the philosophers of the Absurd were consistent in their atheism, there would be no cause for despair. We despair only because we react as if the model we were using were not 'There is no God', but: 'He has gone away, and thus we are abandoned; there is absurdity at the heart of things because we see that the cultural categories and imperatives we inherit do not truly reflect the reality we acknowledge to exist; "Good" and "God" are worse than nothing, they mock our new understanding of the facts'. Perhaps Kant's Analogy put the matter in its true light: man had always conceived of God in quasi-paternal terms, so that the new 'belief' was felt as a loss exactly as if God *had* died, or irresponsibly deserted us. That is why so many sceptical and atheist works of the nineteenth and twentieth centuries take the illogical form of invective or abuse of God: the hysteria of disillusioned seminarists.

The whole case may be repeated with regard to values in things. What is Absurd, properly speaking, is the disparity between our value-making consciousness and the reality we observe with our minds (which now, unalterably, operate upon the scientific empiricist model). Yet this is so only because we insist on framing our values in terms of 'absolutes' in turn interpreted according to the old God-Good formulae. It is notable that when a thinker has succeeded in freeing himself of the constrictions of the old value-system (William Blake, Bernard Shaw and D. H. Lawrence are all examples) value itself has emerged as a new absolute. It is only when the thinker insists on getting answers to the question of value in terms of the old imperatives that Absurdity arises.

What we know today as modernism is really nothing but the evolving form this Romantic predicament takes in the differing social and intellectual circumstances of the early twentieth century. Certainly, modernist art is different from Romantic. But there is no question of going back to where we were before the Romantics messed things up. To believe this is itself the sheerest romanticism. There is a relationship similar probably to that between Romanticism and the Enlightenment, between Romanticism (or late Romanticism) and modernism. There is a change in tone in stance; but the changes take place in territory clearly and unalterably marked out by the preceding generations. Just as the novel of Fielding and Defoe and Richardson lay behind that of Scott and Dickens, so the philosophy of Hume and Berkeley lay before that of Kant and Hegel: in neither case would the latter development have been possible without the former. So it is with modernism. Modernism, for all its anti-Romantic irony and its rejection of the bardic statesmanship of the great Romantic writers, accepts, in philosophy and technique, the necessary changes brought about by the work of the Romantics. We are not free to choose our situation, which has only got 'worse' since the great Romantics died. What we have lost, of course, is just those forms which the great Romantics – supplying themselves at our expense – took to the point of extinction.

5 Romantic Alienation

So far we have studied the Romantic predicament in terms of the language of its poetry, its new sense of 'meaning', and a certain subjectivism of literary content. In all cases, what had been felt before to be shortcomings of Romantic writers, turned out on inspection to be simply characteristics of a particular historical situation. This situation – the Romantic predicament – is beginning to emerge as a series of content-shifts. These shifts can be seen in turn as fallings-away – privations of subject-matter and attitude. Not only the way poets see things, but what they see, is created by the evolution of the historical continuum of which they are part. Erwin Panofsky's perception that the material available to the artist changed dramatically during the Romantic period emerges as more and more important. If the evolution of history robbed the artist of the efficacy of certain traditional iconographies (themes and motifs, once operative and pungent, now decorative and useless), so did it alter the artist's vision of man himself.

Our relations with our fellow-men determine the way we use our language. Not only the manner but the matter of poetry changes in the Romantic period. To follow this change, we must turn to the ways in which poetry is related to society. For the poet is related to society through language, and the changing poetry of the Romantic period registers deeper changes within the societal organisation. Moreover, the sense of depletion, of privation, in the language of poetry, is reflected in the constantly iterated sense of society itself being in a state of 'decay'.[1]

(i) ALIENATION: FROM HOBBES TO ROUSSEAU

What we are confronted with here is, of course, the fact of alienation. It is alienation, in fact, which really constitutes the essence of the Romantic predicament. In its broadest terms, alienation can really be seen as the hidden content of all poetry. It can easily be observed, that the sense of a lost content forms the content of all poetry, of whatever period.[2] On a narrower perspective, we could locate the birth of a definingly modern concept of alienation in the writings of Montaigne or Pascal. Pascal strikes an especially modern note with his description of man separated from the hidden God. This is surely different from the ultimately confident sense of the Christian's traditional awareness of his apartness from God. Pascal's man is recognisably ourselves, and it is significant that he should have made his appearance in the age of Locke and Newton. Yet this existential vision of the human condition was only properly realised in the writings of the Romantic philosopher Søren Kierkegaard. There is something assured about Pascal's wager, a certain air of the *jeu d'esprit* about it, which sets it apart from existentialist *Angst*: its anxiety, such as it is, elegantly solves its own problems, mathematically and logically. As the example of Kierkegaard shows, there is a historical dimension to our modern anxiety and alienation. And for the understanding of his dimension, we must assume a societal framework: the first really modern analysis of our peculiar condition occurs in the sociologicaly orientated writings of Rousseau. It is from Rousseau that the Romantics principally learned the language of alienation.

Hobbes's *Leviathan* (1651) presents us with an unflattering vision of human life as 'solitary, poore, nasty, brutish and short'.[3] This disabused view may reflect the fact of the English Civil War, and the general sense of uncertainty pervading European thought at this time.

Yet Hobbes does not condemn 'society' for the fact that it is so unappetising a beast. On the contrary, Hobbes's experience of civic disturbance in England led him to the contrary view, that it is society that redeems man. Only civilisation and the larger societal organisations make the cave-man palatable: law and 'society' save us from the law of the jungle. This, to be sure, is an over-simplification. As Professor MacPherson has demonstrated, it is not the 'state of nature' which is regarded as in need of correction in Hobbes, but the state of society as it existed in Hobbes's day:

The behaviour of men in Hobbes's model of society is, so to speak, so anti-social, that when he carries this behaviour into his hypothetical state of nature, it is there easily mistaken for a statement of the behaviour of non-social men.[4]

But the point is strengthened by this consideration. It is not merely society which is endorsed in *Leviathan*, but a particularly strong state of society ('sovereignty'), one which will end the disorderly competitiveness of the market-society Hobbes was in fact, as MacPherson shows, describing. Hobbes gives endorsement to the kind of monarchical doctrine favoured by the Stuarts, the difference being that in Hobbes the decision to accede to the law of the sovereign is to be made rationally, and the Stuarts demanded an irrational, quasi-mystical obedience which expressed itself in self-bankrupting economics and self-contradictory politics.

In Hobbes, the state therefore receives a powerfully reasoned endorsement, one which reflects the fear engendered by Civil disorder, and which is to be found repeated variously in literary works such as Dryden's *Absolom and Achitophel, and Samuel*.

Butler's *Huddibras*, and Otway's *Venice Preserved* (to say nothing of *Paradise Lost*: the precise nature of Milton's ambivalence towards these matters has yet to be explored). When we turn to Rousseau, it is the decline from such an endorsement that is so significantly striking. Between *Leviathan* and *Le Contrat Social* (1762) comes Locke, with his *Essay concerning human understanding* and, more pertinently, the *Two Treatises of Government*. There is no doubt that, whether rightly or wrongly, Rousseau and other eighteenth century theorists read Locke's *Treatises* less as a defence of property than as an assertion of the rights of majority (or consensus) rule: Locke's 'Civil society' is practically indistinguishable from Rousseau's *volonté générale*, and was taken in the emerging United States of America to guarantee the rights of little men rather than the property of big men. (The paradoxical nature of American democracy, equally passionate in its defence of capital and of the rights of labour exploited by capital probably derives from this characteristic reading of Locke.)[5]

The theories of Hobbes and Locke reflect the conditions of the seventeenth century, no less in their unhistorical nature than in their actual recommendations. We might say, indeed, that their work demonstrates that in political theory contemporaneity is the best historicity. For the major difference between their work and Rousseau's is that where they present a theory of man that is logical and empirically based upon observation, Rousseau's work draws upon a model which is supposed to be genuinely historical, yet is a figment of the imagination. Hobbes's 'state of nature' is society now: Rousseau's noble savage is supposed to have existed and to exist in less advanced, more fortunate societies now. Hobbes describes, Rousseau idealises: Hobbes analyses, Rousseau rhapsodises. Hobbes and Locke present an analysis of man which is a thinly disguised portrait of contemporary seventeenth century man, and produce recommendations to extend hegemony but also to allow of a flexible extension of property and labour (liberalism), so that there is no hard line between individualistic capitalism and equally individualistic democracy. Rousseau lays down a theory of man which hardly allows of change, and points directly to the dogmatism of communism – idealistic, but inflexible and doctrinaire.

An important and decisive evolutionary turn has taken place between Hobbes's disabused but confident argument for strong 'sovereignty' (the most positive endorsement the State has received in modern times) and Rousseau's view of man as being born free, but living in chains. Rousseau replaces the Hobbesian view of the sovereign state as necessary and desired in its omnipotence, with a strictly Utopian view of a small egalitarian *polis* which is not really a state at all but a larger species of family. Rousseau differs from the classical satirists (Plato, More, Erasmus) in that his critique of society was not designed to purge that society of its defects, but to do away with it altogether. In Rousseau, social man is distinct from 'natural' man: natural man has a beneficent *amour de soi* (roughly equivalent to enlightened self-interest or simply the ingrown sense of life) which deteriorates under pressure of civilisation into *amour propre* – egoistic self-love, competitive and destructive. The very process of self-awareness – *via* the mirror-image, which forms the basis of all our arts – becomes in Rousseau, evil and factitious: the difference between authentic being and this socially conditioned self-consciousness is expressed by Rousseau in the two terms *être* and *paraître*.[6]

What Rousseau has done, plainly, is to drive a wedge between modern man and his 'real' self. The young Marx astutely characterised the process in distinguishing between the man and the citizen. Differing from Rousseau only in putting the blame specifically on the new bourgeois society, Marx observes:

Political emancipation is a reduction of man, on the one hand to a member of civil society, an *independent* and *egoistic* individual, and on the other hand to a *citizen*, to a moral person.[7]

Now Marx's further suggestion, that man will only be completely emancipated when the man has been absorbed into the citizen is thoroughly in accordance both with Rousseau's stipulation that the individual will must be satisfied in some way in the general will (how, it is not said). It also consorts with the whole Utopian stream in modern left-ist thought. From the time that Rousseau made his major observations on the subject, in fact, the fundamental schism between 'man' and 'citizen' becomes a major element of political and social philosophy in Europe. In the philosophy of Kant, there is a fundamental distinction between 'true ego' and 'phenomenal ego' which became a major element in Idealism, under Fichte and Hegel, and persisted in the twentieth century in the various, and variously obscure, attempts by Heidegger and others to establish an 'authentic' mode of being from all sorts of inauthentic sorts. Marx himself drew upon Hegel's concept of *species being*. This means the abstract sum of all those capacities which man possesses and which require satisfaction in group- and societal activities. Only when man's social aptitudes (which are regarded *as no less indissolubly part of his essence*) are realised in meaningful cooperation in society will man be fully free, *i.e.* fully himself.

All of these manoeuvres can, I suggest, be understood as constitutive of what we can in the most general sense call alienation. Extreme versions of alienation-theory, such as those of Fichte in the Romantic period, and of Jacques Lacan in the twentieth century, regard the fundamental divorce between true 'ego' and socially constituted ego as ultimate and final – a fact about the human condition, called by Fichte *Entäusserung*.[8] But this extreme view competes with the less extreme, societally oriented theories of such thinkers as Marx and Rousseau, who regard the particular organisation of society known as capitalism (Marx), or the particular degree of complexity in any highly civilised society (Rousseau), as empirically causing a divorce between man's true or better nature and the 'non-ego' forced upon him by highly competitive and unegalitarian societies. But both kinds of alienation-theory, metaphysical and sociological, belong characteristically to a particular historical period: they are equally expressive of the Romantic predicament. There is now a schism between the man of good will and the facts of political life. Whereas man had been able to fulfil himself and his societal aptitudes in the body of civil society, he is now forced to withdraw from such 'cooperation', which can be sustained only at the expense of his true or authentic being.[9]

By these means we see that the subjectivity characteristic of Romantic art bears a deep sociological significance. It expresses the new condition in which man felt himself to exist (although he did not, as it were, know it yet: the artist's role here as elsewhere is prophetic and proleptic). This condition was early diagnosed by Hegel, who observed that in the arts man had already given of his best.[10] What Hegel meant (or should have meant) is not that the age of the giants is past; nor is the significance of his profound observation exhausted in Schiller's terms of a totality now lost. Its real meaning is better understood in Marx's terms: it is no hypostatised Grecian unity or totality that has been lost, but a capacity to put into use all the elements of which we must feel ourselves to be composed. Such a statement, certainly, implies acceptance of a particular theory of 'humanity', in particular, of a theory asserting man's necessarily social and political nature. In Marx, man is *zoon politikon*: so he is, variously, in Rousseau, Locke and Hobbes. Sociological alienationists depart here from metaphysical ones: against the theory of man as 'intrinsically' or mystically such-and-such, alienation sociology asserts that 'man' is created *at least in part* out of his interaction with others, with his family first, and then with the larger family that is the race or nation. What Hegel saw was that man had lost the capacity to express his political or social nature, and that this nature can in no way be artificially divorced from the rest of him. Alienation, then, gains further definition: modern man has been divorced from the fullest expression of himself because he is himself sundered from himself. The new societal divisions (division of labour, accumulation of capital, machine-assisted work) are mirrored in individual self-division.

(ii) FROM POPE TO WORDSWORTH

We can best appreciate the new condition of literature by comparing the work of Romantic poets such as Wordsworth and Blake, with that of high Augustans such as Pope. The artists of the Augustan period were perhaps the last to be able to celebrate the State. That is, to produce work of high quality which endorses the fact of political power, and presents an image of man as not merely an isolated subjectivity with a 'true' ego, but as a social and political animal whose works and ceremonies have meaningful splendour. This latter fact has caused radical critics a good deal of chagrin: they would like either to show that the Augustans were bad poets, or that their attitude towards a hegemonic power-structure was in some sense ironical or unconsciously subversive. The truth is that we must accept that art for what it is, or draw a line across human history and write off everything produced before that line as vitiated by the fact of its expressing unacceptable ideology. Pope and Johnson, Swift and Gainsborough, Purcell and Vanbrugh, Handel and Reynolds, whatever their complex personal doubts and reservations about particular politicians or sovereigns, present and assume an image of human life as being meaningfully and splendidly fulfilled in the high panoply of power. Purcell's Odes for Queen Mary, Handel's music for the Hanovers, Gainsborough's aristocratic portraits, Vanbrugh's Blenheim and Castle Howard, Pope's *Essays* – these great products of the earlier eighteenth century testify to the acceptance of political power *and affluence* as a proper manifestation of man. The political philosophy (in its broadest possible sense) that unites them is that of Hobbes: the state is seen as a rational and proper compact between men; it is not 'natural', since natural man is, in Pope as in Hobbes, vicious and short-sighted. The 'historical' thesis advanced in the *Essays on Man* gives a brilliantly realised account of man's progress from an early hypostatised innocence, through inevitable corruption by greed and self-interest, to self-transcendence in large social units.

The Augustan artists, then, express in their superbly formal yet human style, a splendid vision of man as a political animal. Yet I am aware that many of my readers must have questioned the apparently bland assumption made about this Style. There is,

for example, a great difference between the political poetry of
Pope and that of Shakespeare. Pope as a Catholic was out of
favour for most of his life. Yet his attacks on the Whigs assume
that a norm has been violated, not that that norm is itself wrong.
The Tories would do better, but the power wielded by the Whigs
is nevertheless regarded as a natural and wholesome exercise of
man's essentially societal nature. Augustan art celebrates a State
which represented in its own constitution a great number of
collaborative efforts, efforts involving a great deal more of the
nation than merely the court and the aristocracy. The sound-
ness of the tone and the confident wholeness testify to Pope's
confidence in being able to speak for man himself, not merely his
class. Yet when we turn back to the Shakespeare of the Histories,
the difference is at once apparent. Shakespeare sounds the full
human diapason, encompassing everything in man's social and
administrative vision of himself, as well as in his private regions.
When a poet cannot celebrate with full confidence the exercise of
man as he is at his most splendid and powerful, then a dimension
has been lost. What we see in Shakespeare is, of course, the last
great paean of the high Renaissance: in Monteverdi's music and
Tintoretto's painting, as well as in *Henry IV* and *Antony and
Cleopatra*, we see the unabashed celebration of wealth – not just
spiritual wealth, but material:

> The barge she sat in, like a burnish'd throne,
> Burn'd on the water. The poop was beaten gold;
> Purple the sails, and so perfumed that
> The winds were love-sick with them; the oars were silver,
> Which to the tune of flutes kept stroke, and made
> The water which they beat to follow faster,
> As amorous of their strokes. For her own person,
> She beggar'd all description. She did lie
> In her pavilion, cloth-of-gold, of tissue,
> O'erpicturing that Venus where we see
> The fancy out-work nature.
>   ('Antony and Cleopatra', Act 2, Scene 2, ll. 195–205)

Already, in the political art of the Augustans, there is a sense of
that inward social disintegration which was in the end to produce
Romanticism and the modern world. This is not to renege upon
my former statements of Augustan magnificence, but merely to

try to describe it more exactly. There is a significant change, for instance, from the fine tone of Shakespeare's Histories, in which political power consorts naturally and beautifully with patriotism, to the bombast of Thomson's 'Rule, Britannia!' *Richard II* does not seem designed to oppress or to intimidate, as Thomson's poem does. The brash assertiveness of 'Rule Britannia'! is paralleled, perhaps, by the very elegance of the characteristic Augustan manner. The glitter of the rationalistic Toryism consummated in Pope's poetry does, perhaps, testify to certain changes that have taken place within English society. Perhaps the artificiality of the neo-classical style – the cult of mask, manners and surface – reflects a divorce within the societal pyramid. It represents perhaps an asseveration, a last bulwark against the coming deluge. Pope saw, with the true conservative's horror, the coming of the 'universal Anarch' (Demos, of course). The last book of *The Dunciad* looks forward to the disruptions which were to end the old order in France and threaten England, bringing in their train the disintegration of the social pyramid, and the disappearance of those cultural standards so confidently defended throughout Pope's work. While the best minds (Pope, Swift, Johnson, Gibbon) held fast to the norms of high art, less exalted but no less vigorous talents were bringing to birth the literary form that was to dominate modern literature and also to typify its new, non-hierarchical standards. The novel of Defoe and Fielding reflects, in its very plot-mechanism, the processes which were even then undermining the politico-cultural bastions adorned by Pope. The real meaning of the 'dissociation of sensibility' lies perhaps in the gradual emergence of the socially divisive low church consciousness in the seventeenth and early eighteenth centuries, creating a new kind of culture with new orders of rhetorical achievement. From this point of view, as from the linguistic point of view, Augustan art, and, with significant variations, the Enlightenment neo-classicism which emanated from France and dominated European culture generally, represents an important transitional stage in the evolution of the societal organisation, away from the quasi-familial pyramidal model in which there was a natural congruency of power and cultural excellence, towards the nineteenth century, where there was a more or less absolute divorce between power and art. The society of 'possessive individualism', in securing or trying to secure, the freedom of the individual from hierarchical domination, also destroyed that cultural congruence, and removed forever the possibility of sounding the full range of man's potentiality in art. Of the old socio-cultural congruence, the splendour of Augustan art is the last evidence in England. We may detect in its over-emphasis on style and appearance the inward uncertainty of a culture already threatened with extinction from below.

The so-called pre-romantics (Gray, Collins, Cowper, Akenside, Dyer) were private, introspective poets in whom, already, the Augustan politicality and splendour were gone. Their poetry is 'personal' rather than subjective, ruminative rather than meditative. They turn aside from society and politics, from the splendour and pageantry of power: they are pained rather than despairing, as if unable or unwilling to confront the facts of the historical situation. They reject the Augustan positiveness, but have no other centre of gravity. The creative mind seems to hang fire, while the inexorable tread of technology and economics brings the modern world into being. At the end of this curious hiatus, the Romantic poet stands revealed as a man set apart both from his fellow-men and from the possibility of political involvement with the power-structure of the society in which he lives. This is alienation. The condition, we note, is the general human one: there is no difference between the artist's position and that of his fellow-men. It is simply that the divorce between the man and the citizen had become more pronounced, and the artist's professional obligation of 'expressing' the heart and mind of social and political, as well as religious and philosophical, man has withered, for good. It has withered, of course, with the 'average' man's sense of belonging in an organic and hierarchical community. There was a heavy price to pay for the division of labour in society, and the fracture of our art-forms was part of it. For the contents that now flow in to replace the lost icons will never have that capacity for fulfilling man's sense of himself as a political and splendid creature: the splendour and the richness have gone for good.

From this state, it was a relatively short step to the subjectivism of Romantic art, so significantly accompanied by political disaffection or outright radicalism. If the social glitter of the Pope style goes along with assertive Toryism, the inward, de-publicised mode of Wordsworth is the expression of a politicality based upon the maximum realisation of individual potentiality.

Political power is regarded as hostile to individuals; it is repressive and exploitative.

It is, of course, impossible to assume a definition of Romanticism which covers all cases, any more than it is to assume such a definition of Augustanism. Indeed the whole purpose of the present book is to try to offer some descriptive statements to replace such definitions. I should wish to describe both Blake and Wordsworth, for instance, as Romantic, not because of any similarity of artistic ideology (they have none), nor thorough philosophical unity (they were at odds on almost every issue), but because they were caught in the same historical predicament and bounded by the same condition. We see this first in their attitudes towards power itself and towards the state. By the end of the eighteenth century, the poet and intellectual alive to his time adopts a series of attitudes which would, to the Augustan, have seemed intolerable Whiggery – the traffic of small, grubby upstarts like Wilkes and Defoe. The Romantic poet consciously identifies the state with oppression, the very possession of political power with the infliction of misery and injustice. He might, as Blake and Wordsworth independently did, share views on current political and social issues with the Whig opposition. He was generally, like Fox, sympathetic to the French revolution, hostile to the British declaration of war against France, appalled by the slave-trade and by the growing malodorousness of urban life, and in general possessed by the conviction that the social order was unequal and exploitative, and the times desolate and decaying. But the Romantic's detachment from political engagement ran deeper than his conscious dislike of particular policies.[11] And here we approach what is perhaps the most serious and difficult problem that can confront the literary or artistic historian. This is the fact that the artist has certain obligations over and above those of the honest intellectual (though he has these, too).

What is important about Augustan art is not merely that it made such-and-such assumptions and endorsed this and that attitude; *it is that it fulfills itself as high art by means of these attitudes and assumptions.* Good art, I have said, cannot be made out of an outworn iconography. Iconography represents living belief and interest. To be serviceable to an artist it must satisfy the artist's commitment to a certain scale – the scale, to use an outworn but serviceable term, of the absolute. The artist has an obligation to his time: without *a* contemporaneity (even if expressed allegorically), the artist can achieve nothing. But although the phenomenal expression of this obligation varies from age to age, it is constant in one thing – its exaction from the artist of the highest expression of which he is capable. Again and again, especially in our own time, the layman or the philosopher has reproached the poet or the painter with obscurity or 'privateness': 'Why don't you write about so-and-so?' they ask. 'So-and-so' is generally some important 'theme' of the age – it may be abortion, it may be the political liberation of a particular society or group within a society (women, or homosexuals or children or the poor or the black). It may be 'the Bomb': the poet should write about the Bomb! The answer is that the poet *should* write about nothing: it is not really within his choice. In a very material sense, it is not the poet who writes the poem, but something else. Not the Unconscious or History, certainly. But the laws of availability are so severe that they can be transgressed only at the penalty of death – execution by second-rateness, though possibly also financial success.

To summarise. Traditionally, the artist's obligation to society had assumed the unity of a group: this could vary in size from the Italian city-state to the Celtic tribe or the modern nation-state. The reach of the artist's aspiration (the extent of his absolute compass) could be co-extensive with the political or religious ambition of the group within which he worked. Now, with the Rousseauistic divorce of the man from the citizen (the true ego from the non-ego, if you like), this political exercise of the poet's sense of the absolute becomes impossible. Man's sense of himself as a subjective individual ceases to cohere with his sense of himself as a citizen: the traditional pun upon the word 'subject' becomes flawed. Man is now a prisoner of societal mechanisms, no longer a willing participant in those mechanisms, which traditionally completed him.

Certainly, such an account, simplified as it must be, makes a number of assumptions which will appear, to many readers, unacceptable, if not actually outrageous. In particular, it appears to suppress the possibility of disaffected sub-groups within the 'organic' quasi-familial unity so blandly assumed to have existed in the 'good old days'. I may, at best, appear to be taking for granted the kind of historical account expressed, at its most benignly magnificent, in G. M. Trevelyan's *English Social History*.

To this order of objection, I make the following reply. My account does not in fact rest upon the non-existence of class-dissent, and even of rebellion, within the social hierarchy. A family may be torn within by dissent and the friction of incompatible interests, yet it remains a family. So it may be with a state or a community. Radical postulations of ideological sub-groups with conflicting interests do not do away with the idea of a quasi-familial state, bulging at the seams with conflict and often bursting open, but still one thing. And, of course, it is radical sociology which has given us the best accounts of such a state. It is in Marx and Engels that we shall find the most convincing depictions (often out-doing Trevelyan in their rhapsodic nostalgia) of an older, superseded pyramidal society, unequal and repressive, but nevertheless felt by its constituent members to be one. The young Marx, whose neo-Hegelian insights into the nature of social history formed the basis for the economic materialism of *Capital*, saw that at some unspecifiable point towards the latter half of the eighteenth century, one kind of social order – pyramidal, quasi-familial – grew into another – democratic, individualistic; that, in his own words, 'The bourgeoisie, wherever it has got the upper hand, has put an end to all feudal, patriarchal, idyllic relations.'[12] The case being argued here demands no more than this.

(iii) THE POLITICALITY OF THE ROMANTIC MOMENT

Once the conception of man as a societal organism has been shattered, the poet is unable to sing man's absolute dimension in political or societal terms. For the Romantics, the possession of political power now involves the exploitation of man, unless, in some way, it can acknowledge and encompass within itself the complete emancipation of man. Unless, that is, it can translate the soul of the man into the aspirations of the citizen, and thus heal the breach within man opened up by the evolution of modern society. Now, this possibility is one of the most important elements in Romanticism and we are justified in calling it Utopian.

It is common among bourgeois mandarins of a liberal persuasion to sneer at the political 'naïveté' of poets such as

Shelley: as if anyone really believed that man could be an angel! And yet there is nothing naïve or contemptible in Shelley's radical idealism. On the contrary, it is not only not naïve, it is an open-eyed acceptance of a hard political fact – that the only 'political' absolute left to man was that of a socialistic egalitarianism. The ideal of the Utopian Left is the transformation of man himself into the ideal synthesis of man and citizen of the kind envisaged variously by Rousseau and Godwin, Shelley and Schiller, Paine and St. Simon, Blake and Heine. There is nothing escapist or ridiculous in such visions. Anything less, indeed, would be less a compromise than a falsification. The Utopian ideal does not depend upon a hazy, and probably false, view of man as a perfectible angel. It is an admission that any form of political organisation which does not allow of the completest possible vision of human development in freedom carries within itself an inherent contradiction: while claiming to define an ideal 'polis', a conservative or reactionary ideology in fact enjoins the repression or oppression of some parts of the community. If we point out that Marxism is itself Utopian, it should be clear in what sense it is being suggested that politics and poetry in the Romantic period become incompatible, as they are not in the world of Shakespeare and (with the reservations outlined above) of Pope. After Rousseau, there are no intellectually respectable reactionary theories of the state. Henceforth there will be only radical quasi-socialistic theories, on the one hand, and refusals to adopt a 'theory' on the other. It is perhaps the most troubling characteristic of the Romantic period not so much that the only inwardly consistent theories of the state are Utopian and open-ended, but that these theories are consistent only in so far as they are open-ended. Recent developments in European communist theory – dropping the insistence of the dictatorship of the proletariat, for instance – suggest the awareness that Marx was in earnest when he suggested in *Capital* that the state itself will eventually wither away.

The ideal of what we can pardonably call the Left is the transformation of man into the ideal synthesis of man-and-citizen – into Angel, in fact. Such a vision, as I have suggested above, is incompatible with the possession of actual power in any of the existing forms, forms based upon hegemonies of wealth and property. The Romantic moment might be defined as that short period when the Utopian vision coincided with the poet's sense of the absolute. For a brief moment, the idea of actual emancipation (real prisoners being released from real prisons, real slaves being liberated from real shackles) is conjoined with the supposed spiritual emancipation: this is the period of Blake's 'Jerusalem', of Shelley's 'Ode to the West Wind', of Beethoven's *Fidelio* and, with interesting qualifications, of the Ninth Symphony; of Byron's 'Prisoner of Chillon' and Delacroix's *Massacre of Chios*. I suggest no exact chronological dovetailing: Wordsworth's *Prelude*, a disabused work which entertains, and then dismisses, the radical alternative, precedes the magnificent panache of Shelley's 'Ode to the West Wind' by a decade. Neither, as the example of Wordsworth suggests itself, do I propose to equate a certain politico-philosophical position (the radical) with a certain artistic strength. It is rather a question of a certain fullness, an openness and vigour of texture, a depth of feeling accompanying a sensitive candour of thought. Wordsworth's great poem (the true epic of Romanticism) turns upon the disillusionment of the radical ideal, yet it can do so without sacrificing the intense exhilaration that is perhaps the most important identifying characteristic of Romantic art in general:

> The horse is taught his manage, and no star
> Of wildest course but treads back his own steps;
> For the spent hurricane the air provides
> As fierce a successor; the tide retreats
> But to return out of its hiding-place
> In the great deep; all things have second birth;
> The earthquake is not satisfied at once; . . .
>
> *(The Prelude*, Bk X)

It is the kind of power and exhilaration represented at its height in this passage (a passage actually divulging within itself the profound disabusement with the radical ideal) which I should wish to advance as the hall-mark of the Romantic moment. Before this, we have the private rumination of the pre-Romantics, changing imperceptibly into the near-philosophical meditations of Akenside's *Pleasures of the Imagination* and Wordsworth's early *Descriptive Sketches*. That writing in itself rests upon the implicit acceptance of the Augustan political and cultural world-view. In music, it is the age of Mozart, the last great product of the Enlightenment aesthetic, often challenging the political establishment of the old régime in its words and thoughts, yet accepting it inwardly in its formal procedures, which remain aristocratic, court-centred and hegemonic.

It is Beethoven, of course, who pushes beyond the Enlightenment aesthetic into the Romantic terrain, just as Wordsworth and Blake, with their overtly radical politics, do in language. It is Beethoven who transforms the formal procedures of Haydn and Mozart into the Romantic, and it is Beethoven – in more daring and overt terms than Mozart dared to use – who also transforms the static, backward-looking ideology of the high Classical era into politically progressive radicalism. In terms of 'form', this meant the retention of the sonata – basis, added to the new subjectivisation of melody and harmony. Theodor Adorno has tried to give the Romantic a (somewhat scornful) socio-political basis as the triumph of the new individualism. 'The autonomy of the musical subject (i.e. the theme or 'tune') took priority over all other considerations and critically excluded the traditional form of objectivisation, at the same time making do with a semblance of objectivisation just as the unrestricted interplay of subjects seemed the best guarantee for society.'[13] The 'traditional form of objectivisation' here means the fugal counterpoint of Bach, whom the Romantics 'critically' ignored. At the same time, Adorno concedes that Beethoven (and, by implication, Schubert) retained his grasp on 'a semblance of objectivisation', for a while, thus holding off the collapse into post-Romantic sprawl. Thus, the aesthetic and the societal run parallel: 'unrestricted interplay of subjects' means bourgeois individualism, which only 'seems', we note, the 'best guarantee for society'. Later, this fine ideal of individual liberty will, according to Adorno, disintegrate into the anarchy of late capitalist individualism, just as the tight yet relaxed formalism of Beethoven will deteriorate into the one-movement extravaganzas of such composers as Strauss and Scriabin.

Adorno's tone is unnecessarily and even suspectly contemptuous: it suggests the necessary subjection of this individualist anarchy to the historically and intellectually justified tyranny of Leftist ideology. But his suggestion of a certain balance having been reached in these years – the three decades of the early Romantic movement – does, I think, carry a good deal of authority. Whether politically overt, like Shelley and Byron, or apparently a-political, like Keats, the great artists of the Romantic moment show forth a power and lucidity (a harmonisation, if you like, of objective and subjective dimensions) which was soon to be lost for good; and this harmonization accompanies the momentary political ideal of a full emancipation of man from societal prisoner to limitless angel.

Clearly, the fading of this vision is to be explained by a variety of causes. Chief among these must be the evident capacity of the new technology actually to achieve – in the foreseeable future – the emancipation of man from the bondage which had hitherto appeared simply as a necessary and unquestionable part of the human condition. Poverty would – men had it from the highest Authority – always be with us. The idea of a complete equality among men had, similarly, always been part of Christian doctrine: in England, especially, there had been a long history of egalitarian agitation. There was nothing new, therefore, in the idea of *liberté*, *égalité* and *fraternité*. Yet at the 'dawning of the new age' – the moment of Romantic revolt – both equality and liberty appeared as actual social possibilities. The old idea that when Eve delved and Adam span 'Who was then the gentleman?' had appeared little more than a theoretical anomaly implicit in Christian doctrine. Ideas are not absolutely free: they are geared to social and historical processes. And it was only when the new technology at last brought into existence the actual possibility that poverty and bondage might be ended for ever, that the idea of them could function as a root-force of art. From this derives the blazing visionary quality of the greatest Romantic art.

But artists are politically unreliable creatures. They are at the same time too conservative (their art deriving too much of its force from a love of the past for them to relish revolution) and too radical: they see beyond the realisation of the limited aims of the political activist or theorist to the desert of fulfillment ahead. The radical vision is never really radical enough for the poet: sooner or later, man asserts his bourgeois nature, and political change will not change man himself. In the immediate circumstances on the other hand, the revolution is too slow: the poet's keen sense of actual life prevents him from being able to live off the future for long. As the Romantic moment passes, and the great vision of brotherhood fades into a more and more actualisable programme, the poet finds himself up against the truth of his predicament. Shelley's zeal and drive alternate with despair and disillusionment:

Rarely, rarely comest thou, spirit of delight.

In the brief space between the coming into existence of a 'new' idea, and its practical applicability, art-forms tend to thrive. As the vision becomes a programme, so the artist gradually begins to withdraw from it, because it no longer satisfies his hunger for the absolute.

This complex yet clear relationship between circumstances and vision helps us to explain otherwise inexplicable facts. Most striking is the fact that political idealism furnishes material for the artist only in those states where the realisation of revolution seems remotest from actuality. Briefly, we can say that in politically and socially backward countries, the artist will tend to align himself with the intellectual Left, because the Leftist ideal of the emancipation of the proletariat or peasantry lies along the grain of his own visionary commitment to the absolute. In more advanced societies, such as England and France in the nineteenth century, the artist tends to identify the radical cause with materialism, and the triumph of democracy grows steadily out of the advance of capitalism. Where there is an appreciable degree of liberal independence and genuine individual liberty, the radical or Leftist cause is left to lesser literary talents or to trade unionists: it appears to the creative writer to be an insufficiently absolute cause. Once again, as in the case of the Augustan poets, the proof is in the quality of the work produced. Shelley wrote fine and bitter political poems, consistent in their radicalism, coherent and well-thought out. Yet these poems ('The Revolt of Islam', for example, or 'The Masque of Anarchy') are not of his best. Only where the politicality can be translated into absolute terms, as in the visionary emancipation envisaged in the 'Ode to the West Wind', does it contribute seriously to Shelley's greatest work. Keats, to take another example, never wrote a socially 'committed' poem like Thomas Hood's 'Song of a Shirt'. Yet fine as Hood's poem is, not only does it not compete with Keats's verse, it does not equal the best of Hood's own: it is in directly derivative works such as 'Autumn', where Keats himself is his mentor, that Hood aspires most plausibly to major status.

Confirmation of this general argument is surely offered by the theme of patriotism. Partiotism has been a source of Great Art, as Shakespeare's Histories alone testify. It is difficult to isolate the point where patriotism ends and some deeper, broader sense of love for the earth begin. All poetry shares a near-religious sense of place: Nature will always lie at the heart of poetry. And Nature will always be nature in a particular place – the poet's 'country'. Where love of the English countryside, for instance, ends, and love of, and pride in, England the political and national entity begins, it may be impossible to establish. This is certainly true of Shakespeare's earlier work, in which the love of the land and its flora merges imperceptibly into the overt patriotism best exemplified in Gaunt's famous speech in *Richard II*. What we can say, I think, is that the power of Gaunt's speech derives from the wholeness of Shakespeare's response to the whole scale of feeling from the most concrete and immediate sensations of natural beauty (evident in the sense of light and fertility breathing through phrases such as 'This precious stone set in a silver sea' and 'This blessed plot') up to the heights of political and administrative power ('This teeming womb of royal kings'). The fecundity of the natural England (the beautiful piece of earth) yields its rulers naturally, and it is the power of this association that binds the whole speech and the whole cycle of History plays together into the most powerful political art that we know of. Here the political and the natural, the mystical and the societal, are at one.

Such a near-mystical sense of place and community informs also, I think, the high drama of seventeenth century France and, of course, every great society has its examples. The point is twofold. First, that we make a great mistake if we condemn patriotism (by calling it 'nationalism') outright; and secondly, that the capacity for artists in given societies to 'use' this emotion varies with circumstances. I have already given the example of Thomson's 'Rule, Britannia!' to show how far the patriotic theme declines between the Elizabethan and Hanoverian periods. By the time we reach Wordsworth and the Romantics, it has all but vanished as a theme for English poets. It can make a sort of appearance, suitably translated into terms of mystic symbolism, as in Blake's 'Jerusalem', where 'England', though identifiable with its 'dark Satanic mills' and its 'green and pleasant' atmosphere, must really be read in non-national terms: it is all mankind that Blake intends to be translated into spirituality.

Otherwise, England is the sated, tyrant-ridden land of Shelley's Sonnet, whose princes are but 'the dregs of their dull race', and in which the people are not the splendid yeomen of Shakespeare, but 'starved and stabbed in their untilled field'. For Shelley, England is tainted by capital and the ruling class, just as his patriotism is poisoned by radicalism: he pities the people of England who 'weave the clothes which (their) oppressors wear'.

This scorn for one's own nation, whether affected or genuine, has become so familiar to us that we often fail to see what is really only a particular feature of a particular set of historical circumstances. This leads us into often tortuous self-contradiction: we leap in atavistic joy if our country wins the World Cup, but maintain a derisive attitude towards her in political matters, often to the detriment of objectivity. The demise of the patriotic ideal is a natural concomitant of a certain degree of social success and political emancipation. This can be proved easily enough by turning to cases of writers working in different sorts of society. In the nineteenth century, we find that patriotism can be a powerful artistic emotion, especially when it is harnessed to oppression. Pushkin, for instance, offers the fascinating example of a poet working in a culture that was at the same time senile and infantile, and in a political society both undeveloped and repressive. Russia inspires Pushkin, much as England inspired Shakespeare, and the power of his work derives from the same union of the quasi-mystical sense of place, the simple pride in nationality. This is also true of Adam Mickiewicz, with the qualification that Poland was, for most of Mickiewicz's life, under foreign domination.

Pan Tadeusz, Mickiewicz's masterpiece, is at once a passionate love-poem to the Polish landscape and its mores, and a profound plea for liberation: the Utopian motif of Romantic politics receives here one of its most magnificent expressions. Again, as in Pushkin and Shakespeare (though obviously with crucial differences) Mickiewcz's simple power stems from the ability to encompass the whole scale of human activity, from the most humble and natural to the most exalted and complex, with none of that intellectual scepticism with which English and French poets were by this time (1837) thoroughly imbued.

Other Romantic poets who drew strength from political oppression were Taras Shevchenko, the Ukrainian, and James Clarence Mangan, the Irish poet. We can go so far as to say that only in undeveloped countries, or in politically deprived countries, can the patriotic theme be used by nineteenth century poets. Political oppression confers upon liberty something of that semi-mystic aura it loses when it actually arrives, and which it needs to be usable by poets. Once a society has submitted to the processes by which the industrial and political revolutions of the eighteenth century gradually transformed Europe, there is no possibility of sounding that pure, strong note which we find variously in Shakespeare's Histories, Mickiewicz's *Pan Tadeusz*, and Taras Shevchenko's *Doomi Moyi*. In an oppressed nation such as Ireland, for instance, the plight of the nation will be still capable of drawing the poet to the height of his powers. This is the case with Mangan's 'Dark Rosaleen' – a poem better, we might suggest without too much whimsy, than Mangan had it in him to write. The run of Mangan's verse is like that of Edgar Allan Poe, tawdrily metrical, at best poor pastiche of the English Romantics. But 'Dark Rosaleen' is very nearly a great poem. In Mangan's time (the eighteen thirties and forties), the nationalist theme had to be expressed covertly. 'Dark Rosaleen' does not mention Ireland or England: it is, to all intents and purposes, a love poem, rather in the perfervid mode of Poe's 'Lenore' and 'Annabel Lee'. The difference is that Mangan's poem is in code, like so many of the poems in the *Danta Gradha*: it is subterranean, and the force exerted by the implicit, ever-present national theme is much greater than that self-induced, slightly phoney hysteria of Poe's love-poems:

> For there was lightning in my blood,
>> My dark Rosaleen!
>> My own Rosaleen!
> Oh! there was lightning in my blood,
> Red lightning lightened through my blood,
>> My dark Rosaleen!

If a man *really* felt like this about a woman, we should think him neurotic. The strange fresh brilliance of Mangan's irresistible piece is evidence of its deeper origins. For Mangan, in fact, Ireland has the same mystic untouchableness as the beloved had for the troubadors. The idea of the Motherland, in short, functions as an absolute.

A hundred years later, James Joyce knew that Mangan's

theme was no longer capable of the absolute dimension without which art cannot properly function. For Joyce, Irish independence was a matter of political practicability: it was obviously going to come in Joyce's own life-time, and relatively early in it, at that. It was left to lesser talents to sing this theme, because the singing would be exhortative, really closer to propaganda than to art. As ordinary man, Joyce had some (qualified) sympathy with the aims of Sinn Fein;[14] as poet and novelist he was not interested. For him, as for Yeats and O'Casey it was more matter of satire than of song.

The real theme of 'Dark Rosaleen' is absolute, mystic, untouchable, and yet it was something that united a whole nation; Joyce could not utilise the national cause, except negatively, as a subordinate formal element, in the *Portrait* and in *Ulysses*. His theme was, at one level, always Ireland, but no longer in the near-mystic nationalist sense of Mangan. The artist at all times, seeks to maintain formal relations with the most absolute, invisible compass his mind is capable of conceiving. His keen detailed sense of intermediate actuality is held in constant tension with the awareness of the absolute of which its expression is really allegorical.

6 The Poet's Sense of Role – 1: the Romantic Predicament

(i) WORDSWORTH AND COLERIDGE

Alienation brought about a further shift in literary contents. To be divorced from the political, military and societal dimensions of human experience (as the poet at the end of the eighteenth century largely was) rendered still more of the traditional materials of literature unavailable to the poet of good faith: it was left to the second-rate poet to write patriotic odes, celebrate the state and hymn martial valour. Shakespeare, Homer, and the folk-epics, all show that there was nothing intrinsically malign, ignoble or absurd in these things. Yet now they join traditional religious belief as contents unusable for the modern poet. The poet loses, moreover, his sense of being able to 'speak for' all men as the quasi-familial sense of social unity has perished along with social evolution. The poet has now to 'express' that sense of isolation which, in greater or less degree, forms part of all men's social experience in the new world.

With the coming of modern democracy and capitalist individualism, the relations between artist and society alter decisively and irrevocably: the thematic content of art now reflects the new condition in which the poet is working. The aristocratic court-culture no longer serves as a focus for intellectual aspiration. Previously, the artist has put his gifts unthinkingly at the service of the cultural hegemony of the society in which he lives. (Milton, who might be thought exceptional, proves the point by putting his gifts at the service of an improved, expanded version of the worldly society: his commonwealth is a radiantly transfigured Christian version of the world.) Art had supported and cohered with the power-structure simply because it did represent the only élite available: the court and aristocracy represented the most refined and evolved consciousness man could produce. Art was part of 'culture', and to be cultured, by

112

definition, was to be part of an easily recognised and indubitable political and civilisational hierarchy.

When this sense of a 'natural' élite passes, as it does with the advent of eighteenth century capitalism and the rise of the middle class, the poet no longer places himself at the disposal of the cultural establishment, in so far as one exists. He is thrown back on himself, his status and nature. He places his own consciousness at the centre of his art, not because he is narcissistic or egocentric, but simply because there is nothing else, and because there are questions which need answering. If the poet can no longer assume the values of a social and cultural hegemony, what is his function? If we compare the poetry of a typical Augustan poet, like Goldsmith, with, say, Wordsworth, the most signal difference that emerges is not so much the greater depth or profundity of Wordsworth's nature-writing, as the fact that his chief inward preoccupation is with the question of the poet's function, his role, his power, his obligations.

This may at first suggest a preoccupation with bardhood. The idea of the bard or poet-as-seer is ancient and is clearly relevant to any consideration of Romanticism. Yet the notion of the poet-priest is itself of less importance than the way in which Romantic poets adapted it to the circumstances of the modern world.[1] The most important figure in this respect, as in many others, is Wordsworth. T. S. Eliot long ago noted the significance of Wordsworth's appropriation of new powers for the poet: 'Wordsworth is really the first, in the unsettled state of affairs in his time, to annex new authority for the poet . . . and to offer a new kind of religious sentiment which it seemed the peculiar prerogative of the poet to interpret.'[2] Yet this priestly appropriation is less important than the peculiarly concrete way in which Wordsworth made the awareness of his bardic powers the subject-matter of his poetry; confirmed, that is, the shift of contents that had been taking place inchoately since Gray and the Schlegels. For the idea of the inspired or possessed bard is particularly significant in pre-Romantic poetry: it appears not only in Gray's ode, 'The Bard', but in the cult of Ossian, and in Schlegel's glorification of Gothic Shakespeare – in the whole *Sturm und Drang* cult of *Genie*. It was perhaps the fact that English poets did not have to 'discover' Shakespeare – even if Young, in an essay which exercised a powerful influence on the *Sturm und Drang*,[3] felt the need to refurbish him – which made it possible for an English poet to exploit the implications of the *Genie*-cult so successfully.

Wordsworth investigated the nature of the poet's powers and the processes of his imagination in three major poems, the 'Lines composed above Tintern Abbey', *The Prelude* and the 'Ode: Intimation of Immortality'. (I shall use the familiar abbreviated titles of the first and third poems throughout.)

In *The Prelude*, the poet establishes the new territory of the poet as the quest for his own theme: the historic shift of contents which lies at the root of Romanticism is intimated in the introduction of *The Prelude*, which brings into the realm of content that inner struggle which we know preceded the composition of *Paradise Lost*. Milton's early doubt that 'that inward gift which is death to hide' will be unfulfilled, is echoed by Wordsworth's fear that he will 'travel towards the grave,/Like a false steward who hath much received/And renders nothing back'. (*Prelude*, Book I, ll. 267–9.) We could have no better illustration of the particular crisis represented in the Romantic predicament than is afforded by the contrast between Milton's brave but confident admission of early disappointment in the sonnet on his twenty-fourth birthday, and Wordsworth's structural use of his doubt and uncertainty in *The Prelude*. Milton presents an apologia, and at the same time a promise that some great task will be fulfilled. Wordsworth makes it clear, from his careful sifting of the traditional sources of poetic structure in Book I of *The Prelude*, that this process of selection is itself to be proferred as theme: *this* is to be the theme of the 'immortal song', not some knightly tale or paean of liberation. I shall refer later to the importance in Wordsworth of the sense of guilt: nowhere is his proneness to pass his days 'in contradiction' more important than here, at the very root and spring of English Romanticism. It is just this somewhat anxious, guilt-laden inability to settle to any noble theme that enables Wordsworth to reject the irrelevant – those tempting traditional themes now put beyond the poet's reach by history and social evolution. His soul in her ambition urges him to take something up, but

> Vain is her wish; where'er she turns she finds
> Impediments from day to day renewed.
>
> (Bk. II, ll. 130–1)

The Prelude, then, eventually takes for its theme its own provenance, for that 'growth of a poet's mind' is but the continuance into the past of the vein which first launches it on its way. From the moment that it did so, Western literature was decisively turned from its earlier course into that channel in which it was to run for more than a hundred years, and still, in some ways, does. For not only the novel of remembrance like *David Copperfield*, but also those more intellectually self-conscious meditations upon the artistic role and vocation – Joyce's *Portrait of the Artist as a Young Man* and Thomas Mann's *Tonio Kröger* – receive here their true insemination. Most spectacularly, it is Proust's *A la Recherche du temps perdu* which shows how deeply and precisely Wordsworth had understood the nature of the modern artist's predicament: not only as the text as self-conscious meditation upon itself, but as the text as ultimately circular, its end returning to its beginning through the agency of remembrance, Proust's novel parallels Wordsworth's poem. It is in *The Prelude* that the obligation the modern poet feels to render account not merely of the nature of experience, but of the act of experiencing, first emerges as the poet's principal theme. In 'Tintern Abbey', Wordsworth had rendered those trance-like states of mind in which the poet 'sees' into the life of things, as he had been traditionally supposed to do; in *The Prelude* he raises to full consciousness the significance of those moments, those numinous illuminations whose arrival he had described so sensitively in the earlier poem: these 'spots of time', 'gleams like the flashing of a shield' are to be his theme now.

In 'Tintern Abbey', we remember also, Wordsworth had referred to Nature as 'unintelligible': that is, as a kind of code or message, as a Book, but one whose leaves are to be interpreted by the poet. It is sometimes said that the world was a book for Dante and those earlier writers who had the support of a coherent world-view, but that for modern writers, lacking such a world-view, it is mere nonsense – opaque thing-ness. Yet both Romanticism and Symbolism, to the contrary, depend upon the conception of nature as a message that can be de-coded or understood by man in the right spiritual condition. Indeed, Romanticism proposed to itself precisely this function of interpreter of nature. To take it to task for this is both illogical and myopic: *mutatis mutandis*, it has been the role of the poet since the birth of literature and religion. Wordsworth's importance is not confined to his appropriation of priestly solemnity. It is rather his intelligent and analytic attitude towards the question of the nature of literary content in his time. Throughout *The Prelude*, we shall find him guessing at the 'meanings' of the book of nature not in a hermetic or arcane spirit, as Christopher Smart had and Gerard de Nerval would, but in full consciousness that there were no mysterious meanings like the answers to riddles, but only the facts of experience and the riddle of value.

Hence, he took it upon himself to describe those moments when

> the earth and common face of Nature spake to me
> Remembrable things

and impressed

> Collateral objects and appearances,
> Albeit lifeless then, and doomed to sleep
> Until maturer seasons called them forth,
> To impregnate and elevate the mind.
>
> (*The Prelude*, I, ll. 593–7)

'Tintern Abbey' suggested three stages in the process of poetic composition: first, the 'glad animal' stage of boyhood, in which the poet was thoughtlessly in Nature, part of it, yet collecting impressions as it were unwittingly; second, the adolescent stage of intellectual and spiritual awakening, in which the poet knows Nature, in the fullest sense; and lastly, the more sober stage, at which the experience and insights of the second phase, now themselves past, are catalysed by conscious recollection and meditation into actual poetry. In *The Prelude*, Wordsworth pursues the implications of this outline:

> And if the vulgar joy by its own weight
> Wearied itself out of the memory,
> The scenes which were a witness of that joy
> Remained in their substantial lineaments
> Depicted in the brain, and to the eye
> Were visible, a daily sight . . .
>
> (*The Prelude*, I, ll. 598–602)

The joy of the experience, we note, is itself, though important, 'vulgar': it is important to see how carefully Wordsworth separates the joy of the experience from the process of 'symbolising' it. The experience is common to all, the cultivating of the capacity to experience and to abstract *the idea of it* from its accidental phenomenal form, remains a professional duty of the poet. The poet, of course, is a man before he is a poet, and not all the experiences that make for poetry are of the ecstatic, numinous sort. *The Prelude* describes the mind's symbolising process in its most general form, as well as the 'growth of a poet's mind'. This is made clear in the passage from which I have just quoted, which ends with an important chain image ('invisible links/Were fastened to the affections'). The chain-image provides the epistemological framework of the whole poem, and links it with the empiricist psychology of the eighteenth century. Much has been made of the alleged failure of Wordsworth's experiment with Hartley's philosophy, and of the importance of the German Idealist influence on the poet.[4] We should be more attentive again, I think, to the positive influence on Wordsworth of the Hume-Hartley account of the mind and its modes of perception. Wordsworth accepted the moral groundwork of human personality in what we call today conditioning – the formation through repetition of responsible chains. In Wordsworth, imagination is treated empiricistically. Later in the poem, Wordsworth described the process by which meaningless elements (the actual circumstances of day-to-day life) become charged with symbolic import under emotional stress. Through association with the sudden death of his father, certain objects, natural and manufactured – 'The single sheep and the one blasted tree,/And the bleak music of that old stone wall' – became for him forever resonant, evocative, so that

> All these were kindred spectacles and sounds
> To which I oft repaired, and thence would drink,
> As at a fountain.

> (*The Prelude*, xii, ll. 324–6)

This is the way things become symbols for us all; no one later was to add much to Wordsworth's description of the process. His account was to serve as a model for – among others – Dickens, Joyce, and Proust. In giving such precise psychological definition to the way mental imagery becomes charged with that emotional significance we call symbolic, Wordsworth also, at the beginning of the nineteenth century, defined the scope and nature of the modern poetic symbol, as something bearing pragmatic relations to ordinary experience, not as conventionally or archetypally significant 'in itself'. When Baudelaire, later in the century, defined symbolism he differed little from Wordsworth: 'In certain semi-supernatural conditions of the spirit, the whole depths of life are revealed within the scene – no matter how commonplace – which one has before one's eyes. This becomes its symbol.'[5] In the course of time, the rhetoric of argument and presentation we find in Wordsworth was to drop away, leaving the symbol, as he had defined it, isolated and itself able to bear the poetic meaning. For Wordsworth had done more than merely define the way in which our mental images assume symbolic meaning. The symbol of the poet is significant in virtue of its numinous power – its association with profound, ecstatic or simply valuable experience. It is not merely moments of emotional stress with which we are concerned, but moments of a particular order of significance. Those 'spots of time', those 'gleams like the flashing of a shield' are isolated by Wordsworth as being of peculiar value to the poet. The image, in other words, has become alienated from its context, so that the poet's value-conferring experience of it becomes a model of the individual's isolated existence within a society void of that human communication which had been lost in the evolution of social organisation by history. Is not Wordsworth here isolating the 'essence' of the poetic vocation, winnowing away the various didactic theological or moralistic husks, leaving it clean and clear? Now, of course, it was history which was doing this – history in its broadest sense of the combination of everything that happened, or, in the more customary extrapolations, the action and interaction of economics, technology and socio-spiritual evolution.

It was Wordsworth's achievement to have penetrated to the heart of the writer's predicament in the new world. He saw, sooner than any other European poet the consequences of the gradual divorcing of the poet from the general social voice, so that the poet could no longer sound that full socio-political diapason, confident that the values he endorsed were in themselves good and right. And, of course, it was man himself who was divorced, set apart from himself and his fellows by that inexorable movement of economics and technology that put the cash-payment (the 'cash-nexus' in Carlyle's term) in place of those subtler, more inwardly realised social relations. Once again we must remember that in concentrating attention on the predicament of the poet, Wordsworth penetrated to the understanding of the general human predicament in the only valid way open to the poet, through the poet's professional isolation, and its attendant spiritual risks. Once more, we approach the question of the subjectivism of the Romantic poets, their apparent inability to address those fundamental questions of human existence without relating them to their own subjective experience. Again we see this subjectivism as the reverse of indulgent – as indeed the only authenticity available to them.

In the case of the poet, the experience of the general human situation took a particularly intense form. It was left to him only to cultivate that capacity for experience of a particular quality and intensity, that capacity which identified him as poet at the same time as it relates him to all men in virtue of their own (perhaps less highly developed) sense of value. Once again, Wordsworth was quicker to see the new dangers open to the poet than anyone else

> We poets begin in joy and gladness
> Whereof in the end come despondency and madness.
>
> ('Resolution and Independence')

The disturbing implication of this couplet is that the 'despondency' described in the earlier part of the poem – entertained in the face of the natural world at its most ravishingly beautiful – is of a type the poet is professionally prone to. In cultivating the susceptibility to intense experience, and, moreover, in setting greater store by these experiences, the poet lays himself open to a more fundamental despair when the experiences begin, with age, with familiarity, with the natural narrowing of the arc of expectation, to lose their radiance. In *The Prelude*, Wordsworth had focused attention on the peculiar significance to the poet of childhood experience: to have associated intense, liberated, joyous experience (sensations) with dawning intellectual self-consciousness is certainly one of Wordsworth's most important contributions to modern thought. (We note again that it is the self-consciousness about the process

– what we can call the apperceptive dimension – that identifies the Wordsworthian poet, not the mere proneness to the experiences. Wordsworth's poetry is itself at the opposite pole from spontaneous gush. Where it appears most spontaneous is where an experience has awakened and completed a longevious process of absorption and assimilation.) The intense short life of the creative artist ('burning himself out', in the cliché) is not a uniquely Romantic phenomenon, but it is a phenomenon that acquired a particular significance in the Romantic period, when those sheltering, structuring resources of earlier art were first shorn away from him. It is from the Romantic period that we can date the origination of the philosophy of youth – the idea that in youth and early adulthood, we experience with an intensity and vigour that gradually pales with ageing.[6] Wordsworth's importance here is not confined to the seminal nature of his treatment of childhood experience, however: still more important than his clear-sighted and sensitive attitude towards childhood is the way he relates childhood and youthful experience to the formation of poetry. Everyone hates ageing. But there is a particular professional anxiety in the regret of the poet, who has hung everything on the exhilaration of those 'spots of time', conscious enjoyment of which is the reward but also the curse of the modern poet's commitment. This dilemma is touched on in 'Resolution and Independence'. More profoundly, it provides the thematic core of the 'Immortality' Ode, a poem fully as important to the evolution of modern poetry as *The Prelude*. Wordsworth speaks for all men in the first five stanzas of the poem, but the pang of loss the verse so beautifully articulates owes its intensity to the especial significance these ecstatic apprehensions have for the poet:

> Whither is fled the visionary gleam?
> Where is it now, the glory and the dream?

So Wordsworth states the dilemma of every modern poet who, bereft, through social alienation, of the political, moral and theological dimensions which had traditionally carried the poet's apprehensions and worn them as 'grace', 'inspiration' or 'wit', finds himself thrown back upon that single identifying quality – the sensitivity to a value in experience which made him poet and not any other thing. We note that the sense of loss has not sprung from any dullness in perception itself. Modern psychologists like Abraham Maslow have diagnosed biological deterioration in the perceptual mechanism with age.[7] But in fact the real poignancy of these marvellous stanzas is that Wordsworth's vision was never more limpid – the world never appeared more wonderfully alive and joyous to his mind. It appears that it is not the capacity to experience itself that declines in quality. What is it, then, that causes the sense of being outside these things ('I see, not feel, how beautiful they are'). The sights remain, and with them the apparent reasons for joy, but the emotion is not forthcoming. Wordsworth has articulated the pang with such consummate clarity, such force and tenderness that these first four stanzas of the 'Immortality' Ode could stand as a complete poem. As such it was read by Coleridge,[8] and became, on Coleridge's reception of the poem, the thesis of a dialectic, one of the most remarkable in all literary history.

The antithesis is Coleridge's riposte. What has happened, Coleridge in effect answers, is that you (Wordsworth) have mistaken the occasion for your joyous exultation in nature for its source:

It were a vain endeavour,
Though I should gaze forever
On that green light that lingers in the west:
I may not hope from outward forms to win
The passion and the life, whose fountains are within.

(Coleridge: 'Dejection; an Ode')

This is a key-metaphor, that of the fountain. It is ambiguous here. It can mean either that fountain which is responsible for the life of those outer phenomena (clouds, storms, trees), or that which provides our own joy in perception. In the light of Coleridge's readings in German Idealism, we can see easily enough that it is the latter meaning which is intended here; but the ambiguity remains. The fountain of consciousness (or Imagination), then, – spontaneous, self-erecting – is itself responsible for the motions of perception itself, as well as of the emotion or *meaning* which seeing things generates in us. 'O Lady! we receive but what we give', Coleridge points out, 'And in our life alone does Nature live.' So far Coleridge is correcting Wordsworth, supplying the element missing from Wordsworth's diagnosis of the predicament. He goes beyond this in the lines that follow, which add to this essentially Idealist account of perception the element of value required to constitute a true response to Wordsworth's picture:

> And would we aught behold, of higher worth,
> That that inanimate cold world allowed
> To the poor loveless ever-anxious crowd,
> Ah! from the soul itself must issue forth
> A light, a glory, a fair luminous cloud
> Enveloping the earth.

This effectively discriminates between that condition of all perception he has described earlier in the poem, and that value-endowed perception of the poet, or the ordinary man in his best moments. (Without these latter, poetry could be read only by poets.) Coleridge works towards his climax with a definition that anticipates much later poetry, in particular that of W. B. Yeats. The 'sweet and potent voice' that must be sent from within the soul in order to confer value on experience – upon the 'inanimate cold world' of man without poetry – is, he now says, 'of its own birth'. (Yeats describes the joy he wishes for his daughter in his famous 'Prayer' as 'self-delighting'.) It requires another half-stanza for Coleridge to trumpet the name of this force from within, self-begotten:

> Joy, virtuous Lady! Joy that ne'er was given,
> Save to the pure, and in their purest hour,
> Life, and Life's effluence, cloud at once and shower,
> Joy, Lady! is the spirit and the power,
> Which wedding Nature to us gives in dower
>   A new Earth and new Heaven,
> Undreamt of by the sensual and the proud –
> Joy is the sweet voice, Joy the luminous cloud –
> We in ourselves rejoice!

Joy is, we note, both 'of its own birth' and given us 'in dower' by 'wedding nature'. Nature provides the *Grundwerk* of our humanness, and the power of Joy is given us by Nature; but we have the choice to lose or sustain it. It is evident, therefore, mostly in children, and it is taken from us by the growth of consciousness. It is at this point, just after the triumphant annunciation of Joy in stanza V of his poem, that Coleridge as it were stitches his antithesis to Wordsworth's thesis. Wordsworth's identifying formula, 'There was a time when . . .', now appears, but as it were, adjusted by the foregoing explication. Now, this formula had itself already been used by Coleridge, in a poem – rather a poor one – which was printed in the *Morning Post* in October 1800, 'The Mad Monk: an Ode in Mrs Ratcliff's manner': 'There was a time when . . .'. Yet so much more pointed and urgent is Wordsworth's exploitation of the motif, that Coleridge's re-use of it in 'Dejection' seems like a conscious allusion to Wordsworth rather than an echo of himself. Certainly, it means much more so viewed. The foregrounding of Wordsworth's thesis has been revealed to us by the incisiveness of Coleridge's analytic intelligence. He now proceeds himself to transform Wordsworth's thesis into his own antithesis:

> There was a time when, though my path was rough,
>> This joy within me dallied with distress,
> And all misfortunes were but as the stuff
>> Whence Fancy made me dreams of happiness . . .

Now when we remember Wordsworth's great 'Ode: Intimations of Immortality', it is very likely of the phrase 'Shades of the prison-house begin to close/Upon the growing boy', that we first think. Yet the principle of the second part of Wordsworth's poem is really given in Coleridge's sixth and seventh stanzas. It is here that the Wordsworthian pattern is first articulated. First, there is the foliage of Hope, then the boring effect of 'afflictions'. What the reader of, say, W. B. Yeats is likely to find most interesting in Coleridge's analysis (and it remains one of the great analyses of modern consciousness) is the structural part played by the idea of dream. The young man turns even his adversities into 'dreams of happiness'. Hope (a form of dream later to be devastatingly analysed in the cycle of Dickens' novels) is generated out of inward vitality, producing foliage 'not my own'. And it is the 'shaping spirit of the Imagination' which shaped the misfortunes into fruits and foliage of Hope. In the seventh stanza, Reality itself is analysed in terms of human thought:

> Hence, viper thoughts, that coil around my mind,
>> Reality's dark dream!

The wild thoughts that afflict the poet, that is to say, constitute reality for him, but they are dreamed by 'Reality'. The poet now turns to the wind raving outside, which has, the poem implies, been playing upon the poet as upon a harp of Aeolus. The balance between external reality and internal appearance is beautifully sustained by Coleridge. He does not say that he is played upon by the wind (he does not, that is, deny responsibility for himself), but his juxtaposition of the internal 'Viper thoughts' as 'Reality's dark dream' and the wild night outside, forces us to accept that man, too, is played upon, and is as helpless as 'Bare craig, or mountain tarn'. The wind is a 'mad Lutanist' who makes a 'devil's yule'. It is then characterised, significantly enough, as an Actor, perfect in all tragic sounds, and 'Mighty poet, e'en to frenzy bold!' What this mighty poet is telling about (to borrow Coleridge's own awkward phrase) is human cataclysm –

With groans, of trampled men, with smarting wounds . . .

Then, in a lull between blasts, it tells a quieter and sadder story, of a lost child – the orphan of war and disruption – who

now moans low in bitter grief and fear,
And now screams loud, and hopes to make her mother hear.

This is the natural father's fear for his child, and it affords Coleridge his transition to his beautiful close, with the child asleep in the house as he writes, and his wishes for her, and for her mother,

friend devoutest of my choice,
Thus mayest thou ever, evermore rejoice.

This, too, is a prayer for a daughter, and the links with Yeats' poem so-called are many and profound.

The synthesis of this dialectic between two great poets is one that has no parallel in any later poetry. Wordsworth's great riposte to Coleridge's antithesis comes in the eight stanzas he appended to the four that he had already written and read to Coleridge. Instead of the prayer for his child that Coleridge offers, Wordsworth offers a great hymn of acceptance in which knowledge of 'human suffering' is conceived as adequate compensation for the loss of that inward joy which, he now accepts (from Coleridge's 'Dejection'), as inevitably wearing out with growth. Like all great odes to joy, Wordsworth's poem is deeply sad, yet it stands as a valid synthesis of the dialectic of joy-and-experience. We notice that the joy – accepted by Wordsworth in Coleridge's diagnosis – does not constitute a synthesis in Coleridge's poem, as it does in Wordsworth's. What Wordsworth does is to take over Coleridge's analysis (the wearing away of the inward capacity with experience and adversity) and incorporate it into a greater design. That numinous joy – which, unnamed, informed the opening four stanzas of 'Intimations of Immortality' – is absorbed into the dialectic, and in the synthesis emerges as a different, deeper kind of joy, one which is not 'given' in dower by nature, but acquired, achieved, by the human mind itself. This is Wordsworth's synthesis. The first term of the dialectic, as it has been articulated by Coleridge, is recapitulated at a higher level of comprehension and generality: innocence breeds experience, and experience, in turn, breeds the new synthesis of the 'Thoughts that do often lie too deep for tears'. Thus, in the 'Immortality' Ode, Wordsworth completes a genuine dialectic, in which the synthesis is not merely a random reaction to the antithesis, but a recapitulation of the original thesis out of the action of the antithesis.

Thus, Coleridge's riposte made no central difference to the situation Wordsworth had articulated. To point out that the sense of the numinous comes from within us, so that Wordsworth's error was to have staked everything on an appreciation of the external world as if *it*, not the human mind (read, Imagination) held the source of joy, was merely to state the dilemma more accurately. The main point is that the 'gleam' is still fled, whether conferred on things by us, or merely apprehended by us. Coleridge's dejection shows that he knew too well the condition Wordsworth had described so beautifully. The power had failed – the power *does* fail – and the poet is left with 'ordinary' reality, that weight of custom that lies upon us, 'Heavy as frost, and deep almost as life.' The poet's predicament is, again, only a particular version of the general human one. In pursuing the implications of his own situation, the poet arrives at general human truth. Coleridge's very analytic precision (manifest in the details of the scene described in his Ode, over-precise, losing the life in the attention to minutiae) is itself typical of the 'new' condition: man seeks to know too much, too closely, and loses the life of the whole.

No less significant was Coleridge's *ennui*, his 'grief without a pang'. It was ordinary humdrumness that beat Coleridge, not marriage or opium. From this time, the relations between poetic experience and 'ordinary' life, with its claims and responsibilities, form part of the subject-matter of poetry. Increasingly, the poet sees his role (as articulated by Wordsworth) in conflict with the demands of ordinary life, because in the new economic structure there is simply no room for him. He has no other role than that of poet, yet he cannot be a poet for man or society in general. It is not a question of patronage: it is rather a question of the fragmentation that had taken place in society under the new socio-economic conditions – the disintegration of the older ties between men, replacing group-relations with possessive individualism, the older bonds of loyalty with the cash-nexus. All men feel – in varying degrees of intensity – the difference between high, rich states of being and the ordinary condition from which they erupt so brilliantly. The poet's total commitment to these 'exceptional' states of consciousness was enforced on him by the development of society away from the more or less homogeneous pyramid of older societal organisation towards the new disintegratedness of modern democratic capitalism. Bereft of mental structures to adorn, decorate, intensify or invest with value, the poet is now left with nothing but his commitment to that capacity for grace, to the luminous apprehension of the experience of value itself.

The 'Immortality' Ode of Wordsworth and the 'Dejection' Ode of Coleridge give the earliest articulations of that schism which was to cause the impassioned despair so characteristic of Romanticism. The crisis is registered, one could say, as it happened, with painful and brilliant clarity, in the opening stanzas of the 'Immortality' Ode, which offer us the structure of joy without the informing content, the reasons for rejoicing without the ability to rejoice. More generally, the two great Odes represent the consequences of the folding-in upon itself which now besets European culture. With all its new awareness of the past, Romanticism collapses in upon itself, contemplates its own workings, again illustrating that structural similarity that obtains between the art of the period and the philosophical method of

Kant. Part, at least, of the profound depression which overcame Coleridge derived, I think, from his feeling of having obscurely transgressed, perhaps 'unconsciously', in making the intuitive creative faculty so nakedly the object of study. His experience was perhaps to be more representative. Reading 'Kubla Khan' and 'The Rime of the Ancient Mariner', it is easier for us to understand the poet's feeling that nothing remained that was worth doing. Coleridge's personal dilemma has been best described by T. S. Eliot:

> He had no vocation for the religious life, for there again somebody like a Muse, or a much higher being, is to be invoked; he was condemned to know that the little poetry he had written was worth more than all he could do with the rest of his life. The author of *Biographia Litteraria* [sic] was already a ruined man. Sometimes, however, to be a 'ruined man' is itself a vocation.[9]

Here, surely, we have the paradigm of the modern poet: having produced work of inexplicable and insuperable brilliance, the poet must choose between settling for middle-age and mediocrity, and killing himself now (by whatever means).[10] This, at any rate, was how the alternatives suggested themselves to the poets who followed Coleridge. Is not 'Kubla Khan', too, the paradigm of the modern poem, the poem which resists any political, philosophical, religious or moral interpretation yet carries its very meaninglessness as its poetic force – as its meaning*ful*ness? Coleridge's poem remained something of a model for Poe's more vulgar incantations and, through Poe's influence in Paris, must be counted one of the most important responses to the new cultural situation, especially when one adds to it an idea dropped with casual brilliance in *Biographia Literaria*. 'A poem of any length neither can be, nor ought to be all poetry', Coleridge observed,[11] and here, surely, is the birthplace of that central nineteenth century notion of the poem that is a poem and nothing else, that does not 'mean' something, but 'is' something. The 'meaninglessness' of 'Kubla Khan' is a direct product of the social, intellectual and political forces at work upon the poet in its age. It constitutes a refusal to be interpreted in terms of any current *Weltanschauung* external to itself, a refusal to be anything but itself – a poem. Set forth, embodied with all the plastic energy required of art by the eighteenth century aestheticians, 'Kubla Khan' is indeed *Zweckmässigkeit ohne Zweck*. This specifically means that the poem is not to be read as 'pure poetry' – as music, as sound, as nonsense; a poem, by definition, is *impure* – it uses the sonic and the referential properties of language in order to consummate meaning. A reduction of poetry to 'pure' poetry – to music, to sound, to form – is an evasion, a spurious claim of autonomy that does not count as response-to-situation. Certain of the Symbolists were later to try this escape-hatch. 'Kubla Khan' ducks none of the burdens assumed by the poet, and its 'autonomy' – such as it is – consists in a valid relationship with the contemporary situation. It acknowledges the poet's position in the modern world by reducing his activity to the exercise of his art, and presenting it as an embodiment of what the world will lack if it excludes the poetic dimension from its experience.

(ii) KEATS, SHELLEY, BYRON

It is the crisis of consciousness dramatised by Wordsworth and Coleridge, I submit, rather than the disaffection with society following the failure of the French Revolution to honour its ideals, which lies behind the 'despair' characteristic of the second generation of Romantic poets. Wordsworth's power, like Turner's, was for the whole, for totality, and from this power derived his awareness of the poet's true place in a world which no longer accepts him as needed – which lacks, in effect, any cultural hierarchy in the old sense. Wordsworth was uniquely gifted to do this. But he was also enabled to do it simply by being English. The contemporary German poet, springing almost nude from a primitive literary terrain with almost no high fine literary realisation within it, was limited in his awareness by the political facts of living in a small semi-feudal or mercantile state or city-state, with none of the complex political and economic and social processes behind it to stimulate him into full consciousness of the artist's true predicament in the coming world. This was inevitable, given the facts of German life, with its narrow isolated principalities, cut off from awareness of the evolutionary process that was in fact transforming modern society.

In France, on the other hand, actual Revolution gave writers the *ignis fatuus* of the 'new age' – that myth of the society open to all the talents which was really only a formula for the military coup, the opportunistic grab, with still less relationship to the real forces that were shaping society than German provincialism. Instead of the concrete apprehension of the real facts of the writer's place in the new world, French poets give us pseudo-Napoleonic grandeur – egotism disguised as subjectivity. But the condition that was coming to all Europe had already arrived in Wordsworth's England. So it is the English poet who sees through Revolutionary ideology to the real facts of the human condition in the technological world: in the poems of Blake and Wordsworth already we see modern man alienated from himself, not only by political and economic repressiveness (these are as much symptoms as causes), but by the facts of technology, the development of the cash-nexus, the emergence from group-consciousness into 'possessive individualism', the dying of God.

The poets born in the 1790s inherited a situation defined pre-eminently by the twin recantations of the 'Immortality' and 'Dejection' Odes. In a profound sense, Wordsworth and Coleridge, in articulating with such ruthless honesty a crisis of consciousness which seemed rooted in the pursuit of poetry itself, had withdrawn from the second wave of English Romantics the possibility of a personal adjustment to the new cultural situation: alienation is now written into the poet's cultural contract with society. It is because of this that the new Romantics indulge alternatively their beautiful despair and their heroic rebelliousness. They take from the older poets the isolation, the sense of having to justify themselves in their poetic vocation, but they lack the social continuity, which afforded – to Wordsworth at least – the capacity to transcend the predicament in understanding it, as at the end of the 'Immortality' Ode. Wordsworth won through to this certitude only after a breakdown of confidence in the very apparatus of poetic feeling, and he did so precisely by making his doubt his theme. After Wordsworth the possibility of this kind of resolution no longer existed. Something – something terrible – was known. The concern with role, with what it is to be a poet, remains, but it has changed its inward tone and direction: the new poets alternately despair and vaunt their sense of importance in protestations whose occasional shrillness betrays the inward uncertainty. There is nevertheless a ripened fullness of feeling and contour in the greatest poetry of the 1820s in England rarely to be matched in Continental Europe. From the 1790s until about 1830, English poetry is supreme in Europe. Coleridge and Wordsworth were apt to be scornful of the lush subjectivism of their younger contemporaries, but there is nothing in their tone of that faint disgust and disapproval inspired in the older Goethe by the plays of Kleist and Eichendorff, for instance.[12] German Romanticism after Goethe – an isthmus-figure, like Wordsworth, Turner, Beethoven, and Goya, with too much of the eighteenth century in him to be knocked off-balance by the Revolution – is a sickly thing, neurotic and over-intense: German poetry leaps from Goethe and Schiller to Heine and Hölderlin with little of that beautiful achieved formal ripeness that lends the Odes of Keats and Shelley their resonance. They rushed feeling, as Heller observed, to the throne vacated by reason.[13]

In the Odes of Keats and Shelley we find, if anywhere, something approaching that equipoise of the objective and subjective T. W. Adorno praised in the sonata form of the mature Beethoven: transitorily, the poet is poised, caught musing between himself and history. In the 'Ode on a Grecian Urn', Keats can wonder – with such a wealth of what Rilke later was to call vertical time that the infinitesimal human moment acquires the stillness of the urn its meditations were inspired by – whether it would be indeed better not to experience at all than to experience so briefly and shoddily. The sheer leisureliness of the Keats poem – it is one of the great formal achievements of European Romanticism – does not so much belie its desperate theme as exploit its irreconcilable tensions by resting upon them, keeping itself effortlessly afloat on surface-tension. This poise was soon to be lost. After the generation of Keats, we find the haunted despair of Leopardi (bitter retrenchment within the poet's means); the faintly paranoid imprisonment of Hölderlin's *Liniensleben* (lines of death, not life); the hectic nightmare of Poe's hallucinogenic ecstasies; the sarcastic balladeering of Heine – in which already there is present that bourgeois-pleasing fluency Baudelaire was to ridicule in George Sand. The timelessness of the Keats Odes represents the true 'moment' of Romanticism, timelessness only to be achieved through meditation on time. The theme of time was a logical continuation of the lines of thought initiated by Wordsworth and Coleridge. To experience powerfully (exquisitely, intensely – poetically) means to experience things for the sake of the experiencing, not for the sake of the social, religious, political or ethical world the experience takes place in. The Romantic experience is lifted by its intensity – and not only by its intensity, by its quality, its very nature, its poeticality – out of temporal and societal schemata. Hence it is both supremely historical and supremely a-historical. It is historical because it is itself of the very essence of the consciousness which makes history History, not just a series of events; it is a-historical in that it defies the before and after implicit in an acceptance of human projects. It has no project but itself: it is not therapy, pleasure, utility. And in this it is most centrally human: it is an assertion, if you like, of sheer value, of sheer humanness – consciousness when it is conscious of nothing but consciousness.

If, in 'La Belle dame sans merci', Keats presents an allegory of sexual experience – promising bliss and bequeathing a parched hangover – such as Shakespeare had illustrated already in the Sonnet 'The expense of spirit in a waste of shame', his treatment of the theme is radically different from the Elizabethan poet's: Keats makes the sexual experience allegorical of all experiencing, thus posing a far more desperate problem than Shakespeare did. Sexual experience, of course, was, from this time on, often to propose itself as a possible modus to the poet. In itself it was to seem to some men a paradigm of the poetic experience. The 'Ode to a Nightingale', on the other hand, sets the poet (as modern experiencer) in relationship to the bird that, never seen, had become, like Wordsworth's cuckoo, a mere voice, a 'high requiem': – it is free only in its consummateness, and is not so much an image of the poet, as an image of what the poet knows he can never become, yet is committed to aspiring to become. The free singer of the 'Ode to a Nightingale', as it were, experiences nothing: in him, the material of all song is fully transformed, embodied as only the poet should be embodied – pure voice, pure rhapsodist. The 'Ode on a Grecian Urn', on the other hand, contrasts the disappointment that human experience bestows with the beauty of a possible realm of experience. The richness of the poem itself, of course, testifies to the complexity of the poet's involvements here: the capacity for fine and powerful sensuous experience was necessary before Keats was even able to identify his theme at all. The quality of the poetic experience – the sense of a dimension of grace and illumination in life absent from ordinary human experience – becomes a paradigm of man's relations with time and the absolute. Paradoxically, the richer and truer the experience, the more bitter is the truth the poem asks us to swallow. The 'Ode on a Grecian Urn' is an exact mirror-image of the experience: it succeeds only in so far as it presents us with a precise image of its own failure, and itself all but teases us out of thought by bringing us to the edge of eternity. Thus its apparent theme – the opposition of 'art' and 'life' – becomes subordinate to the underlying or enfolding theme in which it is embedded. True, Keats gains from using the *objet d'art* as starting-point: even though he could have derived his conclusions from a photograph, had photography been invented, (the lovers would still be the fortunate beings about to kiss in the photograph as well as on the Urn), Keats' choice of the 'eternal' work of art gave him a second tier of meaning. Art persists, but in a curiously tantalising or 'teasing' way. It is no consolation (or at best a *pis aller*) for the painfulness of the human condition, but remains, persists, as an eternal taunting reminder of what we are condemned to. Yet it is also testimony of our will to transcend. This is the Janus-nature of all art. It torments while it consoles. In itself it represents that very consciousness by which we are tormented – without which, indeed, we might be 'happy' (even 'happy, happy'). Thus, to say that the 'Ode on a Grecian Urn' is an ambiguous poem is to say much more than that the poet left his punctuation unclear at the end of the poem.[14] That very lack of care to ensure that the commas were in the right places in itself gives us sufficient indication that the real source of the poem's ambiguity is not here. No, we can take it that what the urn tells us is transmitted to us with the poet's endorsement: what it has of desired calm is sufficiently well suggested in the lines that precede the famous aphorism: in 'the midst of human woe' it will – still – be what it is now for us. The contrast with 'our' misery is too plain to be sabotaged by punctuation. Thus the poem neither emphasises the Yeatsian aesthetic reading ('Go for art, not life, life's too uncomfortable'), nor the Leavisite anti-aesthetic ('Go for life, art's dead, a cold pastoral'). Such readings crudify and distort the Ode's essential ambiguity – an ambiguity the more poignant for being so openly and urgently urged throughout.

It is clear that Keats no longer believed in the redemptive power of Wordsworthian recollection. Romantic poets, after Keats, similarly, no longer believed in the melancholy which Keats evoked to fill the vacuum left by Wordsworth. But they inherited from him his damaging wisdom, his knowledge that for the poet – and, ultimately, for all men – all experience is banal and unsatisfactory. In a sense, therefore, Keats undercuts the tradition he inaugurates. For the most tangible result of the Romantic explorations of the new condition of western man was that cult of intensity later to be taken to its logical extreme by Rimbaud in France, and, in England, rationalised by Pater. The rationale of this 'school' is predictable enough from the findings of the Romantics: most experience (the ordinary kind even so upright a man as Wordsworth found wearisome) is death to the poet; let us therefore commit ourselves to the maximum intensity in headlong pursuit of those moments of epiphanous significance which Wordsworth had been prepared to spend hours (days, months, years – a lifetime) cultivating in order to redeem the sludge of ordinary consciousness. Yet Keats in the 'Ode on a Grecian Urn' has already consigned mere intensity to the realm of the banal. Love – Byron's effective though scorned panacea – is the first thing Keats says clots when tasted. Art (the piper) and religion (the priests) are next in line. What therefore could the poets of mere intensity hope to attain but sensation? And what, ultimately, is more vulgar, more sheerly 'bourgeois' than the cult of sensation? The plot of Keats's poem is the space created by the inoperativeness of the moral and philosophical codes which earlier poets has assumed so tacitly as to constitute poetry's *raison d'être*. The questions asked by the poem – which *are* the poem – could not have been asked by any earlier poet, for whom love, Christianity, God or Duty were sufficient reason for not despairing. The 'Ode on a Grecian Urn' despairs, but for no good reason: it despairs because things are the way they are, not because of any particular disabusement, political or emotional. The 'ways things are' is not wickedness or duplicity, but mere experiencing. This is Keats's shatteringly quiet message, and it is in this way that the poem differs from all earlier poetry, all earlier pronouncements on the human condition.

The beauty of the Keats' poem – its peculiar integrity – lies precisely in its going beyond the fine experience itself to set it in its turn against the absolute of the inviolable. Keats pursued many of the implications in his correspondence, where we find him forever seeking to define the nature of the poet, the quality of his experience. To produce, along with his verse, a body of more or less expository prose – sometimes analytic, sometimes closer to manifesto – is a significant peculiarity of the Romantic and post-Romantic poet. In Shelley, this tended to assume a more polemical form. Shelley was, of course, as Marx acknowledged,[15] the most consistently radical of all the Romantic poets. His revolutionary consciousness was more overtly concerned with actual political life than Blake's; and he did not appear to experience the fundamental disillusionment of Wordsworth and Coleridge, even when the Revolution had failed him. Shelley's political intelligence – so much keener and more penetrating than that of his later liberal detractors – is an important element which cannot be overlooked or slighted in any balanced view of his poetry. But it is the more significant as it goes along with the anguish and despair Shelley inherited as the successor to Wordsworth and Coleridge. The 'honey-dew' and the 'milk of paradise' at the end of 'Kubla Khan', symbolise the peculiar powers the poet had always historically felt, but only now drawn upon, like uncashed credits, to justify the poetic stance. Coleridge had in fact created the 'image' of the poet with more verve and panache than Wordsworth:

> And all should cry, Beware! Beware!
> His flashing eyes, his floating hair!
> Weave a circle round him thrice,
> And close your eyes with holy dread,
> For he on honey-dew hath fed,
> And drunk the milk of Paradise.   ('Kubla Khan')

This magnificent piece of shamanistic high camp – demanding awe and attentiveness from society – is set significantly enough in a confessional context which assumes society's indifference: the 'symphony and song' of the damsel with the dulcimer remain unheard, society remains unimpressed. At the same time, of course, the poem brilliantly enacts the inspired possession whose absence it bewails. Coleridge's regret is transformed by Shelley into something more realistically plaintive:

> Teach me half the gladness
>   That thy brain must know,
> Such harmonious madness
>   From my lips would flow
> The world should listen then – as I am listening now.
>   ('To a Skylark')

Shelley's counterfactual is significantly related to Coleridge's. Coleridge laments that the poet will always just fail to say what he is professionally committed to believing he both could and should say, and it was left to the French Symbolists, under the guidance of Mallarmé, to elaborate this into the doctrines of necessary failure (failure having become the guarantee of integrity).[16] Shelley shifts our attention more knowingly to the poet's sardonic awareness of the absent audience: his utterances, now become superfluous and faintly ridiculous, are typified by the brilliantly baseless effusions about the invisible bird which have preceded Shelley's poignant acknowledgement of the world's neglect. It is in such bitter precisions that the English Romantic poets articulated the new status of poetry in a society whose technology and economic development had simply left it high and dry – a luxury, a superfluity, an absurdity.

The particular authenticity of 'To a Skylark' lies in its refusal to supply itself with a base, a substructure, until, at the end, it is seen to be balanced upon the awareness that it is the modern poet's fate to disgorge such effusions in a social and human vacuum. The relations between the modern poet and the world receive no more poignant articulation than in this contra-position of joyous yet controlled exuberance and pathos. What Shelley *does* in the poem is of the essence of poetic activity itself.

At the other end of Shelley's scale, the 'Ode to the West Wind' harnesses the poet's professional exhilaration ('We poets begin in joy and gladness') to the intellectual radical's concern with freedom in its fullest sense. This poem is perhaps the last work of art in Europe successfully to unite visionary radiance with political idealism: the emancipation of peoples from oppression is given an authentically universal scale. The Romantic poem, we have seen, had to be radical to be politically authentic: to desire anything less than the total liberation of all men, all prisoners – from tyranny, from ignorance, from 'single vision' – was to run counter to the very nature of poetry itself. And the liberation, for Shelley as for Blake, must be of the whole man – body, heart, mind and spirit. The tremendous force of the 'Ode to the West Wind' (made visible by the precision of Shelley's imagery and by his dialectical use of the *terza rima*) is perhaps the last blast of the Revolutionary hurricane in European art. As such, it takes its place alongside Blake's lyrics, Delacroix's greatest canvasses, and Beethoven's middle-period music. All the more poignant, then, is Shelley's confession in the poem of personal disillusionment and fatigue:

> A heavy weight of hours has chained and bowed
> One too like thee: tameless, and swift, and proud.
>
> ('Ode to the West Wind')

(This sort of statement used to cause a certain amount of discomfort among critics: it is enough to observe that it was a true description of the poet, and is structurally endorsed – more, necessitated – by the drive, tone and power of the preceding verse.) The chain that forged character in *The Prelude* has become 'a heavy weight of hours'. To be sure, in his Preface to 'The Revolt of Islam', Shelley explains Romantic despair directly in terms of the failure of the French Revolution to live up to its human possibilities:

> Thus, many of the most ardent and tender-hearted of the worshippers of public good have been morally ruined by what a partial glimpse of the events they deplored appeared to show as the melancholy desolation of all their cherished hopes. Hence gloom and misanthropy have become the characteristics of the age in which we live, the solace of a disappointment that unconsciously finds relief only in the wilful exaggeration of its own despair.[17]

He goes on to say that he thinks that people 'appear . . . to be emerging from their trance. I am aware, methinks, of a slow, gradual, silent change'. Yet 'The Revolt of Islam' is not Shelley at his greatest; it is, by contrast with the satire of the Restoration of the Augustan period, mere polemic – brilliant, but not really poetry. The truth is that Shelley could not here bring himself up to his highest pitch. Emotion runs high during revolutionary periods; people are transfigured, carried above themselves. This transfiguration is not spurious, but it is in a sense irrelevant to the ends of the Revolution itself: though necessary as a means, it is merely instrumental. When the aims of the Revolution are attained, the high idealism becomes an embarrassment; ordinary life supervenes, altered in only superficial respects by the Revolution. French society after a Revolution was now bourgeois, not aristocratic; essentially, men remained un-transfigured. But, 'Unheroic as bourgeois society is', Marx wrote, 'it nevertheless took heroism, sacrifice, terror, civil war, and battles of peoples to bring it into being'.[18] Within the ultimate liberation, the poet is a dissonance – disappointed even at the moment of triumph, as Aleksandr Blok was to be a hundred years later at the successful Revolution in Russia. Shelley's rueful confessions of failure and fatigue, like the great sighs that punctuate the Bacchanalian exultation of the Ninth Symphony, seem now vitally important elements in the paradoxical triumphs of Romanticism. The truth, for the poet, seems already to be inextricably bound up with sadness and disillusionment. The poet is a bad political bet, even when he is as uncompromising in his radicalism as Shelley or Blok. When the Revolution is achieved, when the tyrants are all dead, when no one is exploited by anybody, when all prisons are empty – " 'What then?' sang Plato's ghost, 'what then?' " It was not the 'failure' of the French Revolution that disillusioned the Romantics, but its success.[19]

Shelley's poetry characteristically moves by a constant dialectic of brilliant exultancy and chilling foresight. Whatever the thrilling brilliance of the world revealed to him by his keen sensitivity, his mind remains aware that it cannot *guarantee* that 'spirit of delight'. Often, as in the 'Stanzas written in Dejection near Naples', he depicts the visible scene with a meticulous brilliance that seems to have been afforded him precisely by his despondency: it is as if the despondency bracketed-out the projects and schemes with which human consciousness constantly obscures its experience of the world, and presented him with a kind of existential truth he had no reserves left to gainsay. The intellectual pressure needed to penetrate to these insights into futility came without doubt from the historical momentum of the Revolutionary period: in the midst of the exultant anticipation, the poet is overwhelmed by the sense of his own irrelevancy. Hence the somewhat strident assertions of 'unacknowledged legislatorship' Shelley made in the *Defence of Poetry*. For it was Shelley who formulated the Wordsworthian sense of poetic importance in its most uncompromisingly political form: the poet's utterances are to be 'The trumpet of a prophecy'; their words are to be 'scattered . . . among mankind', to quicken a 'new birth' – the spiritual revolution of which any actual revolution is a treacherous travesty. Yet his triumph of life became the triumph of death. The dying Keats, too, experienced the paralysing suspicion of being a square peg in the round hole of modern society: the Induction to the Revised 'Hyperion' enacts a symbolic rejection of the sumptuous poetic feastings of the *Odes*. Keats now feels he has social obligations which the sheer magnificence of those poems had somehow scanted. He wishes that he could burn as steadily as the evening star, and finally feels that his name is 'writ in water'. There are, of course, terrible personal sufferings behind these last poems of Keats. But they are presided over by an overwhelming sense of cultural discontinuity, of being nowhere in the movement of history, of being useless, ignored, misunderstood.

The arrogance into which these suspicions were leading poets is, of course, most spectacularly manifest in the personality of Byron, or rather in the cult of Byron which swept over Europe after the publication of 'Childe Harold's Pilgrimage' in 1812. Byron has generally been considered by English-speaking critics to be the least important of all the English Romantic poets, and to be fundamentally something of a poseur. Of course, he was in one sense a poseur: but there is no clear demarcation between pose and stance, and every poet – indeed every human being – is in some degree a poseur.[20] It is easy to dismiss Byron as a shallow exhibitionist; but it is a mistake. Exhibitionism itself may appear at first sight morally indefensible, a form of immaturity incompatible with what we may regard as an 'adult' attitude towards life. But in fact, it may be a necessary form of protection: a talented individual may easily resort to a self-conscious arrogance which in fact distorts a basically positive personality. The effort to distinguish himself from those around him may force the poet into unkindness or apparent heartlessness. He may indeed come to regard kindness, sympathy or compassion themselves as traps by which he may betray himself into ordinariness, and so lose his 'integrity'. Such a process of self-discrimination has, I suspect, always been part of the artistic personality in civilised society.

Byron's stance had an overwhelming and electrifying effect on European poets because it crystallised so many tendencies and influences: it was the final acknowledgement of the place the poet held in the modern world. What his heroics really indicated was that the poet had now finally settled into a new posture, a posture that derived ultimately from Wordsworth. For Byron's own verse

– *English Bards and Scotch Reviewers* notwithstanding – incorporated significant elements of the Wordsworthian position. The 'attitude' Byron struck so effectively was not callow arrogance, but a logical continuation of the Wordsworthian preoccupation with role. It was a mode of self-conception, a vehicle not only for the presentation of himself, but for the creation of himself. The Byronic personality created itself in projecting itself. Byron defines his activity himself with the kind of mental precision that always lay within the studied aristocratic negligence:

> 'Tis to create, and in creating live
> A being more intense, that we endow
> With form our fancy, gaining as we give
> The life we image, even as I do now –
>
> ('Childe Harold's Pilgrimage', III, VI)

'To create, and in creating live/A being more intense': this is a definition of the poetic stance it would be not hard, but impossible, to improve upon. The words which follow clinch the dependence of epistemology upon teleology, for Byron is giving to the Coleridgean conception of the formation of the poetic symbol a dynamic purposefulness: 'gaining as we give/The life we image'. The act of collaboration which resulted, for Coleridge, in the creation of the poetic symbol, is here conceived mythopoeically as a means for developing and sustaining the self in its quest for meaningful experience. Byron thus gives to the traditional allegorical quest-motif a daring and important literalness: it is not some parabolic quest of the Soul in search of God or Grail that 'Childe Harold's Pilgrimage' describes, but the wanderings of a poet in a world to which he himself must bring the meaning. For the content of Byron's poetry (its mythic purposiveness), is identifiable with its form, its structure of significant image: it is the dynamic purposiveness, indeed, which makes the image significant. In a second important respect, therefore, we see that Byron is following Wordsworth: it was Wordsworth, we have already seen, who turned the eighteenth century 'descriptive' poem into the poetry of symbol. The Wordsworthian preoccupation with role is paralleled in Byron by a comparable poetic methodology:

> I live not in myself, but I become
> Portion of that around me; and to me
> High mountains are a feeling, but the hum
> Of human cities torture: . . .
>
> ('Childe Harold's Pilgrimage', III, LXXII)

This is somewhat affected (Wordsworth, with more right to, does not scorn cities in this way). Yet the feeling not merely *for* nature but *in* nature is, in these lines and everywhere else in Byron, essentially Wordsworthian. The fabric of Byron's poetry is made up of natural scenes, presented rather than inhabited, yet infused with Byron himself, and free of the pathetic fallacy:

> It is the hush of night, and all between
> Thy margin and the mountains, dusk, yet clear,
> Mellowed and mingling, yet distinctly seen,
> Save darkened Jura, whose capt heights appear
> Precipitously steep; and drawing near,
> There breathes a living fragrance from the shore,
> Of flowers yet fresh with childhood; on the ear
> Drops the light drip of the suspended oar,
> Or chirps the grasshopper one good-night carol more.
>
> ('Childe Harold's Pilgrimage', II, LXXXVI)

Byron's enormous influence abroad derived, in fact, almost as much from the incomparable clarity with which he presented the exotic ambiences his heroes wandered through as from the conscious arrogance of the Byronic stance: not only the Caucasian atmospherics of Pushkin and Lermontov, but the vaguely Balkan wildness of much of Delacroix's pictorial, and Berlioz's musical landscapes, could hardly have materialised without Byron's earlier explorations. It is, in fact, impossible at this stage to separate the role-consciousness of poetry, which gives it so much of its own 'content', from the symbolic landscape which expresses its form. To give us Childe Harold's inward state, Byron did not need to invent allegorical events and symbols, he simply let the landscape of his travels unfold. The poet's purposiveness invests the 'descriptions' with meaning. It is the function of myth to facilitate just this union of meaning and image (of objective and subjective), and Byron's importance in the nineteenth century derives very largely from the conception of the poetic life which he articulated so precisely.

Byron dramatised his alienation and turned it into self-vindication: it is now society that is wrong, not the poet. Byron does not feel it necessary, as Wordsworth clearly had, to explain himself to society, to justify the ways of society to himself, and himself to society. Byron no longer feels part of society, and no longer respects its aims. Thus, Byron's stance showed the poet settling into a new posture that was a logical development of the old. Byron's impact on the Continent was certainly in part due to the fact that he was an aristocrat and an outcast from society, and that the poets he influenced usually lived in politically backward societies. In countries like Spain, Russia, Poland and Germany, poets found in the semi-outcast English lord a suitable model for their own (actual) political alienation.

At the same time, as an aristocrat, Byron was free of the bourgeois concern which nagged Wordsworth and Coleridge. It has often been the practice among critics to treat Byron's aristocratic background somewhat sarcastically. Leavis called him 'the great vulgarisateur'.[21] Arnold Hauser – marginally more objective – got a little closer to the truth about Byron, 'whose rages against the aristocracy that is excommunicating him show how deeply he feels tied to his class, and how much of its authority and attractiveness it still holds for him, in spite of everything': Hauser also regarded Byron as a successful publicist who 'found his real public in the rank of the dissatisfied, resentful, romantically inclined middle class'. Such remarks surely militate against any serious appraisal of Byron's work. It was not merely resentful *petit bourgeois* nobodies who found Byron relevant, but almost every important poet, painter and composer for nearly half a century. Byron united in his person the poet and the aristocrat, the artist and the rebel. Like the artist, the aristocrat was a member of a doomed and politically impotent class; he was outside and 'above' the sordid grubbing for money, and the exercise of what was increasingly felt to be a brutal political power. The aristocrat like the artist is therefore non-responsible, and by extension, irresponsible. At the same time he retains a definite superiority over the bourgeois who now run society. He retains his breeding, his fineness of behaviour, his innocence of petty anxiety; he is visibly and actually superior to the bourgeois, who acknowledges the fact by sending his son to the schools and universities which have helped form the aristocrat himself. The aristocrat has 'style'. Moreover, his hands are now comparatively clean. Though implicated in government, he is not to a great extent involved in the oppressive industry which is stunting the proletariat; it is the middle class who now assume the class-guilt, and along with it the need to sublimate it into Culture.

For reasons of this kind, Byron's 'image' was irresistible not merely to the sons of bourgeois but to men of genius and talent. For the artist, too, was a dispossessed aristocrat, no longer part of the power-structure, no longer strictly necessary, yet also possessing 'style' and an inborn sense of superiority. By an easy and valid shift, the Byronic contempt for the grubbing bourgeois, with their horrible manners and their obsession with money, becomes identified with a generalised disgust with materialism itself. This is something only implicit in Wordsworth, though it is explicit enough in Blake who was more obviously a descendent from the traditional Christian moralists. After Byron, hostility to bourgeois acquisitiveness becomes a central element in Western poetry. At one level, the anti-materialism which develops so rapidly in 19th century poetry could be interpreted as sublimated sour grapes. Forced out of his traditional position within the framework of the community, and unable to compete with the popular novelist or the operetta-composer for a share in the new affluence, the poet falls back upon the medieval Christian disdain for 'mere' worldly goods. There is no real parallel in pre-Wordsworthian poetry for the kind of horror of 'vulgar' wealth which is so pervasive an element of Symbolist aesthetics and polemics. Perhaps the wealth variously 'celebrated' by Shakespeare, Tintoretto and Monteverdi simply *was not vulgar* – vulgarity being, so to speak, a later development of the age which finally divorced power and wealth from the class (the aristocracy) which knew how to deploy them. At any rate, the artist's sense of the vulgarity of bourgeois wealth is essentially a symptom of alienation. It is not a feature of Renaissance art that wealth – no matter how materialistically obtained – is low or beneath celebration. On the contrary, it is mere fuel for the celebration of man himself, and it is the estrangement from this view of himself that really lies within nineteenth century alienation.

At any rate, the aristocratic English poet provided an excellent focus for the angry alienation of European poets in the century. It is a short but deeply significant step from the thrilling zest of Byron's Harold, feeling the mast quiver at his side and the sea bound beneath him like a horse he himself is riding, to Lermontov's most famous lyrice ('Byelyet parus odinoky'):

> Beneath him sparkles brilliant azure,
> Above, the ray of the golden sun . . .
> And he rebellious, longs for storms
> As if in storms lay peace!

Lermontov is on the shore – watching Byron, in effect – and it is by such gradations that the full Romantic culture-hero phases out into the poet of our own time. Lermontov's last line is deeply ambiguous: 'As if in storms lay peace.' This can mean either that the poet-speaker knows otherwise, or simply that there might well be such a solution, and that the poet-speaker might end up as the invisible, unknown seaman will – like Shelley, dead at sea. Lermontov felt constrained at one stage of his short career to emphasise his awareness of the distance between himself and Byron: 'Nyet, Ya i nye Biaron' ('No, I'm no Byron'). His novel, *A Hero of our Time* – one of the milestones of post-Romantic fiction – contained an excellent lampoon of the vulgarised pseudo-Byron (Granitski) along-side a subtle and sympathetic study of the Byronic hero himself (Petchorin). It was a clever piece of insurance: we accept the real hero – cold, lost, antipathetic as he is presented – partly because of the gross parody at his side. Without Petchorin there could have been no Raskonikov, and without Byron no Petchorin.

In a further respect, too, Byron was more sympathetic to Continental European than to English minds: Byron was the only really 'worldly' English poet between Rochester and Auden. The English expect a poet to be a puritan, an unsoiled communer with Nature, a vessel for pure aesthetic emotion. This was especially true, for sociological reasons, in the Victorian era, when the artist was expected to play his role in cleaning up and refining but also, essentially, supporting society. Being more stable and more prosperous than other European nations, England resented the outsider poet. This led, as we shall see, more or less to the preclusion of a genuine artistic *avant garde* in nineteenth century England. It is not something, I think, to which we can respond simply or unequivocally. It was a source of strength and of weakness, as indeed it was a symptom of strength and of weakness. At any rate, the poets of Europe – Pushkin, Heine, Lermontov, Mickiewicz, Nietzsche, Shevchenko, Espronceda, Hoffmannsthal, Blok (the list is not endless but very long) – found in the author of the following lines a perfect model for their own conception of themselves as world-weary libertines and liberating prophets:

> Alas! our young affections run to waste,
> Or water but the desert! whence arise
> But weeds of dark luxuriance, tares of haste,
> Rank at the core, though tempting to the eyes,
> Flowers whose wild odours breathe, but agonies,
> And trees whose gums are poison; such the plants
> Which spring beneath her steps as Passion flies
> O'er the World's wilderness, and vainly pants
> For some celestial fruit forbidden to his wants
>
> ('Childe Harold's Pilgrimage', IV, CXX)

These lines fully justify, in their flexible strength and their rich fatigue, the 'pose' of the 'Childe Harold' poet, and surely supply the root of that 'uneradicable taint of sin' of which Byron later in the poem speaks. The lines might almost, given a sublime enough translator, be translated from *Fleurs du Mal*. The world-weariness of Byron (written off by so much English criticism as immature affectation), like his unslakeable thirst for something 'forbidden to his wants' and his sense of some deep unsatisfactoriness in the very experience he craves – these things are essential elements of Romanticism, which later became vital structural properties of Symbolism.

7 The Poet's Sense of Role – 2: the Symbolist Impasse

Byron's influence upon Baudelaire brings us, of course, to the Poe problem – the enigma of the minor poet who becomes a major influence abroad. In fact, it was probably necessary for a second-rate poet to interpret English Romanticism to the French. The grandiose poverty of French Romanticism stood as a model of vulgarity to French poets of Baudelaire's generation: so bourgeois this Victor Hugo, caught *in flagrante delicto* not once only, in the bedroom, but every time he put pen to paper! There was more to Romanticism than the adoption of elegantly melancholic attitudes, a vague religion of Nature and a bombastic egotism, but a Frenchman of Baudelaire's time, unaware of English poetry, could have been forgiven for doubting it. The Byronic stance, moreover, without the rich epistemological tradition informing it, was easily confused with the Napoleonic egotism of Châteaubriand and Hugo. Hugo, as Walter Benjamin observed, 'saw himself primarily as a genius in a great assembly of geniuses who were his ancestors'.[1] Certainly, Hugo was lucidly aware of the kind of self-conception which Byron had already defined with such zestful precision: 'Every great man', he wrote, 'works on two works – the work he creates as a living person and his spirit-work.'[2] Yet his 'apparitions' of greatness were, as Benjamin notes, 'threadbare,' and Hugo appended theoretical exegeses which were 'meaningless abstractions'[3] – 'Drama', 'Poetry', 'Literature'. Hugo represents the Carlylean heroism of late Romanticism – a mode, strictly speaking, of evading the contemporary, and deferring all problems to the realm of the sublime and the infinite. It will be remarked that none of the great English Romantics hits this note: it is left to Carlyle to do that, and Hugo slides off into the empyrean, on the back of the sonorous Alexandrine, just at the point when he was needed. At any rate, it was not until Baudelaire discovered Poe, and there – through the thought of

Wordsworth, Coleridge and Shelley, that French poetry showed itself capable of taking up the poetic burden in a mature way. Gautier is, of course, an important intermediary, whose significance is connected with his famous concern for precision and economy, but by no means confined to it. We must discount any claims for a 'new classicism' here. The author of *Emaux et Camées* was a contemporary of W. S. Landor, an equally precise and refined craftsman. But any conception of 'classicism' framed in terms of an 'economy' of means or a striving after an impression of hard clarity is to be rejected out of hand. Quite simply, there is no non-Romantic poetry after Wordsworth, for Romanticism is a situation. Society is fractured, man is alienated, poets are all in the same boat. Whether they express themselves in closed quatrains or 'sprawling' free verse depends entirely upon psychological factors; the difference between, say, Rimbaud and Verlaine, or between Gautier and Hugo, has little to do with any 'Classical' ideal, and much to do with psychological endowment. In so far as Gautier and Hugo were confronted by the same historical, social and political facts, they are equally defined by the 'Romantic' situation. Gautier's predilection for the bright finish and the clipped witticism, is something that he owed to his temperament. It assumes a more general significance only when taken in conjunction with the Preface to *Mademoiselle de Maupin*. Then, the craftsman's pride in a kind of formalistic perfection indicates a more distinctly 'political' or ideological attitude; it comes to represent the spiritual standards which Gautier feels the 'bourgeois' to be without. It is at this time, indeed, that the term *bourgeois* begins to assume its modern tone.[4] This fact itself is highly significant. The conscious adoption of the anti-bourgeois standpoint marks a new stage in the modern poet's evolving sense of role; the gap that separates the artist from the rest of organised society, consciousness of which had been so intelligently articulated and explored by the English Romantics, has now deepened and widened. Nineteenth century poets were often accused of inhabiting the ivory tower out of perversity. Yet the concept of the ivory tower is only a logical development of Byronism. When Gautier was writing, the Byron 'pose' had little serious thought behind it in French. It is, nevertheless, significant; the cult of *épater le bourgeois* – the very conception of the 'bourgeois' itself – is an integral part of post-Industrial Revolution culture. The often

irritating attitudinising of so many later nineteenth century poets
expressed in a trivial form the profound alienation of the modern
artist. The very existence of the bohemian is itself a phenomenon
purely characteristic of the democratic-capitalist world-order.
Bohemianism, dandyism, ivory tower-ism, decadence – all these
related syndromes testify to the irreparable culture-split in our
society as certainly as the more serious meditations of a Hopkins
or a Baudelaire.

This whole development is summed-up in the emergence of the
phrase *avant garde*: what we are here concerned with is the
development of a conscious artistic ideology, one which pushes
further and still further the ideas of Romanticism, and does so by
objectifying the sense of isolation, futility and aimlessness so
characteristic of Romanticism, into a definite artistic programme.
It is significant that our terminology at this stage is French.
Having been awoken from their rhetorical slumber by Scott,
Byron, Poe and Shakespeare, the French take the initiative. The
next half-century is theirs, and as their poetry rises so English
poetry declines.

The reasons for this phenomenon are complex enough to forbid
brief encapsulation here. I must, however, give some indication
as to the way in which I would explain the facts, were there
enough space and time. English poetry declined in the Victorian
era not through any loss of vitality or talent (Tennyson is
probably as good a poet as either Heine or Baudelaire), but
because it ceased to carry forward the fruitful discussion of role
characteristic of Romantic poetry. In other words, Tennyson and
Swinburne and Arnold remain (roughly speaking) at the position
reached by Byron, Shelley and Keats. This accounts for the
absence of sheer excitement in Victorian verse, the drop in
intensity, the loss of that sense of being *in medias res* that is so
electric, for instance, in the poetry of Shelley. It is not in itself to
be explained in terms of any long-term disillusionment; the
French Symbolists inherit the same sort of world as Tennyson
and Arnold. To say that the Victorian poets remained at the
position reached by the Romantics is to say that they accepted the
conception of the poet's role which those poets had articulated, in
circumstances where it was no longer quite relevant. They
remained mystic Wordsworths, noble Shelleys, and dewy-eyed
Keatses: they saw in the Romantic stance only a completed thing,
they missed the inward evolution that had kept it alive. In other

words, the Victorians ceased to develop: they ceased exploring their relation to society and their own significance in the universe. This can be summed up by saying that there was no English *avant garde*. There were to be sure, exceptional 'eccentrics' like Hopkins and Francis Thompson, and there is a pale bohemian movement (the pre-Raphaelites), but these only confirm the rule that there is no real English *avant garde*. There was no *avant garde* partly because the political and social history of England was against it. In remaining unthrown by Revolution or military reverse, England kept contact with its own past in a way that was unique in European history. Although the real economic power had been for some considerable time in the hands of the middle classes, the aristocracy still provided the model for behaviour in England. The English middle classes sent their sons, if they could afford it, to Eton or Winchester and thence to Oxford or Cambridge, where they came to resemble the aristocracy. Moreover, the aristocracy itself had been, since the Wars of the Roses at least, continually infused with bourgeois blood: it was by no means the hidebound caste of European society. (This phenomenon, quite as much as the greater social mobility of English society, is what accounts for the highly developed snobbishness of the English.) This appearance of relatively smooth evolution as opposed to brutal revolution was to some extent fraudulent. Nevertheless it did truly reflect a significant continuity of culture and tradition in areas which were important in the formation of a certain social homogeneity. 'In France', as Engels observed, 'the Revolution constituted a complete breach with the traditions of the past.' English law on the other hand is the 'only one which has preserved through ages and transmitted to America and the Colonies, the best part of that old Germanic personal freedom, local self-government and independence from all interference but that of the law courts, which on the continent has been lost during the period of absolute monarchy and has nowhere as yet been fully recovered'.[5] The breach with 'the best of the past', we note, was effected not only by the Revolution itself, but by the tyranny of absolutist monarchy; the important continuity of English life derived as much from the absence of violent political revolution as from the presence of some kind of evolutionary movement within the earlier history that made revolution unnecessary.

Thus it was that the English intellectual in the nineteenth

century found it less easy than his French counterpart to find objective foundation for the contempt for 'society' which his position seemed to require. The political bankruptcy of France, its military impotence and economic sluggishness, to say nothing of the disillusionment after the failure of the Revolution to provide that society open to all the talents it had seemed to promise – all this made it relatively easy for the French intellectual to despise his country: it was not only materialistic and without ideals, it was ineffectual. The English intellectual was confronted by the fact of British hegemony – by the prevailing of British will militarily, economically and territorially. Unbroken, arrogant, the richly-panoplied power-élite of Victorian England could not have been easy to despise. Carlyle and Arnold both speak of British industriousness and effectuality with a certain awe; and Dickens and Ruskin, for all their scorn of English materialism and horror at the effects of the industrial revolution, assume the stance of reformers, not revolutionaries.

Thus, the English poet found himself, as it were, involuntarily part of the Victorian élite: Tennyson, Browning and Arnold were all, in different ways, part of conventional English society in ways unimaginable to a contemporary Frenchman. The 'good' English writer is still inside society; the 'good' French writer is outside, and he formulates his outsiderness into the ideology of the *avant garde*. Yet the English poet is, as we knew from the Romantics, just as alienated as the French. Tennyson was, said T. S. Eliot, 'the most instinctive rebel against the society in which he was the most perfect conformist'. He therefore suffered 'A gloomier end than that of Baudelaire: Tennyson had no *singulier avertissement*. And having turned aside from the journey through the dark night, to become the surface flatterer of his own time, he has been rewarded with the despite of an age that succeeds his own in shallowness.'[6] Eliot is saying – with unsurpassable tact and precision – that Tennyson was just as much a poet of alienation as Baudelaire, but that he refused the burden of defining his alienation except in those allegorical modes subtly suggested by Eliot in the metaphor of the 'dark journey'. When he finally gave up even this degree of engagement with his proper subject-matter (his predicament in the modern world), Tennyson left alienation aside and concerned himself with 'problems' more properly the business of novelists and melodramatists. The French poet does not allow himself to be nudged away from his centre of strength by his alienation. Indeed, the French poet draws strength and inspiration precisely from his need to define his alienation and to justify it, and the need to justify his position remains incumbent on the post-Wordsworthian poet. The later nineteenth century French poet responded in ways which seem to us markedly and specifically modern, yet are in fact simply the logical continuation of Romanticism.

Our sense of a modern tone in late-nineteenth century French poetry is enhanced by contrast with the backward-looking withdrawal of the English Victorians, of course. But the new 'settings' (city streets and bars instead of ruined mills and forsaken gardens), and the 'realism' which replaces the evasive use of allegory are themselves by-products of the alert and intelligent attitude towards role and function which is what really distinguishes the French *avant garde*. The French, in other words, took up the thread of the meditation upon function, purpose, role and position which English poets let fall at the death of Byron. Tennyson is at least as conscious of role as Byron: poems like 'Mariana', 'The Lady of Shallot', 'The Lotus Eaters', 'The Palace of Art' and 'Ulysses' are all, in their allegorical mode, extremely precise attempts to define the poet's position. They succeed in defining and presenting the reasons for not trying, for giving up; they explain the inevitability of melancholy. They explore and articulate the nature both of withdrawal, and of a near-neurotic incapacity for decided participation in any activity outside oneself. But all this takes place well within the territory marked out by the Romantics. Byron would not have been much surprised by Tennyson's *Poems Chiefly Lyrical* of 1842 nor by Swinburne's first *Poems & Ballads* series of 1866. The failure of these major poetic talents to produce major poetic *oeuvres* is not to be explained by any 'failure to mature', or any other psychological incapacity. Neither is it anything to do with Victorian 'hypocrisy' (whatever that may be taken to mean.) It is rather a question of the sort of acceptance of the findings of the later Romantics that is expressed here by Browning:

Past hopes already lay behind.
What need to strive with a life awry?

('The last ride together')

Along with this acceptance of the 'life awry' goes the resignation to failure – 'What hand and brain went ever paired?' In Browning, too, the passion of Shelley is domesticated, as that of Chopin is domesticated in the music of Schumann. 'He' and 'she' are still concerned about whether they vibrate in tune, but rather as young married couples nowadays do:

> I wonder do you feel today
>   As I have felt since, hand in hand,
> We sat down on the grass, to stray
>   In spirit better through the land,
> This morn of Rome and May?

> ('Two in the Campagna')

To call this bourgeoisfied is not to refer especially to the social status of the poet: Keats, Wordsworth and Coleridge are not in this sense bourgeois poets, for all Byron's contempt. It is a matter of the poet's acceptance – albeit in a spirit of socially admirable good humour – of the world and his relations with it. For, at the same time, Browning behaves 'like a poet' – with dashes of 'tempestuous' behaviour and unpredictability – sweeping his lover off her feet, 'romantically' eloping. The poet's conception of himself and of his role has been arrested at a certain point. An alternative to the dashing Shelleyan, is the swan-like character of Tennyson's 'The Poet's Song', who sat him down in a lonely place and

>   chanted a melody loud and sweet,
>   That made the wild swan pause in her song
>   And the lark drop down at his feet.

The twentieth century reader cannot but be disturbed at the Yeatsian cadence with which the poem ends:

> I have sung many songs,
> But never a one so gay,
> For he sings of what the world will be
> When the years have died away

Yeats, indeed, held fast to the Tennysonian conception of poetry and the poet until the 1920s. It is a conception we have seen already, in the closing lines of 'Kubla Khan' and 'To a Skylark'. Keats had already subjected this conception of the poet to searching criticism in the 'Fall of Hyperion'. By Tennyson's time, it had lost its dynamism, and was no longer related vitally to the world in which the poet and his readers actually lived. There is something essentially undefined and uncritical in the notion, an inherent vagueness ('When the years have died away') which stands in direct contrast to the hard, clear treatment of Baudelaire and certain of his Symbolist successors.

Initially, indeed, Baudelaire's conception of the poet's role and nature is taken from Byron as seen by Lamartine. The tone and even the diction of a great deal of the earlier Baudelaire is already present in Lamartine's famous tribute to Byron in 'L'Homme' (1819). Here already is the *mélange* of good and evil, satan and angel, with which we become so familiar in *Fleurs du Mal*: Byron is an 'esprit mystérieux, mortel, ange où démon', he is possessed of a 'fatal génie', his eye, like Satan's 'a mesuré l'abîme,' and his soul, 'y plongeant loin du jour et de Dieu, A dit a l'espérance un éternel adieu!' The poem ends, after a display of some of Baudelaire's own favourite sonorities – 'ténèbres, funebres, triomphe', – with a couplet which might stand as an epigraph for Baudelaire's volume:

> Il triomphe, et sa voix sur un mode infernal,
> Chante l'hymne de gloire, au sombre dieu du mal.
>
> ('L'Homme')

Much of Baudelaire's poetry fails to move beyond the easy paradox of Lamartine's Catholic Satanism, and the somewhat callow Byronism that lies behind it. Poems like the 'Hymne à la Beauté', 'Don Juan aux Enfers', 'Les Litanies de Satan' and 'Le Reniement de Saint Pierre' add nothing to the by-now stale vocabulary of Byronic Romanticism. Nor did Baudelaire ever wholly free himself – as Rimbaud observed –[7] from the weakness of the old rhetoric with its fatally easy grandeur. True, the characteristic Racinian inversions, that run so glibly off Lamartine's tongue, appear less frequently in *Fleurs du Mal*, in which indeed there is a good deal of Byron's deliberate banality:

> Les sanglots des martyrs et des supplicies
> Sont une symphonie enivrante sans doute,

Puisque, malgré le sang que leur volûpté coûte,
Les cieux ne s'en sont encor rassasiés!

('Le Reniement de Saint Pierre')

The facetiousness of the badly rhymed inner couplet is an important adjunct to the 'irony' which pervades the whole poem and indeed the whole volume; but this irony has too often to consort with the sonorously facile rhetoric which is the curse of French poetry from Corneille to Hugo. Rhyme too often dictates sense: the tyrannous Alexandrine encourages the poet to fill its seductive expanses with hollowly reverberating epithets – 'Ténèbreux', 'orageux'.

This residual magniloquence of Baudelaire's reflects the rather inflexible Romantic stance which structures so much of *Fleurs du Mal*. The 'Benediction' nevertheless brings a new acridity to the characteristic Vignyesque conception of the poetic malediction. The poet's mother curses heaven for giving her a poet in broad farcical terms which Byron might, but Vigny certainly would not, have countenanced:

Ah! que n'ai-je mis bas tout un noeud de vipères,
Plutôt que de nourrir cette dérision.

(One remembers at this point Byron's mother's drunken vituperations against her son.) But the poet's own declaration at the end of the poem is unabashed in the nobility of its pretensions. He sees himself as 'ce beau diadème, éblouissant et clair', which is made only of 'pure lumière'. It was Poe, of course, who intervened to give Baudelaire a conception of the poetic vocation still only imprecisely adumbrated in Musset's *Nuits* and Vigny's *Destinées*. To put the matter briefly, English Romanticism, as interpreted by Poe in essays translated by Baudelaire, afforded Baudelaire a sharper and more systematically self-conscious methodology, a finer and yet more critical conception of the poetic stance and the poetic craft, than anything he could have gleaned from Hugo, Vigny or Lamartine. The investigation of the workings of the poetic imagination, the presentation of the poetic personality, and the analysis of the poet's new role in society – all these were tasks more profoundly and more subtly carried out by the English Romantics; it was from them that Baudelaire – and, through him, the Symbolists themselves – derived their new orientation. Certainly, from the time of Baudelaire's discovery of Poe, French poetry began to take over the serious business of relating poetry to society. The most significant element in their new approach was, I have argued, the gradual formulation of the concept of the *avant garde*. Where English poets floundered or idled within the framework of Romanticism, French poets now moved forward, subjecting the characteristically Romantic personality to continuously intelligent criticism, and, in the process, adjusting the poetic stance not only to new circumstances, but to their own awareness of *What had already been said*. This facility of the French for constant adjustment and reaction was later, it is true, to trivialise itself: the *avant garde* became, in the course of the twentieth century, merely the academy for futile experimentation, the new orthodoxy of the professionally unorthodox. At the time of Baudelaire, however, the French genius for ideology served to move western poetry out of its romantic groove, and it did so by discarding the elegant allegorical trappings of Poe and replacing them quite simply with realism. The result of this move can best be seen, again, by comparing Tennyson with Baudelaire. They often have much in common. 'Ulysses' and 'Le Voyage' are clearly parallel 'Childe Harold' poems, and both are in the allegorical mode. Both, moreover, express typical mid-nineteenth century conditions: mankind is idle, either through too much success (as in 'Ulysses') or through the experience of the tediousness of the actual (as in 'Le Voyage'). Both poems, moreover, fail finally to sustain the heroic voice they attempt. Baudelaire falls back on Byron's 'Childe Harolde' manner, with a dash of satanism; Tennyson on the spirit of the public school – 'To strive, to seek, to find, and not to yield'. Both poems, perhaps, honour in their very inconclusiveness the actual predicament of the man of vision and energy who was also cursed with foresight and sensitivity in an age that promised the infinite and gave only commerce or colonial administration. To be able to articulate such a predicament of course required very much more than being ignorantly symptomatic. To have framed the dilemma itself testifies to the greatest insight and intelligence. Yet how decisive is the fact that Baudelaire chooses to place the poem from the start in the 'real' world. His natural address to the reader to reflect on the truth that the world seems bigger to the child poring over maps than it does to the grown man who has actually travelled the world, is irresistible. It insinuates itself into what both poet and reader know to be their common world. Thereafter, Baudelaire can more easily, as if by a series of answers to eagerly-put questions, extend his profound insight into travel so that it includes all experience, and, finally, death, the negative-plate of all experience. The poem is, of course, about experience, in the way first suggested by the English Romantics, but although there is nothing new about Baudelaire's treatment of the theme, his natural manner of assuming the common ground he holds with the reader is very much more persuasive than Tennyson's heroic allegory. We have to pretend not to know that Tennyson is a bourgeois like ourselves. Tennyson's allegories ('The Palace of Art', 'The Lady of Shallott', 'The Lotos Eaters', 'Mariana') are valuable documents in the development of English poetry, yet their failure to state these problems and situations more baldly and 'realistically' meant in the end, I think, that the issues were being kept at arm's length. More, the problems themselves were turned into beauty. Baudelaire's frontal address to the predicament (his placing himself as Charles Baudelaire, disappointed bourgeois, here, now, in a Paris bar, at dusk) in the end opened up for him the greater vision of the general human condition, a condition which always has to be apprehended in its existing concrete terms before it reveals itself as 'universal'. Tennyson's 'Ulysses' is a good equivalent of 'Le Voyage', but there is no poem of Tennyson's, I think, which has the broad power of 'Recueillement' or 'Le Cygne'. Paradoxically – and the paradox is one absolutely central to the understanding of the development of European culture in this period – it is Baudelaire, the impoverished nobody, who gives us the great picture of humanity and can claim some sort of brotherhood with all sufferers, knowing that in the modern world we are all really sufferers. Tennyson, the friend of princes, who read his poems to the Queen and was part of the Establishment, seems still more desolatingly alone than Baudelaire, more despondently outside the true movement of the times.

Emerging from the early Romanticism then – a mélange of Byronic attitudinising and colonialist sensuality – Baudelaire hardened and subtilised the sense of the role until, all 'evil' past, he looked about him in remorse and regret. The street-walking poet of 'Tableaux Parisiens' and 'Le Vin' may have had his

origins in the self-consciously solitary communer-with-nature
that is so familiar a figure in Romanticism. But early exercises
like 'Le Soleil', which flaunt that solitude in the Byronic manner,
are significantly distinct from the later, great poems of despair
and disillusion – 'Le Cygne', 'Le Crépuscule du Soir', 'Les Sept
Vieillards' – in which a new realism has replaced the vague
Romantic glamour. It is the way in which Baudelaire presents an
image of the whole man that makes *Fleurs du Mal* a great and
original volume of poetry, rather than an indulgence in the sense
of 'sin' opened up by Byron.

The failure of English poetry in the middle and late Victorian
era is best expressed in the trivialisation of Baudelaire by
Symonds and Swinburne, who saw in him nothing but a
diabolist, a proto-decadent. We could, in fact, discard the
'naughty' poems in *Fleurs du Mal* – the poems which secured the
book's denunciation and the fastidious disapproval of Henry
James – without affecting Baudelaire's stature. He is significant
not because he dabbled in perverse sex, but because out of *Fleurs
du Mal* emerged a new conception of the poet's role, a hard, bitter
conception, shorn of flamboyance and utterly without the
deliquescent posturing of Baudelaire's English and German
admirers. The poet of *Fleurs du Mal* is bewildered; he stands
bemused amid the senseless harshness of the modern city. In a
poem like 'Le Cygne', the profound, distressed pessimism of
Wordsworth's Sonnet 'The World is too much with us', has
turned into a desolate bewilderment. Accordingly different is the
use of Greek myth in the two poems. Wordsworth finds in the
image of Triton, the pagan sea-god, a noble grandeur dismally
absent from the modern world; Baudelaire, on the other hand,
sees in Andromache a character as trapped and exasperated as he
is himself. And the poem forces us to generalize the case to
include modern man as a whole. *Fleurs du Mal* is, in short,
universal in just this sense: like Dickens's *Little Dorrit*, it presents
an image of the modern city as a vast trap, an intricate prison, in
which there are no gaolers, only prisoners. Thus, the modern
post-Romantic poet's sense of isolation now revealed to him a
profound truth about humanity in general. Only by persisting in
his isolation, by attempting to understand his own alienation,
was Baudelaire at last able to break through to an insight into the
alienation of his fellow-citizens:

Ainsi dans la forêt oú mon esprit s'exile
Un vieux Souvenir sonne à plein souffle du cor!
Je pense aux matelots oubliés dans une île,
Aux captifs, aux vaincus! . . . A bien d'autres encor!

('Le Cygne')

It is just such a general awareness which we find absent from the poetry of the English Victorian poets (excepting only Hopkins). The Victorian poets ceased to try to define their own position. They failed to understand the world around them because they failed to understand their own relations with it (as Dickens, for instance, did not fail). So it is, that the sublimely elegant nostalgia of Baudelaire's 'L'Invitation au Voyage' eventually becomes a negative statement about modern Paris, a painful yet consoling evocation precisely of what is absent from the present. In Baudelaire, the Romantic melancholy is replaced by a bitter sense of waste, the Tennysonian regret by a devouring remorse. It is this acute sense of waste and exasperation which gives body in Baudelaire's verse to the dangerously abstract dichotomies – good-evil, spleen-ideal, salvation-damnation. Baudelaire becomes a great poet only with age and exasperation. What he gave to the following generation was realism and a new sense of the poet's destiny. He himself did not, in fact, live up to – or try to live up to – the heroic cry that concludes 'Le Voyage':

Nous voulons, tant ce feu nous brûle le cerveau,
Plonger au fond du gouffre, Enfer ou Ciel, qu'importe?
Au fond de l'Inconnu pour trouver du nouveau!

('Le Voyage')

As with 'L'Invitation au Voyage', the real force of the poem is what it implies of our present existence, not its vision of an imagined Utopia. The need for the new, the rare, the exciting is, in fact, as important an element of the *avant garde* ideology as the insistence on superior powers – an element we have already noted in the Romantics themselves. The most important idea expressed in Keats's 'Ode on a Grecian Urn', we recall, was not the 'eternality' of art, but, on the contrary, the pitiful inadequacy of 'ordinary' human experience. From this sort of perception, grows first the Byronic world-weariness, then the *ennui* of Baudelaire, and the concomitant contempt for the satisfied bourgeois. It is for this reason that the *avant garde* artist of the late nineteenth century is generally anti-radical in politics. For Baudelaire and Flaubert, as Cesar Grana observes, 'democracy, like the bourgeois spirit which constituted its nurturing force, was nothing but the cultural facade for the powers of "Iron, steam and wheelwork", which dominated the modern world – a psychological contrivance to foster the external and to cater to the external'.[8] The *avant garde* writer from Flaubert to the *décadents*, therefore, on the whole tends to identify socialism with bourgeois acquisitiveness: it is regarded as a concern with the material, the mundane, the unsatisfactorily ordinary. It is only much later that alignment with the proletariat and with communism appears as a means of expressing *dis*-alignment with society. The alignment of artistic progressiveness with political radicalism in countries like Russia, where the different social structure forced the intellectual into opposition, proves the general argument being advanced here. In politically backward countries the artist tends to stand alongside the intellectual as a committed radical, if not as actual revolutionary, because significant dissent from the social orthodoxy inevitably assumed a political cast. In politically more advanced countries, where the achievement of something like social justice seemed possible without revolution, political radicalism or social activism tended to appear as a further manifestation of materialism. On the whole, western writers who are politically radical, tended to be of second or third rank. The first-rate poet held aloof from the activities of the Trade Unions and the Fabians. This not only helps explain the consistent 'convervatism' of the great 20th century writers – Eliot, Perse, Yeats, Rilke, Lawrence, Huxley, Valéry – but also compels us to be cautious in our understanding of the very notion of communism itself, as it functions as an ideal. Recent developments in the Soviet Union suggest that, a certain level of social justice and material prosperity once secured, communism itself may cease to work as an inspiration to the best minds, which now need something else.

Baudelaire's greatest French successor, Rimbaud, took him so seriously as to put into practice what the master had consigned to the realm of hypothesis. Rimbaud tried to live out the desire expressed at the end of 'Le Voyage'. If, as Baudelaire says, the ethical nature ('enfer ou ciel, qu'importe') is secondary to the intensity of the life lived, Rimbaud reasoned, very well then, we will plunge into the abyss. What made Rimbaud's experiment valuable was the intellectual awareness with which it was undertaken. Coleridge discovered opium by accident; Baudelaire documented the waste involved in casual dissipation. Rimbaud, by contrast, underwent his experiences in full intellectual expectation and readiness – pen in hand, in fact. The effect of the spiritual deterioration, therefore, was measured as exactly as the degree of intensity secured by the way. This is why Rimbaud was able to go through the whole experience so rapidly: within three years he had lived what it normally requires half a life-time to experience.

The condition towards which Rimbaud aspired was – without doubt – that of the shaman. His programme of the 'dérèglement raisónne de tous les sens' is parallel at every point to shamanistic lore: the shaman experienced the dismemberment of the body, he ascended to the sky, conversed with spirits, descended into hell, re-emerged as Knower. The shaman, moreover, was chosen; he was of the elect: 'he becomes absent-minded, and dreamy, loves solitude, and has prophetic visions and sometimes seizures that make him unconscious'.[9] Reading Eliade's account of shamanistic experience, we can more easily sympathise perhaps with what otherwise may appear mawkish and facile cult behaviour. For the moods of the shaman are as manifestly those of the 'Poet' of popular imagination as his more painful initiations are those documented in *Les Illuminations* and *Une Saison en Enfer*. The young Stephen Dedalus, Werther, Tonio Kröger, Nietzsche himself – all these real and imaginary culture-heroes show that 'being a poet', like being a shaman, is as much a matter of performing certain rituals, of conforming to certain 'expected' patterns of behaviour as it is of feeling certain emotions and knowing certain Truths.

Unfortunately, however, such knowledge cannot – to paraphrase Karl Jaspers – be made into a possession: Rimbaud's greatness is that he refused the burden of the knowledge he had acquired, and strode out of his shamanhood. For the indispensable element of shamanism is – shamanism; that is, a body of lore and instruction handed on to the novice from the initiates. The shaman receives instruction from the elders; he becomes a doctor who cures souls. This implies the existence of a body of received truth, and that, as we have had cause to note again and again, is what is significantly absent from the world of the modern shaman.

To an extent, we can see the whole of poetic tradition as a tacit and mysterious handing on of divine and semi-divine powers. Kathleen Raine has argued this case in her book *Defending Ancient Springs*.[10] The springs *are* ancient, and from this point of view it is the moralistic bias of much modern writing and theory which is heterodox, not the Romantic Revival. From Dante's hero-worship of Vergil to James Joyce's of Ibsen, we could trace easily enough an unbroken pattern of influence, initiation and imitation as the real body of European poetry, not the critical, ethical bias of so much of our more recent poetry. With such a view I have personally a great deal of sympathy: it seems quite simply, true. But this does not absolve the poet from the peculiar difficulties of his position in the modern world. The knowledge and behaviour of the shaman depends, as I have said, upon the acceptance of certain beliefs. These beliefs have not entirely vanished: on the contrary, they persist in strange and surprising forms. They persist, one might almost say, not as articles of faith, but as a disposition to behave and feel in certain ways towards certain things. Or perhaps one should say, a certain Thing: for the real object of attention is not particular individual things, but the World, Life itself – God. This disposition towards regarding the World as sacred is, in my opinion, the *sine qua non* of all poetry. Yet the very sacredness of the Object itself imposes upon the poet the burden of continuous alertness, lest he make it into an idol, a fetish, and debase the currency of the sacred into that of the religiose. Gary Snyder's shamanistic poetry seems on the whole merely arcane – the exploitation of shamanistic imagery for decorative purposes.[11] Rimbaud's use of drugs has been followed by many, as it was anticipated by Coleridge and Nerval. The shamans were aware of the dangers of narcotics: 'Narcotics are only a vulgar substitute for pure trance . . . Narcotic intoxication is called on to provide an *imitation* of a state that the shaman is no longer capable of attaining otherwise.'[12] *Une Saison en Enfer* acknowledges the factitiousness of the trips made in *Les Illuminations*: at the end of the passage along which Rimbaud struggled mused Keats with his Urn, and there is something demoralising about too much knowledge too quickly gained.

Rimbaud's experiment is, of course, only the most literal and daring enactment of the Romantic poetic myth. It is directly in line with the consistent development I have tried to trace from Wordsworth: the subject-matter of the poetry, here more strikingly than anywhere else, is nothing less than the poetic life, the role and identity of the poet. What Rimbaud tried to do (with devastating consequences for himself and for those who came after him) was to distil and live the quality of Life itself: – which is to say, that intense and meaningful part of existence which he conceived to be what alone makes that existence worthwhile. Everything else he rejected. As Byron had tried to forge himself by creating significant imagery, so Rimbaud thought to turn himself into God. So, – 'I am he who will become God,' because like God, the poet will be all intensity, meaning, purity.

After *Une Saison en Enfer*, what alternatives were open to Rimbaud? He had exhausted the possibilities in *life*: there remained only death, or death-in-life. Rimbaud's last twenty years might have been spent anywhere, anyhow: he was, to all intents and purposes, a corpse. Or a saint: for the asceticism of Harar was as deliberately chosen as the indulgence of Paris, Brussels and London. It would have been easier, of course, for Rimbaud to live comfortably in Paris, – a man of letters, or a business-man. Why did he choose the hell of Abyssinia, if not because that was as implicit a part of the choice he made as an adolescent as the poetry he wrote? For Rimbaud a life of comfort and banality would have discredited the knowledge he had acquired. Perhaps his ascetic life in Harar was the only kind of shamanhood our society allows.

Sooner or later, given only a sufficiently daring mind, Rimbaud's experiment was inevitable. Someone had to try to be a poet, and nothing but a poet. After him, things were more difficult. A bluff had been called. *Une Saison en Enfer* was hard to get round. There was need for deviousness. Two strategies emerged: irony and silence.

Irony is best represented by Jules Laforge and Tristan Corbière, poets with a notorious influence on English and American poets a decade later. These poets parody the heroic stance of Romanticism. In Corbière's 'Le crapaud', the poet-speaker identifies himself with the toad which disgusts his lady. This is a plain derivate of the Baudelairean albatross, the nobly incompetent beast only graceful in flight. The poet forces the lady to look at the poor toad in Corbière's sonnet: it is a wingless nightingale, a nightingale of the mud. It becomes, over the course of the poem an image of the modern poet, until the poet makes the overt identification in the closing phrase: 'Ce crapaudlà, c'est moi.' The heroism of the poem lies in its bitter honesty. And post-Symbolist irony generally has this effect. In Laforgue, it manifests itself in the series of sighs, sobs and complaints which make up the *Complaintes de la lune*, verbose and somewhat shapelessly tart effusions, generally rather thin in their rhetorical construction. At its best, Laforguian irony results in the linguistic density which thrilled the young T. S. Eliot, but which, as Edmund Wilson pointed out in due course, had been a part of English poetry since Shakespeare. It is a literature of the charm of fatigue, which mingles the inherited properties of Romanticism (the moon, the seasons, the Church) with a contemporaneous wit, a sardonic deflationary exhaustion:

> C'est l'automne, l'automne, l'automne,
> Le grand vent et toute sa sequelle
> De represailles! Et de musiques . . . !
> Rideaux tirés, clôture annuelle,
> Chute de feuilles, des Antigones, des Philomeles . . .
> Mon fossoyeur, Alas poor Yorick!
> Les remue a la pellé! . . .

Ennui here has entered the suburbs and the realm of the sheerly ordinary. It is perhaps Laforgue's distinction to have introduced the diction of the sublime into the world of the trivial, the time-bound, and although his irony is clearly a stop-gap measure, it does succeed in stopping the gap, in throwing a frail bridge to the twentieth century: Guillaume Apollinaire and the young T. S. Eliot were among those who crossed it.

In Mallarmé certain absolutes – by definition unattainable – are posited as the only true goals of poetry. *L'azur, silence, blancheur, pierre* – it is such things the poet aspires to.[13] Or rather envies, perhaps: the new note in Mallarmé is resignation, the sophisticated acceptance of failure. Its sophistication is in proportion to the amount of striving the poet understands to be vain. Mallarmé makes further use of the bird-image by which the young Baudelaire had long ago symbolised the life of the poet. Baudelaire's albatross seemed grotesque and ungainly out of its element on deck, persecuted by the crude mob. Mallarmé's swan in 'Le vierge, le vivace et le bel aujourdhui' is assigned its place by its own 'pure brilliance'; it is immobilised in a 'cold dream of contempt', and endures in a 'useless exile'. The Baudelairean axes of the poem are apparent: life for the poet is boredom, exile, misunderstanding, occasionally made splendid by the beautiful sterility of winter. Winter is, predictably, a favourite season for Mallarmé, with its purity, its zero cold, its static brilliance, its negation of life. What is new in the poem is the acknowledgement by the poet that he has earned his pain by his own refusal to sing the realm of life. This theme in fact now becomes increasingly dominant in Symbolist and post-Symbolist poetry, in France culminating in Paul Valéry's despairing cry – 'Il faut tenter de vivre!'

It is remarkable once again how predictable all of these preoccupations are from poems like the 'Ode on a Grecian Urn' and 'Kubla Khan'. There too, the poet's inability to say what mattered was related to his awareness of the sheer mediocrity of 'ordinary' experience. It is from this fundamental Romantic paradox, in fact, that the Symbolist impasse derives. If ordinary experience, is not worth having, then whatever you can say is not worth saying. So they arrived at the exile of Mallarmé – the 'hard forgotten lake', 'the transparent glacier of the flights not flown'. (We need only compare the intelligent precision of Mallarmé's images of his situation, by the way, with the sentimentalism of Tennyson's 'The Poet' to see by how far French poetry had outstripped English at this time.) The tension of Mallarmé's poetry stemmed from his simultaneous awareness of the exquisite beauty of the un-had experience ('the flight not flown'), and of the 'tragic' sterility of the life spent savouring it. Like the swan in the frozen lake, the poet is clamped down by his inability to embark upon 'life', yet he knows that the beauty of experience would be wrecked for him, once tasted. Mallarmé accepts this tragic incompatibility of the quality of actual experience with the high expectation the poet has of it. Hence, he feels justified in doing 'nothing'. His heightened sense of the marvellous, of hope, itself depends upon his knowledge that he will desist from trying to violate the hymen of the future, of possibility. The despair of Romanticism assumes its final bourgeoisified form in the loved regret of Mallarmé; in the cosy interiors (often with their windows open onto distant landscapes whose magic is their very ordinariness) of Bonnard and Vuilliard; in the memory-trips of Marcel Proust; in the sunlit, permanent possibilities of Débussy. Mallarmé's 'Brise Marine' – which explains his later, currently more fashionable excursions into silence – stands in relation to

'Le Voyage', as 'Le Voyage' itself stood to 'Childe Harold's Pilgrimage' and 'Oceano Nox'. Heroic despair turns eventually into comfort-hugging regret. From the great Napoleonic egotist who took on Governments, we proceed through the mute watcher and the grim outsider unreckoned in his lifetime, finally to reach the figure who is most like ourselves – the bourgeois poet, who waits, wife asleep, lamp on, white page before him, and thinks of the shipwrecks he will never experience and the songs of the sailors before embarkations he will never make.

It is this figure, significantly enough, who takes it upon himself to protect the scrolls, the lore and knowledge of poetry, in the most effective way yet devised – silence. It is from Mallarmé that the pervading fascination with silence so overpowering in French thought really derives. This is the impasse of Symbolism.

8 The Absent Experience

In the light of what has been established above, we can define the essence of Romanticism as a sense of territory. In Wordsworth we have the first conscious analysis of the interpenetration of mind with remembered event and scene: it is the power of incident and event, visual and auditory, tactile and olfactory, to awaken those memories, which is the basis of literary symbolism itself. Wordsworth thus emerges as the quintessential Romantic (and, indeed, 'modern') poet, not merely in the movement of his verse – the great swell of Romantic profundity – but in all other respects. What we see in his poetry is the transmutation of Hartleyan associationism into poetry. Wordsworth's flirtation with Hartley, as we have seen, was not the pseudo-science of the ignorant amateur, but the true poet's quick recognition of the relevant structural aid. It is, to the contrary, the Idealist importations of Coleridge which fog things up in *The Prelude*. Hartley did the trick for Wordsworth as Aquinas did for Dante. Certainly it is fragmentary and fleeting: the Dantesque wholeness (as we are so sick of being reminded) is not there. But this is as it should be, since the essence so skilfully caught is itself so fleeting and fragmentary. The cement Hartley gave to Wordsworth's impressional apparatus effected the transition from young man lost to great poet, and gave him the means to launch his deepest Vaughan-inspired themes. The association of memory with event, of past with present, is the very medium of poetry, at once its instrument and its *raison d'être*. This being so, can we isolate a theme or thematic nucleus which is the essence of Symbolism and indeed of Romanticism itself? I believe we can: it is the theme of absent or lost experience.

It is a theme which emerges only slowly out of the poetry of the nineteenth century, finally to become the mode of Symbolism itself. Its roots indeed go back beyond Romanticism. There are lines and images in Shakespeare which lend themselves to such an interpretation: what we are concerned with is a process of cogitation upon certain ideas, long since mined, until they

165

emerge themselves as fully thematic, rather than as illustration of some wider conception. From this point of view it would be better to begin with Edmund Waller's 'Song' ('Go, lovely rose') than with anything from Shakespeare. Here, in a lyric now neglected but long celebrated as among the finest things produced by the English genius, we find the idea of the absent experience not only mined but minted. The flower is handled in the emblematic seventeenth century way. It is merely instrumental: the poet wishes to convince the lady who wastes the poet's time along with her own that if she does not mend her ways she will simply perish unnoticed. She will perish anyway – the rose is bidden to tell her that too; but just as Marvell wishes to get through to the coy mistress by making her see that she will die, and they had better make the best of what time they are allowed, so Waller wills the flower to enact the lady's own fast-fadingness before her eyes. The poem is a central seventeenth century love-lyric, and held its place for so long precisely through its skill in consummating so many strands of the century's thought. It was well-known enough before its publication in the *Poems* of 1645 to have been plagiarised at least once (by William Chamberlayne: 'Like beauteous flowers which vainly waste the scent/Of odours in untainted deserts'). Yet there is something new in Waller's thought, when he bids the rose remind the lady that if it (the rose) had grown in a desert it would have died un-praised. It is a conventional enough piece of reasoning, no more but no less partial than Marvell's unscrupulously witty ratiocinations in 'To his Coy Mistress'. Yet the power of image – pure image – is nowhere more strikingly illustrated than in Waller's lovely picture:

> That hadst thou sprung
> In deserts, where no men abide,
> Thou must have uncommended died.

In the lines that follow, Waller provides a conventionally adroit generalisation:

> Small is the worth
> Of beauty from the light retired: . . .

Such abstract moralisations are the very life of seventeenth century poetry. Yet the picture in the preceding lines has an effect which goes beyond the meaning of this thought. Now the picture is, in fact, a factitious one. By which I mean simply that Waller cheats: roses do not grow in deserts, and the effect in his lines is gained from the degree of the counterfeit. It will stand us in good stead when dealing with the poetry of the Romantics, and still more the Symbolists, to remember that Waller's picture is not of the Kodak variety, but of the kind experienced, in an extreme form, in the art of surrealism. Over the course of Waller's lyric, the girl becomes the rose: when she blushes, we see *its* hue, and it is from such substitutions that the life of metaphor derives. (In the same way, George Herbert speaks of the rose whose 'angry and brave hue/Bids the rash gazer wipe his eye'. So many things are confused so skilfully in Herbert's lines that it is hard, if not impossible, to extricate them. The gazer is rash because he might get pricked by the thorns, yet this is transposed metaphysically to the excess of the flower's beauty and it is this that causes the tear.)

A good indication of the relevance of Waller's idea is Pope's adaptation of it in *The Rape of the Lock* (1711):

There kept my charms concealed from mortal eye,
Like Roses that in Deserts bloom and die.

(IV, 157–8)

Waller's image and his rationale are taken up more profitably, however, in another poem which exercised a profound influence upon the Romantics. This is Gray's 'Elegy written in a country churchyard' of 1751. Here the idea which in Waller had been part of a persuasive argument is expanded to provide a framework for a whole social philosophy. The 'Elegy' is of course an axial poem, one of the points upon which English poetry pivots from the Augustan to the Romantic. Johnson significantly liked only its Epitaph, that is to say, its overtly Augustan generalisations. Gray's poem allows such an interpretation fairly enough, yet it is, in a sense, also a cheat. The Augustan social manner is used by Gray as a tail or an anchor for the superb series of images which enshrine his central thought. Already in those atmospheric opening stanzas we have the beginnings of that symbolic landscaping which Mill praised Tennyson for producing. Shakespeare is a mine of images which later poetry has not scrupled to rifle, much like peasants taking the stones from an old abbey to shore up their roofs and walls. It is Hamlet's

Yorick speech which Gray borrows from here, with its mordant yet haunting speculations – 'Where be your gibes now, your gambols, your songs, your flashes of merriment that were wont to set the table on a roar?' Milton is here too in his 'Lycidas' vein –

> One morn I missed him from on the custom'd hill
> Along the heath and near his fav'rite tree . . .
> Another came; nor yet beside the rill,
> Nor up the lawn, nor at the wood was he;
>
> The next with dirges due in sad array
> Slow thro' the churchyard path we saw him born.

Yet the poem's most spectacular debt is to Waller:

> Full many a gem of purest ray serene,
> The dark unfathom'd caves of ocean bear:
> Full many a flower is born to blush unseen,
> And waste its sweetness on the desert air.

What Gray has done is to take Waller's lovely image and transpose it to a higher philosophical level: where Waller marshalled the image into a logical argument limited in its effect by the emotional situation which brought it into existence, Gray muses upon it for its own sake. Waller's meaning has been altered along with his mood: the subjunctive '*hadst* thou sprung' becomes the indicative 'is born to blush unseen'. Yet the image is what is important, not the Truth it illustrates. Now, of course, this image is a verbal one: Waller's is partly made up of its strategic prosody, the placing of 'sprung' in particular. Gray has his flower 'blush', thus introducing a whole range of emotional and psychological factors, and it is said to 'waste' its sweetness, thus implying regret. As with Waller's cheat (roses growing in deserts), Gray's cheat also largely constitutes the poetic effect of the image.[1] The pictorial effect of an image in poetry is, of course, always verbal. Yet there is a difference between Waller's rose in the desert and his moralisations. There is a difference, equally, between Gray's gem at the bottom of the sea, his rose blushing in the desert, and his Augustan generalisations: even the pictures that follow ('Some village Hampden', and so on) are homiletic vignettes rather than images in the modern sense. This does not mean that Gray writes better poetry in one stanza than in another. On the contrary, the greatness of the 'Elegy' lies in its formal completeness: what Gray wished to say overlapped with the moral values of Augustan society. What we are concerned with is the emergence, the discovery of an idea, an idea that lies about, yet lies hidden, a kind of poetic open secret. And the process of discovery requires the mediation of poets of high quality: there are no accidents hereabouts.

At any rate, the 'use' of Gray's images, or their relevance to later poets, is not confined to the fact that Baudelaire chose to make a translation of them, trusting so much to their power and pregnancy as to let them stand on their own as a poem, with the atmospheric support of some lines of Longfellow.[2] The idea of the beautiful thing unexperienced because wasting unperceived in a wilderness, or at the bottom of the sea, appears in Romanticism so profoundly transformed as to be generally pervasive. In Wordsworth, it is consciously exploited in relatively unimportant poems, in particular 'Admonition to a traveller', 'To the Highland girl of Inversneyde', and 'Yarrow unvisited'; where it is interestingly related to the idea of territory. The 'lovely cottage', in the 'Admonition', has not only its own stream and fields, it has 'almost its own sky'. Both poems are tourist poems, but astringently so: Wordsworth is not going to let us get away with our wish-fulfilment fantasies. The cottage and its setting are a 'precious leaf'. But if we – the reader sophisticated enough to be reading the poem – were given it, it

> from the day
> On which it should be touch'd would melt away!

Similarly, in the Inversneyde poem, the simple Highland girl in her simple rustic setting, appears as the embodiment of all that is desirable in life. Yet she is, the poet acknowledges, 'but as a wave/Of the wild sea'. Her true function – for the poet, and, through him, for the reader – is to be remembered. He is therefore, 'though pleased at heart', not 'loth from her to part'. Wordsworth's hardmindedness goes along with an evident susceptibility: the poem is warm and rich in its celebration of the 'lovely spot'. He does not indulge in the emotion aroused by the scenes – emotion which became thematic for a later generation of poets. Yet he has performed the function of bringing the implicit content of Gray's and Waller's images to the surface. The beauty of contemplating the *idea* of the precious thing which is beyond experiencing, is that through language we can be there, where the poet says we cannot be: we are invisible witnesses of the un-experienced. Such a capacity, it is important to note, is purely literary: neither music nor painting can in the same way refer to the inexpressible or depict the inexperiencable. It is this capacity of language which has been so difficult to handle theoretically. Yet it is also the source of what is poetical in a great deal of verse. This is the case with the poems of Waller and Gray. What Wordsworth does is to press forward the implications of the idea: let us, he says, leave this precious leaf untouched, because once we touch it, it will 'melt away'. Clearly this is deeply related to Wordsworth's own greatest themes: the loss of the visionary power with age, and the meaning of certain precious experiences. Yet it is characteristic of his deep clear-mindedness here, too, to have articulated what had earlier been inchoate – too successfully perhaps for the peace of mind of his inheritors. Wordsworth and Coleridge between them found out too much for comfort.

It was Keats, at any rate, in the 'Ode on a Grecian Urn' who made the most important contribution to the development of Wordsworth's idea. The uncomfortable implication of Wordsworth's poem is that the 'precious leaf', Yarrow River, and the Highland girl are, like everything else worth experiencing, better not experienced. Wordsworth's greatest poetry had explored the implications of the poet's professional dedication to intense and meaningful experience, and to discriminating between such experience and the seemingly valueless residue of life. 'Admonition to a traveller', 'Yarrow unvisited', and 'The Highland girl of Inversneyde' touch on a parallel theme – the relation between beauty and experience itself. Wordsworth's implication goes further than he intended. 'Wise passiveness in time' made it possible for Wordsworth himself to derive a lifetime's sustenance from the intensity and richness of certain luminous experiences, and to redeem these experiences in Time by recollection. For his successors, memory was inclined to be a burden rather than a boon. For Proust, who tried more systemically than anyone else to construct a philosophical system from a Wordsworthian theory of remembrance, Time and the past were finally to be the source of anxiety rather than of illumination, a reminder of necessary failure, until acceptance of failure itself seemed to provide a kind of release. The past, like the reality it promises to disclose, remains beyond reach.

Yet the conclusion which the second generation of Romantic poets in England drew from Wordsworth is uncomfortably implicit in their originals. Wordsworth may say that memory will reward us, for not touching the object more than the experience (through love, contact, habitation) would. But the suggestion, that the experience is better not had, remains a crippling one.

Keats's 'Ode on a Grecian Urn' is a miraculous interweaving of these Wordsworthian motifs. Wordsworth's greatest poetry explored the poet's experience of the numinous – those 'spots of time' that open up the meaning of life so that we 'see into the life of things'. Yet he had never refrained from admitting that, for him, ordinary human life was a 'heavy and a weary weight'. The image of weight is nearly always contrasted with that of the chain in Wordsworth: if the chain links man's experiences together into a morality, the weight 'Heavy as frost and deep almost as life', is no less than the burden of ordinary life, with all its wearisome obligations and responsibilities. It needed very little to convert this into a dichotomy of the beautiful and the banal: the French adjective has come to stand for a whole ideology, and has acquired in the process a somewhat petulant air. But it is an important element in the poetic development of the nineteenth century. Wordsworth's poetry as a whole adumbrates an important difference between the numinous and the merely phenomenal, between the poetic-and-meaningful and the merely ordinary. It is clear that this is the fundamental problem in a culture deprived of those traditional beliefs which had sustained it. What Keats does in the 'Ode on a Grecian Urn' is to extend the territory of the banal to include everything that is actually experienced.

Each generation, I have argued, supplies itself at the expense of the next. This will be found to be a law of all conscious intellectual activity: the mind displaces its own weight in the contents proposed to itself through heritage. It is thus in a process of perpetually altering its frontiers with reality. Just as Wordsworth used his insight into the experience of the 'precious leaf' to give weight to a redemptive theory of recollection, so Keats adumbrated his beautiful and marvellously complete structure of experience in order to articulate a sense of richness in

life and experience, from which what we normally call sadness is
ruthlessly excluded. By doing so he gutted that so-poetic sadness
and melancholy of their real poetic meaning: although poets in
England, France, Italy and Germany were to go on proclaiming
their sadness, their *tristesse*, their *Wehmut* and their *noia* for
another fifty or seventy years, it is noteworthy that the serious
poets refrain from this increasingly decorative and narcissistic
celebration of sadness. Instead, we find the poet concerned with
the formulation of images (symbols) equivalent to that absent
meaning of which Keats's great Ode had declared the existence.
Increasingly, we find that the empiricism of the English
Romantics becomes the norm of poetic methodology.
Paradoxically, it was English poets who held onto the
conversational, discursive side of Romantic subjectivism
(Browning and Arnold, in particular), where French poets
exclude the discursive voice, and develop the real symbolism
implicit in Wordsworth and Keats and explicit in the early
Tennyson. We can see the difference between English and French
poetry at the middle of the nineteenth century in the entire
absence from Baudelaire of those long discursive narrative poems
of Tennyson's, in which Themes and Problems are discussed.
For it is not in any shirking of Contemporary Problems that
English poetry declines: Tennyson's 'Locksley Hall Revisited' is
more overt in its condemnation of Victorian capitalism than
anything by Baudelaire. Yet our sense of a greater modernity in
the French poet is not unjustified. Tennyson's contemporaneity
in 'Locksley Hall Revisited' is of an extensional variety – a
matter of recognisable Themes being referred to and discussed,
with appropriate emotional and intellectual judgements. The
contemporaneity of 'Chant d'Automne' and 'L'Aube Spirituelle'
and of 'Le Cygne' is intensional – a matter of the reverberation of
recognising the human predicament in its most inward form.

   Baudelaire's contribution to the formulation of Symbolism is
often discussed as if it were largely confined to the 'mystic'
vaguenesses of 'Correspondances'. This has led to an excessively
hermetic conception of Symbolism. It is true that the forest of this
famous sonnet – evoked with such tremulous richness –
anticipates the forest in which Maeterlinck's and Débussy's
Pelleas and Melisande pursue their predictably fated love, and
that in a sense the forest as symbol of the unconscious or the
unknown dominates the whole century. It is there of course in

Shakespeare, whose *A Midsummer Night's Dream* exercised such a profound influence upon Weber and Mendelssohn. But the important implication of Baudelaire's poem is that it is from nature that the listening poet (the poem assumes the vigilant attention of the poet) gleans whatever glimpses or hints of meaning that will come his way. There is no sense in the poem of Nerval's hermetic disclosures: the 'confuses paroles' are the numinous illuminations isolated by Wordsworth, and soon to give birth to Rimbaud's *Illuminations*. Baudelaire's poem gives greater definition to the situation of the poet (and of man in general) as excluded from a world of paradisal meaningfulness by nothing but the human predicament. Thus, Baudelaire replaces the rich melancholia, already parodied by Keats, with the *ennui* that is to dominate French writing for a hundred years. It is neither the modern city (though this has its role), nor capitalism that makes human life intolerable; it is merely being human. In Baudelaire the alternative of intensity is undertaken with remorseless scepticism: 'an oasis of horror in a desert of boredom': – that is what Pleasure affords its hunter.

Gradually, over the course of the century, the image or idea of the lost paradise gains ground in the poet's world. Rimbaud's whole life might be interpreted in terms of the quest for the lost Eden: his final destination in Abyssinia itself parodies the quest. His poetry is full of images of the lost paradise – the abandoned château, the quay on which the child stares out on potentiality. Little by little, the image of exclusion and abandonment receives definition. The absent experience of Waller and Gray, conceived in terms of scenes which cannot, by definition be witnessed, but can be imagined, is explored along two separate axes – that of time and that of space. To the child poring over maps, Baudelaire says in 'Le Voyage', the world is bigger and more mysterious than it is to the traveller looking back on what he has witnessed. Thus grows the idea of the *poésie des salons de départ* – with its mystique of beautiful train-journeys never embarked upon, of tickets not used, of waiting-rooms redolent of lives and voyages.[3] How beautiful, in fact, not to live at all: this is the logical end of such speculations. In Mallarmé's 'Brise Marine', it is 'cruels espoirs' that desolate the poet: taking his cue from Baudelaire, Mallarmé finally concludes that it is expectation which deludes us. What is the Symbolist doctrine of language, then, but a last stockade of metaphysics behind which the poet can protect his soul from the *ennui* of actual experience? Let us, *qua* philosophers of language pretend we are concerned only with what cannot be expressed; let us savour our disappointment at leisure within the haven of a comfortable society dedicated to the pursuit of aesthetics. 'Un coup de dés n'abolira le hasard'. Let us therefore not throw the dice at all, but forever savour the possibilities in the nirvana of statistical relations, forever secure, forever unsatisfied. It is easy to see how such a doctrine dissolved the Rimbaudian heroics: what is the purpose of destroying yourself, if the knowledge so achieved only reinforces your disillusionment? This doctrine did not outlive the social structure of the late nineteenth century: it received its last testaments in the poetry of Paul Valéry and the fiction of Virginia Woolf. Before economics ground it out of existence, however, Symbolism preserved a mirage of independence. Many passed through Baudelaire's *piliers*, or imagined they had, somewhat pitifully building out of weakness and indulgence their own Baudelairean sunsets and twilights. What better figure to represent the time than Loris, Hugo von Hoffmannstahl's beautiful young aristocrat, who dipped his hands in a bowl of precious stones when he wrote his lyrics? In von Hoffmannstahls' early poetry, the allegoric mode of Tennyson has become more localised, in a final wishfulfilling fantasy, enacting the desire for a world which 'exists for the sake of the fullness of beauty, for the sake of love', yet in terms realistic enough to suggest the life of perpetual peace in beautiful surroundings which Rilke was later, with somewhat harrowing results, to procure for himself:

> High railings, yew-hedges,
> No longer gilded coats of arms,
> Sphinxes through the thicket gleaming,
> The gates swing open with a creak.
> With drowsy waterfalls,
> And drowsy Tritons,
> Rococo, charmingly adjust,
> See – Canaletto's Vienna
> Vienna seventeen sixty.
> Green, brown still ponds,
> By smooth white marble framed,
> Gold and silver fish play
> In the reflections of the water nymphs.   ('Prologue to *Anatol*')

Here, surely, is the embodiment of the park of Symbolism. The park, like the château within it, is empty because the aristocracy has been hunted out by economics and social progress. One way or another this idea haunts French art over the early decades of the twentieth century; in various transformations, it dominates Western literature as a whole. In Kipling's poem 'The Way through the Woods', for instance, it is given temporal terms; the 'lost domain' is the past:

> They shut the road through the woods
> Seventy years ago.
> Weather and rain have undone it again,
> And now you would never know
> There was once a road through the woods
> Before they planted the trees.

But the past is significantly aristocratic and leisured:

> . . . if you enter the woods
> Of a summer evening late,
> When the night-airs cools on the trout-ringed pools
> You will hear the beat of a horse's feet
> And the splash of a skirt in the dew,
> Steadily cantering through
> The misty solitudes,
> As though they perfectly knew
> The old road lost through the woods . . .
> But there is no road through the woods!

Here the whole poem is the evocation of the beautiful life known not to exist: the poem is an enactment both of the past and of the desire to re-invoke the past. In Rupert Brooke, Kipling's young contemporary, this love of the past takes the paradoxical form of a nostalgia for the present: in Brooke, the English society so loved by the poet is already conceived as being in the past. History completed Brooke's *oeuvre*, justifying its fondness by precisely destroying that life the young poet had luxuriated in, as if always on a protracted embarkation-leave.

In fiction, this nostalgia for the aristocratic past-within-the-present is paralleled in Alain-Fournier's *Le Grand Meaulnes*. Here the means of realist fiction are exploited, with brilliant success, to create that perfectly realised verbal symbol capable of implying the absent experience. The symbol of the 'lost domain' (as Frank Davison called his translation of the novel)[4] – the aristocratic house full of magically attractive people enjoying an enchanted life islanded from the dull reality – is given its poignancy by the context of Flaubertian realism within which it is set. The opening of the novel almost parodies that of *Madame Bovary*, with the arrival of the new boy, the parade of teachers, the country squalor and a tone of generally loved dreariness. In Alain-Fournier's book, there is a deliberate attempt to heighten Meaulnes' arrival: everything seems to be suspended, routines are disturbed, schedules unmet: life itself is held in abeyance. And the hero, when he arrives – gangling, all-negotiating, a plausible hero, in effect – is given the task of finding the lost domain by mischance: the path to the mysterious house is cleverly overlaid with accidents, path leads to missed path, unexpected wall to wall, gate to hidden gate, until the way is properly obscured. The pathos of the book lies precisely in this subtle realism: it is all so actual, so Dutch, that the beautiful house of happy revellers in *commedia dell'arte* fancy-dress recedes back into the hinterland of consciousness as soon as Meaulnes leaves. We accept it as a symbol of all our longing, as we could not had the novelist descended to those heavily allegoric means of Goethe or Hawthorne.

Alain-Fournier's success, then, depended upon exploiting the properties of realism against itself: if, for a moment, we disbelieve the narrator's good faith, the effect is lost. The writer could not, in other words afford either to retreat too far into Symbolism, in the manner of Goethe's *Wahlverwandschaften*, which insists on being read as 'allegory', as conscious literary symbol. Yet neither could he come too far in the opposite direction and treat the domain as a place we might find if we got out the maps. His effect, certainly, is one which reflects a particular stage of travel-technology: in an earlier age, when travel was that much more difficult and the next parish like a foreign country, there would be nothing strange in Meaulnes being unable to 'get back'; in a later, when France had been shrunk by better roads and faster cars, by helicopters, television and telephones, again, the domain would simply be too easily found. In much the same way, Kipling succeeds in evoking the marvellous unreachableness of the unnamed house in the Downs in 'They': 'One view called me to another; one hill top to its fellow, half across the county, and since I could answer at no more trouble than the snapping forward of a lever, I let the county flow under my wheels'. The motor-car here becomes the vehicle of poetry, for perhaps the only time in its history, being both effective enough to make movement dream-like, easing narrator and reader into the unknown and unknowable domain, yet fallible enough, later, to break down, and make retracement impossible. Kipling exploits the mechanical unreliability of early motor-cars as an instrument of investigation. It enables the narrator here to reach 'hidden villages where bees, the only things awake, boomed in eighty-foot lindens that overhung grey Norman churches; miraculous brooks diving under stone bridges built for heavier traffic than would ever vex them again; tithe barns larger than their churches, and an old smithy that cried out aloud how it had once been a hall of the Knights of the Temple'. But its progress is slow enough for him to get lost, finally landing him in the unknown, encouraging him to shut off power, and slide 'over the whirled leaves, expecting every moment to meet a keeper; but I only heard a jay, far off, arguing against the silence under the twilight of the trees.' It is a quintessence of England which Kipling has so richly evoked, yet it is also a quintessence of nowhere: he finds himself in front of an 'ancient house of lichened stone, with mullioned windows and roofs of rose-red tile.' He half-expects Shakespeare and Queen Elizabeth to emerge and invite him to tea. Later, when he leaves, he looks back to see the house but, 'the crumpled hills interlaced so jealously that I could not see where the house had lain.' Neither does the Ordnance Survey enlighten him later.

The story expresses both the conservative's longing to preserve the past, free from development, and at the same time constitutes a symbol of the unattainable: nowadays, the story simply could not ride the divide between fact and fantasy with such delicate poise: the reader would wonder why the house was not part of the National Trust, with a Motor-way running past it.

It is in such adaptations to existing technologies and conditions that a writer displays his sense of the absolute. Alejo Carpentier's novel *The Lost Steps* presents something like the Meaulnes dilemma in terms of an intellectual's attempt to re-find a lost paradise which he had stumbled across by accident in the jungles of Central America. Though worthy, the novel exists only on the level of moral debate, with none of the metaphysical implications of *Le Grand Meaulnes*: Carpentier's lost paradise is simply too matter-of-factly described, in the manner of superior travel-journalism, to retain any of the glamour of the distant or unattainable.

The poet cannot use the realism of the novelist's plausible narrative in order to evoke his symbols of the unattainable. Instead, he must confine himself to the minutiae of daily experience or observation: paradoxically, it is poetry which exacts the more sober dedication to the empirical facts. The poets of the first two decades of this century are particularly rich in exploiting the metaphysical possibilities in the actual. Once again, we note that the true metaphysical dimension of modern writing is derived through keeping faith with the new pragmatic realism of Romantic subjectivism, not through any appeal to the supra-real. Rilke, Robert Frost, Edward Thomas and Boris Pasternak – different poets in so many ways – are united by a common faithfulness to experiential data, and by an equally striking skill in deriving metaphysical dimensions from their perceptions. They are all poets of an easy, yet rich, density – sometimes excessive in their faithfulness to the programme of poetic work which Rilke, historically the first of them, proposed for himself in writing his *Neue Gedichte*, as 'outwardness' or objectivity.

There is between Robert Frost's first volume, *A Boy's Will*, and his next two, *North of Boston* and *Mountain Interval*, the same sort of relationship as exists between Rilke's *Stundenbuch* and *Neue Gedichte*. Frost, too, later cuts out the extravagant 'personal' rhetoric of the late Romantic poem, and lets his perceptions stand on their own, producing a subtle detonation in the reader's consciousness as the gap between perceived object and 'meaning' comes home to him. By consuming the meaning into fantasy, early poems such as 'Ghost House' waste the potentiality of dereliction which Kipling had exploited so skilfully in 'The road through the woods'. Kipling, we remember, held his poem fast to its negative – 'But there is no road through the woods'. There is no indulgence of fantasy here, merely a legitimate reverie on the past. Frost's development was to be through a similar hardening. Perhaps the most remarkable of his evocations of absence is 'The Road not taken'. Here the fascination with the unexperienced is given particularly concrete form. By taking the image of the path, like Kipling, Frost is able to build up a whole metaphysics of possibility. The poet sees two paths ahead of him in a forest (it is the forest of Symbolism, despite its ordinariness). The effect of the poem depends upn the fact that he cannot – logically – take both paths. Even if he went down one, and stopped, went back and then went down the other, this would be still different from what would have happened if he had kept along one, or the other. For the roads exist in time, as well as in space, and, of course, he could not in fact take them both, even one after another, for one road leads to another, and then another, then another, and so on, until death. The curious magic of this poem derives from the fact that there is no particular reason for choosing one road rather than the other, and this, by implication, expands into a general doctrine of choices – one of which Keats would have approved. This doctrine is that there is no particular reason for making one choice rather than another: it amounts to the same thing in the end. The road *not* taken gives the poem its title, we note, not the road taken. The road not taken remains suspended in possibility, because you can't get back to it. The poet's final rationale is exquisite in its irony:

> I shall be telling this with a sigh
> Somewhere ages and ages hence:
> Two roads diverged in a wood and I –
> I took the one less travelled by,
> And that has made all the difference.

The way is open for a masterly mis-reading: this, the reader might feel, is the poet's age-old choice of unpopularity, of originality at the expense of being understood, the eschewal of well-worn ways, even with visions of starving in an attic. At a later stage of his life, Frost would write poetry quite as bad as this would be: 'I have been one acquainted with the night' is fully as callow an utterance as the one I have foisted onto an imaginary bad reader of 'The road not taken.' The mis-reading is, of course, disqualified by Frost himself earlier in the poem: first he says that he chose the one he did choose because it seemed less worn ('it was grassy and wanted wear'). But he immediately cancels this false reason for the choice – 'Though as for that the passing there/Had worn them really about the same.' So *that* is not the basis of the poem's curious power. Frost was always the master at catching those tiny evanescent movements of consciousness – our false impressions of things, our delusions and spurious reasons: here he manages to convey precisely that aura of reasonableness we confer upon our, in fact irrational, choices. The meaning of the poem is that there was no reason for taking one path rather than the other, and *yet* – here is the poem's metaphysical detonation – that groundless choice 'has made all the difference'. This is magical because literally true: way does lead on to way, our lives are made up of innumerable tiny decisions and acts, which taken severally mean little, yet taken in sum mean everything. At the end of the poem with 'all the difference', the reader's mind plays back over that unknown and unknowable territory, the life that lay at the end of the road not taken, the life not lived, the experiences not had.

It is plain from these examples that to speak of 'symbol' in the context of post-Romantic writing is not to confine one's reference to single words or concepts: a symbol can be as loose and varied a narrative structure as the domain in *Le Grand Meaulnes*, the path in the woods in Kipling's poem (not itself the symbol, but the focus for a narrative reverie), or the congeries of possibilities that constitute a life and especially an anti-life – the life not lived – in Frost's. The master-symbol in this tradition, if we can so speak of it, is the evocation of the hypothetical empty town 'emptied of its folk this pious morn' in Keats's great Ode. The series of empty towns, deserted estates, abandoned châteaux and untaken paths, by which post-Romantic and Symbolist poets have tried to express the absent experience, begins here. There are also, however, symbols more literally symbolic, in the sense of being single objects, foci of attention or longing. These too can be either spatial or temporal.

In Virginia Woolf's *To the Lighthouse*, for instance, the dimension of the symbolism is spatial. Woolf exploits the visual symbol, constantly present to the eye: the lighthouse is the symbol of the remote and therefore the paradisal, precisely as such things are in our actual lives. The symbol grows into our consciousness without our being aware of the fact. Yet again, as in Kipling and Alain-Fournier, the symbol has its societal dimension, and thereby, a temporal one. The major theme of Virginia Woolf's fiction as a whole, perhaps, is the gradual disintegration of the old way of life – the weekends at Bourton, the coming-out parties, the yearly holidays in Cornwall or

Scotland. *The Years* expresses this theme most overtly, with its final long party, almost like a gathering of *l'ancien régime* awaiting execution. In *To the Lighthouse*, Woolf first establishes the indefinable symbolism of the lighthouse itself – a quintessentially Symbolist motif, expressing the unattainable element in all our lives. Then 'Time Passes', and the unattainable is attained – only to resolve into hard rock, devoid of magic or interest. Thus, the lighthouse regains its magic symbolic status – it stands for the lost, the unredeemable, the absolute – precisely at the moment when it appears to forsake it.

Woolf's use of the visual symbol derives, of course, from the nineteenth century poets. There is a whole series of such images, going back to Lermontov's marvellous sail to which we have referred: 'Byelyet parus odinoky' – 'a white sail gleams on the sea'. The sail in Lermontov's poem symbolises that lost unattainable goal Othello glimpses when he knows he is about to die:

> Here is my journey's end, here is the very butt
> And sea-mark of my utmost sail.

Once again, we see Shakespeare as a giant repository or quarry of such symbols. The significance of Lermontov's poem is that it shows the way forward to the modern poet's use of such images – as actual things seen in the actual world. By such means, the modern poetic symbol, empirical, actualised, begins to stand for the values and absent experiences which always lie within poetry. Mallarmé exploits this kind of symbolism when he speaks of 'l'adieu suprême des mouchoirs'; it is the staple diet of all Rilke's imagery.

The Symbolist motif of the sail appears in both Hart Crane and T. S. Eliot as symbolic of the absolute, the unattainable for which poetry expresses its constant thirst. In Crane, this is related to a life of more or less deliberate self-brutalisation, so that it acquires an air of preternatural grace:

> Flung into April's inmost day.

Eliot exploits the sail image in 'Ash Wednesday' at a point where he wishes to express the 'wavering' of the ordinary man, trapped in the ordinary banality of his daily consciousness – 'In this brief transit where the dreams cross/The dream-crossed twilight between birth and dying' – when he glimpses the absolute, what has escaped him:

> From the wide window towards the granite shore
> The white sails still fly seaward, seaward flying
> Unbroken wings
> And the lost heart stiffens and rejoices . . .

Eliot had earlier used the image of the yacht at the end of *The Waste Land*, where it stood for the skilfully gentle persuasions of the lover. Here also it appears to stand for the missed opportunity, the glamorous full love that somehow had to be forsaken before it could be valued. This is perhaps the defining element of the Romantic: and it is at this point that the man-in-street's usage meets up with the most serious and exact meaning of the word. A Romantic, in popular usage, is a man who longs for the unrealisable, chases dreams or prefers the ideal to the real, even when he knows the ideal can never be gained. It is important, I believe, to recognise the serious originals within such popular stereotypes, to recognise indeed that these stereotypes are but dim reflections of literary originals. Fitzgerald's Gatsby is a case in point: Fitzgerald wisely makes his hero stretch his hand out not for the moon, but for a mundane green light at the end of a pier. His love-goddess is diaphanous – an apparition, in her merely plutocratic ease and good manners, not because she is too good for this life, but because she is simply inadequate to Gatsby's vision: Daisy is just ordinary, yet she retains that vague glamour which is what Fitzgerald-Gatsby really longed to know. Unfortunately, our literary criticism has been so moralistic that it castigates Gatsby for being 'unreal', instead of seeing in him a type of the longing which really underlies all art. For the moment has come to state what has really all along been implicit – that these various Romantic devices, motifs and themes are all modes of presenting the absolute, the absolute which is the true point of aspiration in all art. In the modern world, the absolute is to be referred to only through the pragmatically realised symbol: the symbol becomes the vehicles of a longing for the absolute. If this diction – longing, absolute, unattainable – suggests that the search is a delicate one requiring a precious sensibility rather than a powerful intelligence, let Eliot's own *Four Quartets* supply the answer: *Four*

Quartets shows, in its deliberate, almost matter-of-fact rationality, that the theme at the heart of Romantic literature is strong enough to withstand the assaults of the most analytic of intellects. The whole of the sequence is a series of raids and disquisitions upon the unnameable, a constant act of raising visible images of the invisible. It is Eliot, in fact, who provides what is perhaps the master-image of the whole tradition. Not merely the past is unreachable, but the future, Eliot says: it is a 'faded song',

> a Royal Rose or a lavender spray
> Of wistful regret for those who are not yet here to regret,
> Pressed between yellow leaves of a book that has never been opened.

Alienation, and the various content-shifts I have tried to describe above, threw Romantic and post-Romantic poets back upon this central preoccupation of all poetry: it becomes their fundamental theme, and their identity as poets depends upon it. As the example of T. S. Eliot suggests, however, the theme had to be re-worked in the twentieth century: its continuation presents certain difficulties. It was clear from Mallarmé, that a new Platonism must emerge in western poetry: the philosophy of Plato expresses that distaste for the merely actual in the most uncompromising way. Again and again, what we call neo-Platonist movements in western literature reveal the deep-seated preoccupation with the absolute endemic to all poetry. The motif of the sail as longing for the absolute and the unattainable, receives perhaps its definitive statement in Paul Valéry's poem 'Le Cimetière Marin'. Mallarmé, we remember, had really suggested that it was, after all, better not to live: it is better to dwell forever uncommitted, unrealised in possibility. It is this bitter knowledge that lies behind Valéry's poem. Not without significance, Valéry returns to the graveyard, where, two hundred years before, Thomas Gray had really inaugurated the modern treatment of these themes. It is a different kind of graveyard, of course, one where the dead are lucky enough to have their mystery warmed and dried by the sun. In all this great perfection of death that is the Midi, the conscious live man is the only fault, for the dead have already joined forces with the great force of the sun and the absolute. The gift of life, Valéry observes has gone into the flowers. How closely, now, Valéry

approximates to the tone and cadence of Gray may be gleaned
from the following lines:

> Ou sont des morts les phrases familiers,
> L'Art personnel, les âmes singulières?
> La larve file ou se forment les pleurs.

The careful precision with which Valéry packs his own Elegy in a
churchyard has perhaps too much of the traditional materials of
'literature' for the poem to shake free of itself and bring to a
proper climax the tradition on which it so freely draws.
Certainly, the stanza which follows the Yorick-esque lines I have
just quoted amounts to no more than an eloquent *rechaufée* of
literary rumination on 'the Dead'. Yet the poem is poised upon
the silence of Mallarmé, and it is framed by a *correspondance*, at
once simple and profound, which does succeed in consummating
– if that is the word to describe this ecstasy of impotence – a
certain tendency in French writing. The poem opens with the
image of birds on a roof,

> Ce toit tranquille, ou marchent des colombes,
> Entre les pins palpite, entre les tombes; . . .

which will turn out to be sails (*focs* – literally jib-sails), pecking on
the same tranquil roof:

> Rompez d'eaux rejouies
> Ce toit tranquille ou picoraient des focs!

This is a *correspondance* of truly ineffable subtlety: yet the
exclamation mark with which the poet is obliged to end his poem,
like the series of imperative verbs preceding it (three in the
previous two lines), testifies to desperation, rather than despair,
perhaps. Is this not the final *frisson* of the Symbolist agony?
Trapped in his own metaphors (the sea is variously a panther-
skin, a riding-cloak, and an absolute Hydra drunk with its blue
flesh), the poet resists drowning in their suffocating
anthropomorphism only by dint of shouting: 'Il faut tenter de
vivre!' To make full sense of this cry, we must go back to
Mallarmé, to Laforgue, casting sidewise glances towards Eliot,
Thomas Mann and Joyce, all of them held spell-bound by the

metaphysics of Romanticism. Perhaps Valéry's own poem, 'Au platane', illustrates the point better than any other, however. Valéry's plane-tree has its foot retained 'par la force du site': the poet sees in it the perfect symbol of the poet and of man himself, helpless, slightly ridiculous and heroic, held back from action, wasting itself in beautiful but impotent gestures of rage and abandon. Here too Valéry reaches his inevitable cul-de-sac in the impotent imperative: 'Ose gémir', he adjures the tree, even 'Flagelle-toi!' There seems to me, finally, something a fraction absurd in the solemnity with which Valéry exalts the tree as 'puissant personnage d'un parc'. Is there not here an approach to the tone if not of Mrs. Leo Hunter, at least that of Jules Laforgue? So often the pretext for evasion, Laforgue's irony might have been welcome here. It is no wonder that French writers, haunted so recently by the ghost of rhetoric should have found it necessary as late as 1954, finally to denounce metaphor and the sublime in the programme of the *nouveau roman*.[5]

If Valéry puts a final and belated full-stop to the Symbolist tradition in verse, Proust does so no less eloquently in prose. (In fact the difference here is more notional than real, and this is of some interest: it seems impossible to discuss writers such as Joyce and Virginia Woolf in terms radically different from those in which one discusses Eliot and Valéry, and such a rapprochement is historically important.)[6] With Marcel's final meditations upon the objects and foci of his recollection, the tradition which began effectively with Wordsworth comes to an end. Mention of Wordsworth at this point is inevitable, of course: the overall structure, as well as the internal content, of *The Prelude* closely foreshadow that of *A la recherche du temps perdu*. In both, there is the preoccupation with memory as source of significance, the narrative arc leading from childhood through crisis to recollection, the 'spots of time' as source at once of mystery and of wonder, the concentration on objects (the *madeleine*, for instance) as focus of attention; above all, the final redemption of time through memory. All these elements of the Proustian metaphysics are familiar structural properties of *The Prelude*. But between the powerful explorer and cartographer of the Romantic predicament, for whom the very act of discovering these despairs and inexpressibilities redeemed their pain, and the virtuoso of recollection confined to his cork-lined room and condemned by the very clarity of Romantic geography to perform upon their findings miracles of variation, came a whole century of thought and performance. What is important in Proust is not the way he conceived of time and memory – he had little to add to what Wordsworth, Dickens, George Eliot and others had already established – but the actual content of his variations. There are no new 'laws' to be encountered in Proust: all that is valuable is the contour and rhythm of evocation and recollection. For the essential element of Proust's version of the Romantic quest is its acceptance of defeat. This is, of course, in the spirit of Mallarmé and of Bergson. It is noteworthy that Proust was so sure of the extent of his territory (unlike the Romantics, for whom limitlessness is less a spiritual temptation than an experience of frontiers) that he wrote the same book twice, sufficiently confident of his powers to pack away so beautiful a work as *Jean Santeuil*. The same is true of the younger James Joyce, whose *Portrait of the Artist as a young man* rests content with the end-point of *Stephen Hero*, and retreats back to the source in childhood of that spirituality whose nature is known.

There is a sense of intellectual adventure in the earlier essays absent from the finished masterpieces. It is in *Jean Santeuil* that we find Proust testing the receptors of his own intellect, and reaching out for the frontiers of experience in the full Romantic manner: with naïve clarity, he tests the verity of alienation: 'In a word, does pleasure necessarily accompany beauty, as Descartes believed that certainty accompanied truth, and is perhaps as well its criterion?'[7] In a word, the answer was no. What is the artist to do, then, on earth – live, or 'merely' write? Proust's answer runs along lines parallel to Yeats's: the one thing has to be sacrificed for the other to come into being:

> If I could have that, says Balzac in one of his stories, I would not write novels, I would make them out of it. And yet whenever an artist puts his happiness into his life instead of into his art, he experiences a deception and almost a remorse which warns him with certainty that he is wrong.[8]

Balzac of course knew the answer, too; but he merely knew that happiness generally fails to become available at our will: it is a Shelleyan knowledge. Proust's position is different: the Romantic acquaintance with defeat has, through acceptance and familiarity, turned into an ideological instrument. What Proust is articulating in *Jean Santeiul* is the symbolist impasse as we have seen it in Mallarmé and Eliot.

In *A la recherche du temps perdu*, this position – if we can so term it – forms a vital structural element of the whole. It is overtly treated in the Combray section of *Du côté de Chez Swann*: reflection on the 'lack of harmony between our impressions and their normal form of expression' leads Marcel to remember his sense of impotence at being unable to 'interpret', capture or otherwise do justice to, the ravishing beauty of nature on a particularly balmy autumn evening. His only 'response' is to shake his umbrella and shout, 'Zut, zut, zut, zut!' Yet he immediately feels as artist the obligation to do more than this, 'to try to see more clear into my ecstasy'.[9] We could have no better instance of the Symbolist *impasse*. Here is the basic situation of Romanticism: our 'enjoyment' of the sunset is the source of our sense of significance – of value, just as the beauty of nature is the source of our numinous experiencing. The Romantic Agony is that these moments fade and cease occurring to us. The Symbolist *impasse* is that our verbal responses or records of these experiences always seems to let something – and that the most important thing – escape. The predicament that enfolds both conditions is the knowledge that we are the source of our own values, but we can still – reasonably – ask the question, is what we value really valuable? Proust's anguished inability to 'say it all' is, of course, essentially Symbolist. Equally symptomatic is Marcel's feeling that the woman he then fantasises about would in fact satisfy him less than the dreaming landscape: 'But if this desire that a woman should appear added for me something more exalting than the charms of nature, they in their turn enlarged what I might, in the woman's charm, have found too much restricted.' This is a motif we can find repeated everywhere in the art of Proust's period, most notably in the poetry of Rilke, for whom the actual woman desired in the act of love stands in the way of the experience for which she is the pretext or instrument.

It is not surprising that Proust – this virtuoso performer on all the Romantic themes – should arrive finally at the accident as redemptive force (though force is just what it is not). *La mémoire involontaire* has of course in itself nothing especially new: in Bergson and Comte, and indeed in the empiricists themselves, memory is generally treated as being beyond conscious control. We cannot in general choose to remember, and the processes of association by which the forgotten tune or name is brought to mind must remain more or less inchoate. Once again, what distinguishes Proust is less the originality of his contribution than the emphasis he chooses to place upon particular ideas. If language inevitably falsifies, so consciousness, precisely in consolidating itself, denies what we may feel to be the 'essential' element of experience. The artist's role is now conceived in terms of the disrobing of false consciousness:

> This work of the artist, to seek to discern something different underneath material, experience, words, is exactly the reverse of the process which, during every minute that we live with our attention diverted from ourselves, is being carried out within us by pride, passion, intelligence and also by our habits, when they hide our true impressions from us by burying them under the mass of nomenclatures and practical aims which we erroneously call life.
>
> *Remembrance of things past* (Scott-Moncrieff, II 1013)[10]

Here is the final resting-place of Symbolism, and in effect of Romanticism itself. Not only Proust's own but also Freudian analysis, and existentialism, seek to defeat these names and practical goals by which man in his fallen, conscious state seeks to disguise his nakedness from himself. Freud had already taught western man to mistrust his own utterances or, at best, to treat them as codes to be unriddled for their 'real' meaning. Existentialism, in its Sartrean form especially, diagnosed as bad faith all attempts to build an authentic life on the assumptions and constructive procedures of consciousness. Society, as the realised form of consciousness, becomes the repository of the lie, a crude and brutal falsification of the 'real'. But, of course, the unriddling of man's conscious utterances must be conducted according to some code or other. Reading Freud's analysis of monotheism and of taboo customs in terms of an identical code, the Oedipus situation, we can hardly refrain from a gasp of disbelief and weary boredom.[11] 'Not that again! Really, is that all there has ever been in human history? Surely we are not so small?' Freud is reductive in his vision, and lacks even that fading, ragged vision of Utopia which from time redeems the no less reductive unriddlings of Marxism, which also joins Proust in refusing to grant any human dignity to the names and goals man has proposed for himself. That is the Romantic predicament.

It is clear that the position finally reached by Proust in *Temps retrouvé* is the inevitable cul-de-sac, womb and grave at once, which always lay at the end of that corridor stumbled upon by Keats in his own prosecution of the accident. Negative Capability was his name for it, and we would do well perhaps to rehearse its properties again: '*Negative Capability*, that is when man is capable of being in uncertainties, mysteries, doubts, without any irritable reaching after fact and reason.'[12]

That there should, in the search for enlightenment, be no 'irritable reaching after fact and reason' has troubled many a critic of Keats, yet is not his implied opposition of reason and imagination at the root of Symbolism, in general, and of Proust in particular? We cannot, of course, turn Proust into Wisdom: it would be a grim irony if the reward of this master of evasion and disintegration, whose researches led directly to Surrealism, on the one hand, and to Sartrean existentialism on the other, should suffer the indignity of positivisation. Gabriel Josipovici treats Proust as therapeutic:

> Such an art [that which Marcel envisages in *Temps Retrouvé*] must reveal and make sensible the *laws* which govern existence, those formal laws which remain constant no matter how much chance and coincidence there may be in a man's choice of friends and love-objects, places to live in and works of art to admire.[13]

And reading such art, we can learn that words are 'only symbols, inadequate substitutes for a desire which only the creation of this particular artifact will appease':

> It is up to the reader to let the words echo in his mind, from that opening sentence to the closing one, as they echo in the mind of the man who sits in his cork lined room, night after night and day after day, writing himself into total consciousness of himself, sacrificing everything to this end, yet in reality sacrificing what he knows to be of no importance, since it is only in the act of writing that the lost unity will be restored, the lost paradise regained.[14]

This is not so much a description of the aims of the 'heroic tradition' instituted by Wordsworth, as a press-release for it. There could be no more extravagant expression of the religion of art, and almost every article of the Symbolist creed is rehearsed here: the world and experience are of no consequence, the world is valued only in that it will end in a book, the artist sacrifices himself to the production of this book, the reading and writing of which replaces actual living. Actual living is a crude irrelevancy now, a rallying-cry for the (by now middle-aged) followers of F. R. Leavis and D. H. Lawrence. The way is clear for a simple polarisation: modernist Proustians, disdainful of life and experience and their cognate literatures on the one hand, raw Leavisite enemies of Proustian decadence, Lawrence's poems their ammunition, on the other. Must we settle for this foolish gang-warfare? Isn't it rather the case that the work of art only happens (and we must agree that it does happen, and cannot be planned) at the frontiers between experience and that fund of memory and consciousness which is man himself, that without such a re-encounter, art cannot come into being, and that for Proust this re-encounter, happened to be with memory and the past? Mr Josipovici's attempt to place the experience of writing and reading literature at the heart of all wisdom, almost as if life itself cannot be lived without the aid of art, except as a brutal farce, belongs, it seems to me, to the backwaters of Symbolism. The truth is that Proust supplied himself at the expense of the future, fitting himself for the long journey into the dark with every means at his disposal: in the end, love, death and mother all coalesce in the dark warmth of his disease. Proust could not have been more explicit and frank in his espousal of the Romantic myth: 'Cette idée de la mort', Marcel says, a few pages before the end of his long voyage towards Time, 'cette idee de la mort s'installa definitivement en moi comme un amour'.[15]

Gabriel Josipovici dismisses the particularities of Proust's personal situation (the mother-fixation, say) in favour of some 'universal factor' which will enable us to understand ourselves as members of a series and as subject to certain 'laws' of consciousness to understand which, in turn, is to understand everything. This turns out to mean acknowledging that our lives are more or less contingent (they might have been otherwise), that we are going to die, and that our particular projects, friends, acts and emotions are incidental – accidental, so that we should not take them too seriously: we might have been otherwise, it is not Wendy or Susan (or George) I really love, it is myself displaced by them. Understand this, and we are safe, unfooled by the illusion of immortality and necessity under which mankind in general labours. This is the Gospel according to St. Marcel – or is it, St. Gabriel? For the most remarkable thing about Proust is his concreteness – yes, concreteness: these essays in recollection, these assemblages of contingencies, these swirls and filigrees of detail and scene, are life itself to him. His essential medium is reverie-istic: we have notice of this in that monstrous fifty-eight line 'sentence' evoking past rooms in the *Ouverture*.[16] It is the genius for imagining event and scene that gives Proust's marvellous prose its life – the image of the traveller hurrying towards the nearest station, for instance, or the shirts with the turned-down collars in the fantasy about history that follows a little later. Such things tell us that Proust lived in the past in a form which is exaggerated in its intensity but otherwise true of all poets. For him the re-encounter was always with the past, and was experienced within the confines of an emotionally inhibiting, but artistically fertile, subjectivity.

This being so, it is certainly misguided to cry pathological or decadent; but it is much more misguided to erect this terminal introversion – morbid, surely, in a medical sense (or shall we say, chronic?) – into a possible wisdom. It is clear that we have in Proust a final rumination on all the basic themes of Romanticism and Symbolism: we have touched on each of his major themes already in dealing with Wordsworth, Keats, Baudelaire, Rimbaud, Mallarmé, Frost and Eliot. It is equally clear that the authenticity of the Romantic and Symbolist writers' treatment of these themes lay often in the sense of discovery and re-encounter with which they were stumbled upon. It is apparent, by the time we get to Proust, that this sense of discovery – the meeting-place of consciousness and experience which is Truth – has itself been turned into a possession. Proust was himself redeemed from falsity here only by the extent of his love of his own past, and, ultimately, of his own mother. There is, I submit, a fundamental difference between the love of the mother, which, like Kafka's love of his father, was life itself for Proust, and core to his art – and those *amours*, with which Marcel's steps are littered in the pages of the long and often laborious trek from childhood to death which is *A la recherche du temps perdu*. These *amours* are mere Romantic mythology: it is easy for the credulous reader to feel that Proust demonstrates in his novel, in Josipovici's words that there is 'an ineradicable contradiction set up in the very heart of love'.[17] This conclusion is supposed to derive from the fact that in each love we feel that something – the most important thing – has escaped, the body we possess in making love is not the soul, and so on. This is basic Romantic fare, first adumbrated in the mediaeval stories that launched the Tristan myth, articulated with marvellous delicacy and tact by Keats, done to death by every French writer of the next hundred years, and raped necrophiliacally by directors like Truffaut and writers like Françoise Sagan and Philippe Sollers and Boris Vian.

The point is of some importance since there is an undoubted parallel between the conception of the absent experience as I have outlined it in these pages, and that quality in human sexuality which Freud extrapolated as lying outside the reach of satisfaction: 'we must reckon', Freud wrote, 'with the possibility that something in the nature of the sexual instinct itself is unfavourable to the realisation of complete satisfaction'.[18] This is basic Romantic lore, of the sort purveyed in Denis De Rougemont's study of the Tristan myth, *Passion and Society*. Freud's famous question 'Was will das Weib?' becomes, then, not a rhetorical question, assuming the charmed, exasperated reply, but a way into an understanding of all sexuality. For the answer is, she wants nothing that can be satisfied: she wants desire itself. This brings normal sexuality very close to the art-function as I have tried to describe it in this chapter: from this point of view, this characteristic restlessness of human consciousness, preventing full satisfaction even in coitus, and refusing to be identified with any organic or biological processes, can receive its highest gratification only in art, which has as its motive-power precisely the realisation of the unrealisable.

It is this view of Freud which has been taken up by Jacques Lacán.[19] According to Lacan, all the terms used in describing sexual situations ('male', 'female', 'love') belong to the realm of fantasy only: each fantasises the other. Language never fixes meanings, it only serves as the medium for fantasisation. This 'analysis' of language is itself no more than a late Romantic fantasy, its deadness revealed in its progressively more ghostly findings – term after term being eviscerated until nothing is left but the monotonous egotism of M. Lacan. There comes a point in prosecuting any intellectual system when the reality of the real must be acknowledged in contact or collision; it is this sense of collision which is so devastatingly absent from recent French culture.

This is an albatross French literature needs to rid itself of. Certainly, it is one we can do without ourselves. It is not for this jaded Romantic knowingness that we read and re-read Proust. The reason why Marcel experiences exasperation in the experience of love is that he does not really love anybody. The Romantic love-myth thrives upon itself: armed with its increasingly cynical lore, it is easy for the 'lover' to keep himself in reserve, safe in the belief that it is himself he is really loving, that love itself is more important than the girl he is 'making love' to, that the act is doomed to disappoint him, and so on. This fore-knowledge makes a great deal of *A la recherche du temps perdu* laborious reading, no more illuminating in its wearisomely predictable diagnoses than the precocious worldliness of a Radiguet. The same is true for the laboured social observation, those heavy efforts at satire and humour (there can be no less humorous writer in the history of literature), the overdone social observation by which Proust seeks to prove himself novelist rather than mere reverie-ist. This great work carries a heavy duty of social *materia*, much like those scherzos and adagios of modern composers out to compete with Brahms and Beethoven as symphonists.

D. H. Lawrence rejected the lore of Romantic love and replaced it with an exploration which refused the easy polarities of a decadent Romanticism: love – making love – is neither the effort to possess the soul of the beloved (something Lawrence wittily dismissed in his essay on Poe),[20] nor the cynical enjoyment of her body. It is rather something else, something unknown and to be re-encountered. I do not want to replace the Gospel according to St. Marcel with that of St. David-Herbert (though I would certainly choose it, if forced to take one or the other). I am concerned with the art produced: it is the life of Lawrence's art – its art-ness – that proves his rejection of these stale Romantic properties correct: out of his work came a new 'realism', a realism that attests itself not by any accuracy or consonance with a reality outside itself (all art lives by that), but by the familiar freshness and excitement which is always the sign of new art. That excitement was there in Romanticism, it was there in

Baudelaire's new realism, and in Mallarmé's withdrawal into silence (experienced as it is with such icy zest). Such a freshness – which tells us that 'reality' has been re-encountered by the artist – is signally absent from those cultural traditions which have clung on to the ragged ghost of Romanticism and thus betrayed the inner spirit of Romanticism, or tried to escape it through a sterile and cerebral experimentalism. A new realism is likely to take the form of a more accessible idiom, I think, than those practised by the official *avant garde*. The 'new fiction', like the *nouveau roman*, has watery blood in its veins, and age in its very conception.

Thus, the new art is more likely to be recognised by that breath of life which is the evidence of a genuine adaptation to the new situation we find ourselves in, than by its manipulation of the intellectual devices encouraged by the neo-modernist criticism. This, of course, means rejecting the neo-modernist view of traditional realist fiction as revealing 'a world ruled entirely by chance and, what is more, a world quite unaware of this fact, a world which takes its "given" and necessary quality for granted'.[21] The Victorian novelists show in a number of ways that they are fully aware that they are constructing fictions, sometimes by allowing the reader parity of status with themselves, sometimes even by giving alternate endings to their books. The elimination of the direct authorial persona was a formal evolution, the development towards the so-called 'art-novel', which is the fictional equivalent of the symbolic poetry inaugurated by the Romantics. The assumption behind this fiction is that the realistic details presented are indeed symbols, and that the entire construct is to be read in the light of Symbolism. This is, as we have seen above, how modern writers were obliged to work, given the elimination of so much of their iconographic resources by cultural evolution. There is no intrinsic difference between the realist fiction of the nineteenth century and the drama of the Elizabethans, the epics of the Renaissance or of Homeric Greece: the differences are those forced upon the writer by cultural evolution, the necessity to adapt to new circumstances. The twentieth century writer's sense of technical alienation – manifest in Brecht's *Verfremdungseffekt*, for instance, or the shattered perspectives of Cubism or Eliot's *Waste Land* – are themselves evidence of adaptation to a new situation. It is absurd to erect this characteristic need to shatter those expectations of the readership bred on realist fiction and painting into an artistic law applicable to all art of all periods. The Victorians presented their novels realistically not because they thought them 'necessitated' or 'given', but because they were wise enough to know that the work of art is always a raid on the inarticulate by means of verbal representation, that commitment to the image in art parallels the commitment to emotion and experience in life, and that without both neither can be satisfactory. The argument of this book has been that history – cultural, political and philosophical – has forced upon modern writers a particular kind of image, one more or less devoid of those iconographical elements Panofsky describes in the painting of the high Renaissance, and therefore dependent upon itself for its significance. The Victorians made less song and dance about it than our neo-modernist theorists, but they were perfectly aware of the difference between their representation of the real and the real itself. As their rich harmonies and orchestral effects amply testify, they knew that new ways would have to be discovered of making the elements of the realistic art-object *tell*: so we find, alongside the increasingly object-oriented poetry of the Symbolists, the resourceful symbolism of the Ibsen play and the Dickens novel. What we cannot do – ever – is make these symbolic artefacts into a possession. Whatever we learn from them – and we learn from them much of what we can know about our own moral and spiritual experience – must be learned through the experience of the images themselves, in all their fullness and variety. They are no 'laws' of imagination or consciousness to be 'got', enabling us to sit back full of wise appreciation. Each experience of the work of art is a gamble and a hazard, and there are no short-cuts to its rewards.

The present circumstances forbid the continuation of fictional realism in the forms perfected by the Victorians. But it is mere hubris to think that we can master the 'human condition' to such an extent that we can, by adopting a knowing attitude towards our fictions, get outside it and exist in a dream of omniscience. The one thing we can be sure of is that works of art – our surest source of illumination in the long run – lose all vestige of value once taken as doctrines of behaviour. We can only proceed by attacking the situation in which we exist, and this means seeing it for what it is. In the present context, this means dropping this foolish air of superiority over the great artists of the nineteenth century: the work of art is a tactical triumph over an immediate difficulty, and this triumph is to be achieved only by the most honest effort to 'deal with' those concerns which seem of the greatest importance. That the nineteenth century realists – from Balzac to Zola, from Scott to Dickens, from Gogol to Tolstoy – did this with immense skill and intelligence, to say nothing of their good faith, is beyond doubt. What is perhaps more in need of emphasis, is that their attack on the situation does not basically differ from those made, in their differing historical circumstances, by Homer and Dante, Shakespeare and Cervantes. In no case, can we find any evidence that great art has been produced without the artists concerned committing themselves to the expression and analysis of current feeling and thought with the maximum force. There were, I submit, no alternative modes available to writers in the nineteenth century than those variously adopted by the Romantic subjectivist poets and Realist prose writers. Only by committing himself totally to the situation in which he lives is the artist able to transcend it. Ultimately, the work of art makes the actual theme or plot chosen irrelevant. But this transcendance can only be achieved through an absolute commitment to the immediate, either in the form of concreteness of image in an increasingly object-dominated poetry, or of a fiction fully absorbed by the manners and appearance of a world deprived of its traditional modes of transcendance. Only through the most honest and courageous commitment to the facts of consciousness, as we see it variously in Joyce's *Ulysses*, Lawrence's later tales and poems, or in Proust's recollection, can modern writers achieve that release from the merely phenomenal or the contingent, which it is the purpose of art to achieve. To reduce this subtle, complex and exciting process to an intellectual abstraction, as many neo-modernist critics have done, is to take the business of art out of the world and into the seminar.

Notes

CHAPTER 1   DEFINING ROMANTICISM

1. See for instance T. E. Hulme's *Speculations* (London, 1924), where the modernist anti-humanism really begins. A typical recent off-shoot is G. Josipovici, *The World and the Book* (London, 1971).
2. See Jacques Barzun, *Romanticism and the modern ego* (Boston, 1943), for a defence of the industriousness and care of Romantic artists.
3. See Herbert Read's *The True Voice of Feeling: studies in English Romantic poetry* (London, 1953), for the most extreme statement of this hyper-Romantic view.
4. See for instance Northrop Frye's collection, *Romanticism Re-considered: Selected Papers from the English Institute* (New York, 1963). A. O. Lovejoy's essay 'On the discrimination of Romanticism', *Essays in the History of Ideas* (Baltimore, 1948) examines some of the problems involved.
5. See Heinrich Wölfflin, *Renaissance and Barock*, tr. P. Murray (London, 1964); *Principles of Art History* tr. D. M. Hottinger (London, 1932).
6. Wilhelm Worringer, *Abstraction and Empathy*, tr. M. Bullock (London, 1948).
7. See P. Wyndham Lewis, *The Demon of Progress in the Arts* (London, 1954).
8. John Stuart Mill, 'What is poetry', *Early Essays* ed. J. W. M. Gibbs (London, 1897) p. 208.
9. Mill, ibid., p. 208.
10. José Ortega y Gasset, *The Dehumanisation of Art and other Essays on Art, Culture and Literature*, tr. H. Wey (Princeton, 1968) p. 25.
11. G. Josipovici, *The world and the book* (London, 1971) p. 186.
12. Josipovici, ibid., p. 6, also p. 287.
13. Josipovici, ibid., p. 309.
14. Josipovici, ibid., p. 199: 'Had "Las Meninas" not been reworked by him, we would have taken it for granted and thus in a sense failed to see it.'
15. C. Brooks, *Modern Poetry and the Tradition* (Chapel Hill, 1939).
16. P. Ackroyd, *Notes for a New Culture, an Essay on Modernism* (London, 1976).
17. Ackroyd, ibid., p. 54.
18. Ackroyd, ibid., p. 13.
19. Ackroyd, ibid., p. 13.
20. Ackroyd, ibid., p. 13.
21. Ackroyd, ibid., p. 25.
22. See, for instance, Marcel Cohen, *Language: its Evolution Structure and Evolution*, tr. L. Muller (Miami, 1970).
23. Quoted in E. Cassirer, 'The evolution of religious ideas', *Language and Myth*, tr. S. K. Langer (New York, 1946) p. 33.

24. Cassirer, ibid., p. 58.
25. Cassirer, ibid., p. 73.
26. F. W. Nietzsche. *Götzendämmerung* (Leipzig, 1930) p. 98.
27. George Steiner, 'The language animal', *Encounter*, vol. 33 (Aug. 1969) pp. 7–24.
28. Josipovici, op. cit., p. 41.
29. See F. A. Yates, *Giordana Bruno and the Hermetic Tradition* (London, 1964).
30. F. de Saussure, *Cours de linguistique générale* (Paris, 1962).
31. See F. C. Copleston, *A History of Philosophy* (London, 1946), vol. I, 'Greece and Rome', pp. 72–5; also C. Bailey, *The Greek Atomists and Epicurus* (New York, 1964). For Indian thought, see D. Chattopradhaya, *Indian Philosophy* (New Delhi, 1964) pp. 184, *et seq.*
32. D. Hume, *Enquiries Concerning the Human Understanding*, 'Enquiry I', Section XII, part III, p. 165. ed. L. A. Selby-Bigge (Oxford, 1955).
33. See Erich Heller, 'The hazard of modern poetry', *The Disinherited Mind* (London, 1952): 'Lost will be that unity of word and deed, of picture and thing, of the bread and the glorified body', p. 266. Heller's remains the finest statement of the position more familiarly associated nowadays with Michel Foucault.
34. Aristotle, *Rhetorica*, tr. W. Rhys Roberts, Bk. I, 22, p. 1395b. *Works*. ed. W. D. Ross, Vol. XI (Oxford, 1959).
35. See D. L. Clark, *Rhetoric in Graeco-Roman Education* (London, 1937).
36. See W. J. Ong, *Ramus: Method and the Decay of Dialogue* (Harvard, 1958).
37. M. Foucault, 'The prose of the world', *The Order of Things*, tr. A. Sheridan (London, 1970).
38. J. Huizinga, 'Symbolism in its decline', *The Waning of the Middle Ages* (London, 1924).
39. See F. C. Copleston, *A History of Philosophy*, vol. II, pp. 527–9 (London, 1966).
40. E. Heller, op. cit., p. 282.

CHAPTER 2   ROMANTIC SUBJECTIVITY

1. I have discussed this problem at some length in my book *Counter-modernism in current critical theory*. Some of that material will perforce be repeated here.
2. Erwin Panofsky, 'Introduction to the study of Renaissance art', *Meaning in the Visual Arts* (Harmondsworth, 1970).
3. *Counter-modernism*, pp. 53–6.
4. T. S. Eliot, 'Hamlet', *Selected Prose*, ed. F. Kermode (London, 1975); L. C. Knights, *Hamlet and other Shakespearean essays* (Cambridge, 1979).
5. See Ernest Jones, *Hamlet and Oedipus* (New York, 1954).
6. Pierre Macherey, *A Theory of Literary Production* tr. G. Wall (London, 1978) p. 61: 'We have defined literary discourse as parody, as a contestation of language rather than a presentation of reality.'
7. M. Foucault, *The Archaeology of Knowledge*, tr. A. Sheridan-Smith (London, 1972) p. 122; T. Eagleton, *Criticism and ideology* (London, 1975) p. 58.
8. M. Foucault, *Language–Counter-memory, Practice* (Cornell, 1977) pp. 137–8.
9. J-P. Sartre, *Problem of Method*, tr. H. E. Barnes (London, 1963).

10. See for instance, Herbert Read, *The Meaning of Art* (London, 1935) pp. 69–70.

11. T. S. Eliot, 'The frontiers of criticism', *On Poetry and Poets* (London, 1957) p. 117.

12. R. Jakobson, 'Linguistics and Poetics', T. Sebeok (ed.) *Style in Language* (Cambridge, Mass. 1960) p. 356.

13. Marx observes:

> Only in the eighteenth century . . . do the various forms of social connectedness confront the individual as a mere means towards his private purposes. . . . But the epoch which produces this standpoint, that of the isolated individual is also precisely that of the hitherto most developed social (from this standpoint, general) relations.
>
> *Grundisse: Foundations of the Critique of Political Economy,* tr. M. Nicolaus, (Harmondsworth, 1973) p. 84

14. E. Durkheim, *The Division of Labour in Society*, tr. G. Simpson (London, 1933), chap. 2, 'Mechanical Solidarity through likeness', p. 76 *et seq.*

15. Durkheim, ibid., p. 136.

16. Durkheim, ibid., p. 354.

17. J. Huizinga, op. cit., pp. 47–8.

18. Huizinga, ibid., p. 53.

19. This term has already been used, by Philip Hobsbaum, in a book called *A Theory of Communication* (London, 1970) pp. 47 *et seq.* I did not know of Mr Hobsbaum's concept when I chose my own word. I have retained 'availability', since my use of it is totally different from Mr Hobsbaum's, and it still seems the best word for my purposes.

20. Panofsky, op. cit., p. 58.

21. Panofsky, ibid., p. 58.

CHAPTER 3   ROMANTIC LANGUAGE: RISE OF OBJECT-DOMINANCE

1. I. A. Richards, *Principles of Literary criticism* (London, 1922) p. 250. Richards approves of the 'Ode to a Nightingale' and 'Proud Maisie', however.

2. W. Empson, *Seven Types of ambiguity* (London, 1930) p. 21.

3. Empson, ibid., p. 21.

4. Empson, ibid., p. 24.

5. F. R. Leavis, *Revaluation* (London, 1936); see for instance Leavis's account of Shelley, pp. 203–32.

6. Sir Thomas Browne, 'The Garden of Cyrus', *Religio Medici and Other Writings* (London, 1906) p. 205.

7. See p. 21 above.

8. Antonio de Machado, *Antologia de su prosa*, vol. II 'Literatura y arte', ed. A. de Albernoz (Madrid, 1970) p. 139.

9. Rosemond Tuve, *Elizabethan and Metaphysical Imagery* (Chicago, 1947) p. 25.

10. S. T. Coleridge, *Lectures and Notes on Shakespeare and other English Poets* (London, 1893) p. 525.

11. E. Darwin, *The Botanic Garden* (London, 1799), vol. II, 'The Loves of the Plants', p. 63.

12. Dorothy Wordsworth, *Journals*, ed. E. de Selincourt (London, 1959) p. 131.

13. J. S. Mill, op. cit., p. 242.

14. R. Jakobson, 'Two aspects of language and two types of aphasic disturbance', *Selected Writings*, vol. II (The Hague, 1971) p. 255.

15. R. Barthes, *S/Z*, tr. S. Wall (London, 1970) pp. 12–13.

16. D. Lodge, *The Modes of modern writing* (London, 1975) p. 92.

17. Lodge, ibid., pp. 112–13.

18. Ernest Fenollosa, *The Chinese Written Character as a Medium for Poetry* (San Francisco, 1968) p. 5.

19. Quoted in A. C. Grahame, *Poems of the late T'ang*, (Harmondsworth, 1977) opposite dedication.

20. Makoto Ueda, *Zeami, Basho, Yeats, Pound – a study in Japanese and English poetics* (The Hague, 1965) p. 38.

21. See for instance, R. H. Brower and E. Miner, *Japanese Court Poetry* (London, 1955). Also, W. G. Aston, *A History of Japanese Literature* (London, 1899).

22. F. S. Flint, quoted in N. Stock, *The Life of Ezra Pound* (London, 1970), p. 132.

23. S. Mallarmé, 'La musique et les lettres', *Oeuvres Complètes* (Paris, 1945), ed. H. Mondor et G. Jean-Aubry, p. 645.

24. E. Pound, *Gaudier-Brzeska – a memoir* (London, 1916) p. 103.

25. Ueda, op. cit., p. 17.

26. Ueda, op. cit., p. 27.

27. S. Mallarmé, op. cit., p. 647.

28. M. Bowra, *The Heritage of Symbolism* (London, 1943) p. 147.

29. Josipovici, op. cit., p. 29.

30. Josipovici, op. cit., p. 30.

31. See Copleston, op. cit., vol. III, pp. 527–9.

32. Huizinga, op. cit., p. 196.

CHAPTER 4   MEANING AND MEANINGFULNESS

1. Josipovici, op. cit., p. 126.

2. Josipovici, op. cit., p. 127.

3. Josipovici, op. cit., p. 29.

4. Josipovici, op. cit., p. 132.

5. Josipovici, op. cit., p. 132.

6. Josipovici, op. cit., p. 30.

7. See Mircea Eliade, *Shamanism*, tr. W. Trask (London, 1964) ch. 1.

8. J. Hick, *Faith and Knowledge* (London, 1967) p. 3.

9. The best representative of such a view is Colin Wilson: see his early 'outsider' series, especially, *The Age of Defeat* (London, 1959) and *Beyond the Outsider* (London, 1964), *Religion and the Rebel* (London, 1957).

10. See Eliade, op. cit., p. 9.
11. G. Lukács, *The Historical Novel*, tr. H. and S. Mitchell (London, 1962) p. 20 (also *et seq.*).
12. S. Kierkegaard, *Either/Or*, tr. W. Lowrie (Princeton, 1959) vol. II, pp. 136 *et seq.* See also Josipovici's free adaptation of Kierkegaard's ideas, op. cit., pp. 188–9.
13. See Harold Bloom's treatment of the quest theme in his book, *Yeats* (New York, 1970) pp. 7–22.

CHAPTER 5   ROMANTIC ALIENATION

1. See for instance J. C. F. Schiller, *On the Aesthetic Education of Man*, ed. and tr. E. M. Wilkinson and L. Willoughby (Oxford, 1967), 'Humanity has lost its dignity', p. 57. See also J. Israel for a general account of this aspect of Romantic despair, *Alienation from Marx to Modern Sociology* (Boston, 1971) pp. 24–7.
2. Perhaps this helps explain the unresolved contradiction in Plato's aesthetics between Corybantic possession and iron utility.
3. T. Hobbes, *Leviathan*, part I, ch. 13 (London, 1973) p. 67.
4. C. B. MacPherson, *The Political Theory of Possessive Individualism: Hobbes to Locke* (Oxford, 1962) p. 22.
5. See Jürgen Habermas, *Theory and Practice*, tr. J. Viertel (London, 1974) p. 92 *et seq.*
6. J-J. Rousseau, *The Political Writings of Jean-Jacques Rousseau*, ed. C. E. Vaugh, 3 vols (Cambridge, 1915) vol. I, pp. 173–90.
7. K. Marx, Marx-Engels, *Gesammtausgabe* (Berlin, 1962) section 1, vol. II, p. 599.
8. See R. Tucker, *Philosophy and Myth in Karl Marx* (Cambridge, 1961) p. 34 *et seq.*
9. Habermas, ch. 4, 'Natural Law' and 'Revolution', discusses the relations between the two things.
10. G. W. F. Hegel, *Vorlesungen über die Aesthetik* (Stuttgart-Bad Sannstatt, 1964) vol. II, 'De Romantische Kunstform', pp. 120 ff.
11. For the Romantics' political beliefs, see T. R. Edwards, *Imagination and Poetry: a Study of Poetry on Public Themes* (London, 1971).
12. K. Marx and F. Engels, *The Manifesto of the Communist Party*, part 1, 'Bourgeois and proletarians', Moscow, 1959, p. 48.
13. T. W. Adorno, *Prisms*, tr. S. and S. Weber (London, 1967) p. 157.
14. Joyce's politics have been studied in detail by D. Manganiello, *Joyce's Politics* (London, 1980): 'Joyce's attitude to the Easter Rising was complex', p. 172. The principles now entertained were 'not entirely those which Joyce had earlier entertained', p. 163. Insisting on retaining British citizenship, Joyce remained ambivalent to the end of his life.

CHAPTER 6 1: THE ROMANTIC PREDICAMENT

1. I discuss this theme at length in my forthcoming book *The Heroic Tradition*.
2. T. S. Eliot, *The Use of Poetry and the use of criticism* (London, 1933) p. 87. Eliot's essays here remain the finest critical study of these matters.
3. E. Young, 'Conjectures on Original Composition' (London, 1759). See E. Purdie (ed.), *Von deutscher Kunst und Art* (Oxford, 1924), Purdies's Introduction (pp. 25–6) discusses Young's influence on German writers.
4. See S. T. Coleridge, *Biographia Literaria*, ed. A. Symons (London, 1906) chs IV to VII. Also ch. XXII: 'If Mr. Wordsworth's have set forth principles of poetry which his arguments are insufficient to support let him be set right by the confutation of those arguments, and by the substitution of more philosophical principles', p. 232.
5. C. Baudelaire, 'Fusées', *Oeuvres Complètes* (Paris, 1975) p. 659.
6. Henry Vaughan is of course Wordsworth's ancestor here: 'Happy those early days! when I/Shined in my angel-infancy' ('The Retreat').
7. See A. Maslow, *The farther reaches of human nature* (New York, 1971).
8. M. Moorman, *William Wordsworth: a Biography* (Oxford, 1957) vol. I, 'The early years', p. 528.
9. T. S. Eliot, op. cit., p. 69.
10. Coleridge, op. cit., p. 165.
11. Erich Heller writes: that Goethe's 'irritation with them was so intense because he himself already knew the temptation' (op. cit., p. 283).
12. Heller, op. cit., p. 285.
13. E. Wassermann ably refutes the more facile accounts of Keats's poem. 'The "Ode on a Grecian Urn" ', in J. Bate, *Keats, A collection of critical essays* (Englewood Cliffs, N.J., 1964).
14. See also B. Brecht, 'Weite and Vielfalt der realistischen Schreibweise', *Versuche* 13 (Berlin, 1954) pp. 97–107.
15. See J.-P. Sartre, *Qu'est-ce que la litterature?* (Paris, 1948) p. 187.
16. P. B. Shelley, Preface to 'The Revolt of Islam', *The Poems of Shelley*, ed. T. Hutchinson (Oxford, 1960).
17. K. Marx, *The eighteenth Brumaire of Louis Napoleon: Selected Works of Karl Marx and Friedrich Engels* (Moscow, 1968) p. 98.
18. W. H. Auden takes up Shelley's implications in his brilliant tour de force 'Spain 1937':

> Tomorrow, for the young, the poets exploding like bombs,
> The walks by the lake, the winter of perfect communion;
> > Tomorrow the bicycle races
> Through the suburbs on summer evenings: but today the struggle.
>
> Today the inevitable increase in the chances of death;
> The conscious acceptance of guilt in the fact of murder;
> > Today the expending of powers
> On the flat ephemeral pamphlet and the boring meeting.

Today the makeshift consolations: the shared cigarette;
The cards in the candle-lit barn and the scraping concert,
            The masculine jokes; today the
Fumbled and unsatisfactory embrace before hurting.

The stars are dead; the animals will not look:
We are left alone with our day, and the time is short and
            History to the defeated
May say Alas, but cannot help or pardon.

19. I have investigated this question in *The Heroic Tradition*.
20. F. R. Leavis, *Revaluation*, p. 107 and p. 115.
21. A. Hauser, *The Social History of Art*, vol. II (London, 1962) p. 202.

CHAPTER 7   2: THE SYMBOLIST IMPASSE

1. W. Benjamin, *Charles Baudelaire: a Lyric Poet of the Era of High Capitalism*, tr. by H. Zohn (London, 1973) p. 63.
2. V. Hugo, 'Jersey Notes', quoted in Benjamin, ibid., p. 63.
3. Benjamin, ibid., p. 63.
4. See for instance, C. Grana, *Modernity and its discontents* (New York, 1957); 'Hatred of the bourgeoisie was the beginning of all virtue', p. 113.
5. F. Engels, *Anti-Dühring, Karl Marx, Friedrich Engels Werke,* band 20 (Berlin, 1962) p. 102.
6. T. S. Eliot, 'In Memoriam', *Selected Prose*, ed. F. Kermode (London 1975) p. 247.
7. J.-A. Rimbaud, 'Unfortunately (Baudelaire) lived in too artistic a *milieu* and his literary form, so often praised, is trivial. Unknown discoveries demand new literary forms'. Quoted in E. Starkie, *Arthur Rimbaud* (London, 1937) p. 124.
8. C. Grana, op. cit., p. 113.
9. M. Eliade, op. cit., p. 19.
10. K. Raine, *Defending Ancient Springs* (Oxford, 1967). Miss Raine's arguments are devoid of any historical orientation, the arcane being proffered as of an absolute and transmittable value.
11. See G. Snyder, 'Myths and texts', in *A Range of Poems* (London, 1966). These poems use shamanistic material – myths and lore – without reaching the quasi-shamanistic intensity of Rimbaud, or of, say Hughes's *Crow*, which is far closer to the spirit of shamanism.
12. Eliade, op. cit., p. 401.
13. Cf. Benjamin: 'At the end of this development may be found Mallarmé and the theory of *poésie pure*. There the cause of his own class has become so far removed from the poet that the problem of a literature without an object becomes the centre of discussion. This discussion takes place not least in Mallarmé's poems, which revolve about *blanc, absence, silence*', p. 106.

CHAPTER 8   THE ABSENT EXPERIENCE

1. This point is apt to be missed – exquisitely – by an excessively empirically-minded criticism: 'How can a gem emit any kind of a ray if denied access to an original light-source?', Philip Hobsbaum, *Tradition and Experiment in English Poetry* (London, 1979), p. 47 f.
2. The poem is 'Le Guignon', of which lines 4–8 are translated almost word for word from Longfellow's 'Psalm of Life' (an insufferably moralistic re-doing of Horace), and lines 9–14 from Gray's 'Elegy'.
3. That this kind of thinking still persists is evident from, for instance, Gregory Corso, 'Must one stay home to keep Rome Rome?' *Selected Poems* (London, 1962) p. 28.
4. Alain-Fournier, *The Lost Domain*, tr. F. Davison (Oxford, 1954).
5. Alain Robbe-Grillet, *Snapshots and Towards a New Novel*, tr. B. Wright (London, 1965) p. 78 *et seq.*
6. D. Lodge op. cit., p. 125 *et seq.*, tries to describe such a rapprochement as the gradual triumph of metaphor over metonymy in the writing of novelists such as Lawrence and Joyce. My reasons for dissenting from this view are sufficiently indicated above (pp. 58–61). Metaphor had always figured importantly in realist fiction, and the use of a more overt metaphoric symbolism (*The Golden Bowl*, *The Rainbow*) returns to earlier examples such as Goethe's *Die Wahlverwandshaten*, and Hawthorne's heavily allegoric *Scarlet Letter*. Jakobson's dichotomy again fails to illuminate the real nature of the development.
7. M. Proust, *Jean Santeuil*, vol. II (Paris, 1952) p. 253.
8. Proust, ibid., p. 253.
9. M. Proust, 'Swann's Way', *Remembrance of things past*, tr. C. K. Scott-Moncrieff (New York, 1934) vol. I, p. 213.
10. Proust, *Temps retrouvés, A la recherche du temps perdu,* p. 49.
11. S. Freud, *Totem and taboo*, tr. A. A. Brill (Harmondsworth, 1938), 'In other words, we should succeed in making it probable that the totemic system resulted from the conditions underlying the Oedipus complex', p. 204.
12. J. Keats, *Selected Poems and Letters*, ed. R. Gittings (London, 1966), p. 40.
13. Josipovici, op. cit., p. 22.
14. Josipovici, op. cit., p. 24.
15. Proust, *Temps retrouvés*, p. 253.
16. The sentence comes out at fifty three lines in Scott-Moncrieff, *Remembrance of things past*, vol. I (New York, 1934) p. 7.
17. Josipovici, op. cit., p. 12.
18. S. Freud, *The Standard Edition of the Complete Psychological Works*, 24 vols (London, 1953–74) vol. XI, pp. 188–9.
19. Jacques Lacan, *Ecrits* (Paris, 1966), especially 'Le stade du miroir', and 'Fonction et champ de la parole et du langage en psychanalyse'. Curiously, Lacan has given comfort to some feminists – Juliet Mitchell and Jacqueline Rose, for instance (*Feminine Sexuality*, London, 1982). Lacan assigns a humiliating role to women: their femaleness being forced upon them by men. It leads to some odd conclusions: 'the status of the phallus is a fraud',

Ms Rose states (p. 40). Try telling that to the rape-victim. Mss Rose and Mitchell glean from Lacan the solitary card of feminine subjugation. They could have got that from Engels *Origin of the family*, without having their very existence reasoned away by masculine conceit.

20. D. H. Lawrence, 'Edgar Allen Poe', *Selected Literary Criticism*, ed. A. Beal (London, 1965) pp. 334–7.

21. Josipovici, op. cit., p. 20. This view has been widely taken up by critics of a radical persuasion. See for instance Janet Wolff, *The Social Production of Art* (London, 1981) pp. 124–9.

Index

Modern criticism has generally been inclined to ascribe to Romantic poetry a culpable subjectivism and, almost as often, an unrewardingly thin texture. *The Romantic Predicament* suggests that if we define Romanticism in terms of its historical situation, we find that it is no more subjective than classical art. Romantic artists did not choose their predicament, nor is their characteristic subjectivism the result of wilful narcissism. Romantic language, with its characteristic concentration on the image, like the generally "personal" tone of its poetic products, is similarly responsive to historical development: the Romantic poet preys upon the outer in order to acquire the meaningfulness which was given in earlier literature.

An entirely new picture of Romantic achievement therefore begins to emerge. Far from being uninterestingly flat and mawkishly subjectivist, Romantic lyric poetry is seen as the only valid response to a situation in which humanity was thrust into individualism by the same forces which transfigured societal organization and technological methods. The Romantic predicament, moreover, is essentially of our own making; until we see Romanticism straight we shall be condemned to mythologize ourselves.